Enda O'Coineen

The Unsinkable Entrepreneur

Published by Kilcullen Limited
One Haigh Terrace
Dun Laoghaire
Co. Dublin
Ireland

Visit www.unsinkable-entrepreneur.com

10 9 8 7 6 5 4 3 2

First published by The Mercier Press Limited in 2005
This updated edition published 2009

ISBN 978-0-9516662-1-0

Profits from this publication go toward the Ocean Youth Trust Charity,
registered charity number XR36870

Printed in Ireland by W&G Baird
Cover design and layout by Create (www.create.ie)

The first publication of this book generated many personal emails from all over the world. Reading them made the publication worthwhile and was a stimulus to produce the second edition.

Many thanks to all for their kind words. Keep them coming at enda@unsinkable-entrepreneur.com

---

"In Toronto I finally managed to get myself your book after a deuce of attempts, and were it not a night seeping into the next day, I'd have finished it in one go"

- Adam Daniel Mezei

"I just read your book last night, well started last night and finished about two hours ago. It was very, very interesting for me and I could see lots of parallels in what I am trying to do here in Krakow. P.S. I loved the Warsaw stuff!"

- John Naughton

"Those who can't do teach... I have to deal with so many academics living in Kinsale and so recognised some of the characters."

- Peadar Mac Gabhann

"It has been an inspiration at a time when I need a boost with plans for my business. It is also very entertaining."

- Robert Shaw

"What a breath of fresh air from the 'normal' businessy type books; it's pragmatic approach, honesty, encouragement, coupled with real life recounts of your business 'adventures', had me captivated. I'm sure I will refer to it for years to come."

- Gerry Cahill

"Brings back memories when I worked in Dun Laoghaire in the 1980s and nothing stirred except the birds...."

- Gerry Kilduff

"I like the corporate culture parts. At one time in Vermont I had even used my Anthropology degree a little consulting on corporate culture and it made me think of that."

- Robert Sanford

"...But, in all of Eason's, I found myself picking up your book...Suddenly I didn't feel so alone or out of my depth. I went home and finished your book that evening and was even more invigorated to try and start out on my own."

- Daire Whelan

"I am a Dutch person and set up my own business in Ireland. I can understand in another country, especially when you do not speak the language. I spoke the language and still didn't always understand what went on exactly... Thanks for sharing your knowledge with me!"

- Kenneth Buchholtz

"It's a good story and we have number of beliefs in common. I would like to put some of your story on our Crazy Goals website (www.crazygoals.co.uk) perhaps the Atlantic crossing in the dinghy as an example of Crazy Goaling at its best!"

- Tim Powell

"It was extremely enjoyable and very much to the point in terms of the backbone required for a true Entrepreneur."

- Gary Walsh

"Life is full of ups and downs, especially for an Entrepreneur, and when you are on a down, sometimes it is hard to have faith and confidence in yourself. Your book has given me a second wind. A lot of inspiration and I thank you for that."

- Mark F. Dolan

Contents

Acknowledgements *7*
Foreword by Howard H. Stevenson *9*
Preface *11*
What I thought was 'Stamp Collecting' *13*
The Greening of the Dragon *20*
The Rabbitts of Galway *33*
Alcohol, the Army and Academics *42*
Across the Atlantic... *52*
My First Business *67*
Sailing around the World *83*
Sea Change *92*
Executive... *100*
Entrepreneurship in Organisations *115*
The Corporate Life *128*
Torn Curtain *137*
Prague, Year Zero *149*
Counter-revolutionary *165*
Setbacks *182*
'I am from Central' – the Czech and Slovak Credit Bureaux *193*
Globix Telecom and eTel *208*
Investor and Entrepreneur again *222*
Finally, and in conclusion *243*
Index *258*
About the Author *263*

Acknowledgements

No entrepreneur has ever succeeded without the help and goodwill of others. Success is creating a 'win-win' for all wherever possible, and whereas I have not always been successful, like most I try and do the best I can. However, the reality is that no matter how hard you try, when you're out front doing stuff, not everybody will be happy all of the time. I hope I at least managed to get the balance right!

I'd like to dedicate my thoughts in this book to the following people. My son Cormac 'Skipper' B, his mother Lucie, and to my three wonderful daughters Roisin, Aisling and Saoirse. To have inherited by birth a restless entrepreneur Dad is a tough calling, and also to their wonderful mother Suzanna, who shared that calling for a long time. To Nicola Mitchell and her delightful children, Anna, Louis and Joe for sharing part of their lives.

To my brothers and sisters, Pauline, Mairead, Mona, Cormac, Eoin, Annmarie and Frances, to their partners, their children and a very large extended family which includes over seventy first cousins and over twenty-five nieces and nephews together with my late parents Maureen and Charlie. Such are the size of Irish families, that it's an adventure and a joy in itself getting to know them all and I always like to help them along where I can.

In particular to Dermot Doyle for his friendship, understanding and assistance in editing the book, to Linda Duffy, and all the staff at Create for their work on the book cover, layout and design. Also Sharon Hutchinson for her proofreading and Conor Lynch for his illustrations regarding leverage.

To the following human beings (and indeed those life forms on other planets) together with everybody else I have had the good fortune to have had contact with. This small acknowledgement is in gratitude for support, encouragement, help and assistance, big and small, along the way. And whereas business relationships ebb and flow like the tide, good ones also become personal friendships.

In no particular order, *John Killeen, David Beattie, Tim Gunning, Jerry and Jimmy Dowling, Brian Lynch, Ewan Gibb, George Formandl, Richard Klecka, Robert Nemec, Jana Ridanova, Karel and Crystina Bukova, Michael White, Alastair Hammond, Shane Woodroffe, Scott Baker, Eamon Conneely, Jamie Boag, Ian Walker, Johnny Smullen, Maria Moynihan Lee, Martin Stachník, Mirek Zanaska, Frantsiek Hala, Zdenek Stuchlik, Josef Krepinsky, Jaroslav Jirman, Jiri Rasner, Zbynek Dvorak, Barbora Roubalova, Pavel Rozsypal, Hana LiÏanová, Peter Novotny, Tom Fitzpatrick, Michal Mika, Jonathan Wilkinson, Johan Huurman, Tony Mullet, Enda Kelly, Tony O'Reilly, Denis O'Brien, Richard Branson, Dag Pyke, Dermot Desmond, Paddy Cooney, Trevor McClintock, Wesley Armstrong, Marian Broderick, Norman Barry, Winkie Nixon, Denis and Mary Doyle, David Baines, Bill Cullen, Conal Forbes, Cyril Forbes, Dirk Nauta, Joe English, Killian Bushe, Harry Cudmore, Hugh Coveney, Howard Kilroy, Frank Gaughan, Feargal Quinn, John Bourke, Chuck Feeney, Des Burke Kennedy, Tom Power, Robert Dix, Ron Holland, Charlie Haughey, Paul Murphy, Susi Huber, Jim Irwin, Linda Scott Irwin, Tom Doyle, Colm Hendrick, Neil O'Dowd, Gay Mitchell, Peter McGibney, Katka Krizek, Jimmy McShane, Frank Haughton, Petr Kucera, Daniela Kafkova, Ian Smith, Michael O'Brien, Larry Howell, Carlo Gherardi, Frabazio Fraboni, Jack Stack, Thomas Denmark, Honza Denmark, Andrea Leprisova, Matt Starr, Radek Brnak, Sean Melly, David Hardwicke, Bernard Sommers, James McCollum, Hana Svehlackova, Peter Bastable, Billy Kane, Klaus Tebbe, Michal Pozar, Pádraig Ó Ceidigh, Jan Urban, Declan Dolan, Michael Clarke, Frank Heath, Sean McVeigh, Bryan Maguire, Sarah Newman, Andrew Collins, Paul Brosnan, Declan Kennedy, Peter Allen, Ajit Virk, Harpal Randhawa, Charlie Bergen, Rob Shesol, Chris Craig, Hugh Bailey, Jimmy Fitzpatrick, Peter and John Donnolly, Sean Lemass, Des Kelleher, Alena Mandelickova, David Wherry, Brid Korby, Ales Kratochvíl, Zdenek Sluka, Jana Stastny, Richard Duggan, Orla O'Malley, Ruairi and Killian Lannen, Michell Cheesman, John McDonald, Tony Tennyson, Roger Lacey, Maureen and John Rabbitt, Kaisa Kado, Anna Mackey, Kevin Moore, Aidan Higgins, Gerry Brennan, Catherine Maybury, Barbora Roubalova, Alan Burnside, Marie O'Neill, Shelia Pimm, Noel Johnstone, Ashley Hunter, Fiona Johnstone, Gerry Bell, Nigel Mansley, Paul Rowan, Robin Hogg, William 'Chip' Dowering III, Cathal Friel, Roger Conan, James Coyle, Conor Daly, David Becvar, Dave Flynn, Vladimir Skolout, Seamus O'Tiernaigh, Dick Phillips, Eamon Gilmore, Jim Fahy, Niall Mulqueen, David O'Brien, Vladimir Ezr, Vibjorn Madsen, Eva Skorepova. Patrick and Brigetta Hess, Karel Gott, Ken Rogers, Liavan Mallin, Maria Surboeck, Micheál Ó hAmhláin, Nick Koumarianos, Olga Magliocco, Owen and Martin O'Malley, Paolo Boido, Dave Parker, Roger Lacey, Declan Ryan, Skip Mansfield, Radek Brnak, Dick Phillips, Ivana Bozdichova, Ged Pierce, Michael Cotter, Gerard O'Hare, Tom Roche, John Coyle and John Flaherty.*

Foreword

Although Enda O'Coineen questions the ability of academics to teach entrepreneurship, he does it in such an engaging style that this academic read on. So should you, the reader. The lessons for the fledgling entrepreneur are real, important and understandable. More importantly perhaps, this book helps the reader to understand the interaction between the person and the opportunity.

In the over thirty years that I have been teaching and engaging in entrepreneurship, Enda's lessons have been taught to me in a more painful way. We say that the school colours for the entrepreneur are black and blue and the school yell is ouch! By reading this book you can avoid some of the pitfalls. You can also have fun!

Among the important lessons that he teaches are some that are universal – you will do better doing the things you like. Entrepreneurship often involves parts of the day that are not in your favourites category like his first experience with sales. He wisely observes that unless you like what you do, it will be hard to get the energy to do it well.

His experience emphasises another important lesson for the budding entrepreneur: it is about others. His stories illustrate the power of empathy as he deals with suppliers, customers, financiers and employees in ways that make them winners even while he is winning big. Whether in his boats or his business he is a fortunate entrepreneur who recognises the role that others have had in his success.

As the book gets into the issues of change, I felt a brotherhood. People don't mind change (for others). His fun lessons focus on the fact that all business is about the customer, but all implementation is about getting other people to agree on a definition of success, see how success benefits them and then helping them to succeed.

In this book you will understand better than many academic treatises the role of environment and culture. As he moves from his own backyard to the woolly wild east, he learns new lessons that will stick in your mind and hopefully change your behaviour if you intend to build a business.

He reminds me of the story told by an American presidential candidate, Bill Bradley, about a dinner at which he was the guest of honour. As the waiter came around, he asked for a second pat of butter. The waiter said, 'No!' Bradley importuned the waiter by asking him if he knew who he (Bradley) was. The waiter answered, 'No!' The waiter asked Bradley if he knew who he was. Bradley answered, 'No!' The waiter responded that he was in charge of the butter.

Understanding who is in charge of the butter is important in all entrepreneurial settings. The more unlike the setting is to those in your experience, the more you have to learn who is in charge of the butter. This book will both remind you of that rule and offer you guidance as to the sources of the answer to that vital question.

The lessons learned about people, opportunity, deals and context provide a useful framework for those interested in entrepreneurship and a fun read for those who wish right now to be only spectators.

After years of studying and doing, this professor of entrepreneurship recommends highly that you enjoy the journey, but take notes. It is much more fun than most textbooks.

Howard H. Stevenson
Sarofim-Rock Professor of Business Administration
Former Chair of Entrepreneurship
Harvard Business School
Senior Associate Provost
Harvard University

Preface

When you do things in life, very often it is only afterwards that you actually realise what happened – the when, the where, the why and the whom.

There are good reasons for this. If I had logically analysed in advance the risks and the rewards of everything I have done whether it amounted to a failure or a success – little would have happened. Attempting to understand the unknowns would have paralysed me, an impossible task because, until such time as a thing is encountered, an unknown remains exactly that – unknown. Most of the time I just did things because I wanted to and they felt right.

In this regard being an entrepreneur is more akin to being an artist than being an engineer, doctor or scientist. Professionals of that category, and indeed most categories, are used to operating with standardised environments. Legislation, guidelines or procedure determine the boundaries of their actions. By contrast an artist draws from his or her muse, the fleeting excitement that has no definable origin. Depending on your belief system you may ascribe it to divine inspiration or a chemical imbalance in the brain. Wherever the feeling comes from, it urges them to create. To do.

This art of entrepreneurship is the ability to see an opportunity and follow it through with the creative skills that can mould information, finance and, most importantly, people into a living, breathing, sustainable entity.

My enterprises span from a nineteenth-century style adventure across the North Atlantic to a technology-led information business of the future. The one common trait of all my experiments, both successful and unsuccessful, is that they have dealt with the unknown. Don't get me wrong, I have always tried to minimise the risk by learning as much as I could before setting out. But ultimately there had to be a leap of faith, an abstract belief without any fundamental proof that I could do whatever it was that lay ahead of me. It's been a great adventure and it is what I wish to share.

It was only after I had crossed the Atlantic – alone in a sixteen-foot dinghy at the age of twenty-one – that I got to understand my deep inner sense of adventure and of being challenged – and could start to work out what had driven me to attempt such a venture. Many times people have regarded me as being 'lost at sea'. In fact I have always known where I am, it's simply been a place most other people don't understand. 'The problem,' as one psychologist said to me, 'is we find you distressingly sane.'

In *The Unsinkable Entrepreneur* I will identify the traits of the entrepreneurial art and what it takes to be one, sane or otherwise. I have had the benefit of sharing other people's experiences and learning from them, now I want to make my own contribution to the knowledge-driven world of the twenty-first century.

Most importantly, I have learned that to be a successful entrepreneur you may harvest other peoples experiences, distil the information and data available, take the best of what you learn and use it, but – *and this is the big but* – you cannot copy. The art of entrepreneurship is in itself the ultimate contribution. The style, character and effort that you add will be personal to you and you only.

If we are to thrive and prosper as a species in the real and virtual worlds, the art of entrepreneurship must be recognised and nurtured. So go forth, create and let me know how you get on.

You'll find me at enda@kilcullen.cz!

Chapter one

What I thought was 'Stamp Collecting'

It's appropriate at this stage – before I talk about making money – to add a note on what we might consider doing with it once we have it. For example losing it through social investing! This may seem a little bit like putting the cart before the horse, but it's not. What you do with your wealth once you've made it says a lot about who you are, and what type of entrepreneur you are as well. The very best entrepreneurs do not hoard wealth. They believe 100 per cent that if the proverbial dung were to hit the fan, they could make it all back again and more. They choose to circulate their money, both into new ventures and philanthropic causes, and sometimes a combination of the two.

In my early days I had no understanding of either the words 'philanthropy' (which I thought was some sort of stamp collecting) or 'entrepreneur' (which was just some posh French word). In line with the purist 'Saints and Scholars' mentality of my Jesuit-led secondary school, I was consequently chucked out of French class and 'demoted' to Commerce class instead. Such was the culture of a stiflingly anti-business Ireland. Intellectual prowess was held in far higher regard than economic contribution.

However, to quote Abraham Lincoln's blunt words, 'you cannot help the poor by becoming one of them.' Adding poverty to poverty does not lessen poverty. Adding wealth to poverty does. The reality is that philanthropy is the last and highest level of entrepreneurship. Giving back to society, preferably in a sustainable, far-reaching way, is essentially 'adding value' to humanity. You are empowering others to reach their potential, and by doing so, enriching the world for subsequent generations.

Additionally – unless your religious beliefs extend to you being buried like an Egyptian king with tons of gold melted into your coffin, zillions of bucks of ornaments, and a massive pyramid to boot – you can't take it with you.

Plus I'm sure most major religions would agree that if your welfare in the afterlife is your concern, then distributing more of what you have in this one is probably the way to go...

An extraordinary example is that shown by Chuck Feeney, whom I had the pleasure of meeting in the early 1990s quite by accident. He was the first real philanthropist I ever met, although I didn't realise the extent of his giving at the time, and a model for us all.

A reclusive Irish-American entrepreneur, he accumulated a fortune through his chain of Duty Free Shoppers outlets and in 1988 was listed (somewhat tardily) as the twenty-third richest American alive by *Forbes Magazine*. As if that was not enough of an accomplishment, Chuck then decided to give it all away secretly during his lifetime. When we met, I was raising money for my entry in the BOC single-handed round-the-world race and also the youth sail training vessel, the *Pride of Galway* which I ran with John Killeen – a forerunner to Ocean Youth Trust Ireland founded some years later.

While Chuck passed on the opportunity to support either at the time, I was still honoured to spend time with him at his attic office in Saville Row in London, a meeting arranged by his secretary and partner Helga Flaiz, whom he later went on to marry. A very private individual, it was a privilege to be able to spend time with him – though at the time, like almost everyone else, I had absolutely no idea of the true depth of his giving.

Unknown to the world, he'd already transferred the entirety of his wealth (approximately $4 billion) to a foundation in Bermuda called Atlantic Philanthropies. When disbursing the funds, he used the power of leverage to get better returns for his contributions. He would offer seed money of, for example, $10 million for a hospital project on the condition that the national government match the $10 million and then raise another $10 million. This guaranteed buy-in from the government from the very beginning, and ensured that a $30 million facility would eventually be built.

My connection to Chuck is that he'd arrived in Prague at the same time as myself and subsequently set up a retail outlet there. While he was there he stayed in a bed and breakfast run by the family of Jan Urban, who Chuck assisted (I think) to go to Harvard University. Jan Urban subsequently ended up working for Simply Mortgages, the mortgage broking firm that I set up, and this is how the connection was made.

However, for the Irish people at large, Chuck's influence has been all around us for decades. Particularly in the university sector, which was heavily funded by Chuck, and also in the peace process in Northern Ireland, where Chuck played a hugely significant (and extremely discreet) role. He even funded (I think!) rooms where my daughter Rosin went to college. On a worldwide scale his foundation has been similarly influential, positively touching the lives of millions of people in Vietnam, Australia, South Africa and the USA amongst others.

Chuck's story is superbly brought together by Conor O'Cleary's biography, *The Billionaire Who Wasn't*, which I would highly recommend you read. Material things are just that, material. Wealth is not judged by the size of your car or the number of big houses you have to live in – and I now don't feel embarrassed by my usually modest living. ('Oh, you're not driving a 1994 car!' as my daughter Saoirse exclaimed with disgust on seeing my well-used Honda Civic... She was only thirteen at the time so she can be forgiven.)

Anyway, after looking after my own family, if that's possible, I can only aspire to a tiny fraction of what Chuck Feeney has done. He is an extraordinary role model. While ego and personal drive are hugely important to success, Feeney's life is a brilliant example of what can be achieved when personal pride is put to one side.

Also, after reading his book, I somehow feel there are others out there thinking the same and who are not bothered or impressed by wealth, but are simply motivated by achievement.

One time I remember, it was about four in the morning and I was sitting in Tretter's Bar in Prague with Sean Mulryan and Paddy Kelly, then very successful property developers. Paddy had already agreed a €10,000 donation to my youth charity but when I put it to Sean he responded with all the subtlety of a sledgehammer. 'Well you can go and fuck off!' he said. 'The youth of Ireland do not need it!'

This startled me a little but, as the cocktails flowed, Sean explained how he put €500,000 into a new orphanage in South America. He didn't 'trust the shaggers' to take care of the project, so he sent his own supervisor to make sure it was built correctly. Sean won my respect as a 'doer'.

Aidan Heavey of Tullow Oil gives another excellent example.

Aidan recently spent time with villagers around Lake Albert in Uganda which, with Ghana, is one of Tullow Oil's main prospects. 'You would find there are thirty people a month around the lake dying of cholera, which you can do something about by drilling a well for clean water,' Aidan said. 'On average, twenty-five per cent of the babies would also die at birth due to lack of hygiene, but it was the simplest thing in the world to solve. We just built a little clinic.'

Aidan also recommended building a road to the lake so fishermen could transport and sell their catch, as well as grow sunflowers for their oil and keep bees to make honey from the flowers. It was a wonderfully organic combination.

But he is most proud of the project to save fishermen's lives. 'Thousands of people drowned in the lakes because there were no rescue boats or life jackets,' he explained. Since the villagers made their own clothes, Aidan set up a local plant to make life vests, but then still found that the men were reluctant to wear them. Why?

'The men were stubborn so we concentrated on the women and kids instead through an insurance scheme. If the men died wearing a life jacket they would get a sum of money. They would also get a sum of money if they were rescued wearing a life vest.'

This way the wives beat the hell out of their husband's macho attitudes and made them wear the jackets. Fifty-five people were saved in one month! As a person with strong maritime interests this story has a particular resonance with me. It is an excellent example of a low impact project that had a high impact outcome.

To put it all more simply, philanthropy is undertaking entrepreneurial activity that has no personal economic return. If it does so in some indirect way, well and good, but that should not be the starting point. Sometimes it's logical. Sometimes not.

Anyway, call it what you may, the old-fashioned concept of giving back to the community is one that my father preached to me, just as his father and his father's father before him. Being a contrarian, I did not listen at the time, but my sister Pauline and other family members reminded me of it. So, I try to do my best in the area in which I'm most interested and experienced, which is sailing. On a personal level (and charitable activities are something which are very personal to each of us) I feel most involved when I'm putting something into my local community, and linking it to a global community rather than *vice versa*.

Oddly enough this relates to everything from my role in EnWest, where we have successfully completed a much needed oil terminal – an industry I never thought I would be involved with – to founding the Let's Do It Global organisation and the various events which came under its umbrella.

Overall, these components were put together in order to get the Volvo Ocean Race to Galway, which meant fielding an entry to the race, our charismatic *Green Dragon*, and to make sure that we maintain the knowledge base for future generations, establishing a youth program and global network.

The entire 'Global' experience has been totally mad in time demands, totally crazy regarding the ambition of the projects (many thought it would be impossible), and very expensive to get going. Not only that, but in an earlier attempt to raise funding I was almost charged for corporate espionage! Beat that for commitment... But before I give the story here as a cautionary tale, I will just conclude my thoughts on philanthropy.

Life is a wonderful and bizarre thing that can lead us in many directions. Each hour, day, week and month can be exciting – mixed in with the necessary mundane – because you never know where it will all lead. You never really know what's going to happen next, but sure as light is day, you can influence it by thought, action, attitude, perseverance and being positive. And one of the best ways to remain positive, focused and active is to devote yourself to a charitable cause that's close to your heart. The skills and attitudes that you develop ultimately assist in other challenges in your life, providing a positive loop that strengthens your spirit, your soul and your character. These are benefits that you just cannot get from purely business transactions.

And the marvellous thing about it all is that the more you give the more you get! That may seem hard to grasp as you read it here, but if you devote yourself to a charitable cause, you too will come to understand what I mean. I hope you'll give it a try and find out for yourself.

Getting back to my brush with law, it came about when I was working on an entry for the last Volvo Ocean Race – a logical follow on from the 1989-90 Whitbread race which is described later in this book.

From past experiences I had determined that it was best not to go public without a core sponsor. Unless you have a commitment in advance of at least €10 million it is simply madness to undertake such a challenge.

And I was tantalisingly close to just such a commitment. I was chasing €16 million of funding and even had top boat builder Killian Bushe lined up, who had built our first boat twenty years ago and the Ericsson and ABN AMRO boats of the 2005-06 race.

Then everything went rapidly pear-shaped. It all started (or finished, depending on how you look at it) during the last few days of a holiday with my partner Lucie and our son Cormac on Miami Beach in Florida. I received an email with the schedule of a high level corporate meeting in Bonn of a company which I'd been pursuing for support. The company in question was massive, had €40 billion in turnover and over 350,000 employees worldwide. However, it had come together at incredible speed as a result of many mergers and acquisitions and had a lot going on internally – hence the need to get the decision makers together under one roof.

This seemed like a perfect opportunity for me as I had been unable to get to the key players. For the company's part, a sponsored entry into the race was a fantastic marketing opportunity, both internally to the various different teams and operations, and externally to the world as a burgeoning conglomerate. Plus, the budget of €16 million was well within their means. I had the support of one executive within senior management, but the decision was split between four global regions, and I needed to get the backing of two or three board members to seal the deal.

My patron had sent me the schedule with the opinion that this was the optimum time to pitch the idea to the right people. Several airline connections later, and Miami beach sand still trickling from my sandals, I arrived in a Bonn store to kit out in proper attire (cuff links, pinstripes etc.), my pitch readied for the corporate royalty.

This year the rigid German feel of the proceedings was being supposedly relaxed for a dynamic, free and easy American-style culture, and the top hundred executives would be conducting their presentations and business in English. While fascinated to be at the heart of such a high-level corporate meeting, none of the strategies, business plans, upcoming acquisitions, restructuring plans and so forth were of commercial value to me. My sole focus was to get a sponsor for our yacht, and I used the opportunity to get talking.

But I had walked into the inner sanctum of a hugely powerful company and its seething corporate politics can be very dangerous. With all the mergers and what not going on things must have been even more treacherous than usual, and whilst I was pitching the sponsorship one executive saw an opportunity to shaft a rival, which he did so – by reporting me to security.

The company's security officials first put me under surveillance (on reflection, I probably did seem quite suspicious. I was constantly on the phone for one thing, trying to sort out my partner's problems in Miami where I'd left her). Then, like a lightning bolt, several security men approached me from different directions and escorted me out of the conference to much embarrassment, indignity and indeed drama.

I was subsequently interrogated in a way that would have made the Gestapo proud. My hotel room was searched and my computer and phone were confiscated. I thought I could handle my own problems so out of loyalty I refused to give the names of the executives I'd been dealing with. Unfortunately, this tack made things look even worse than they already were. Not only that, once they came to realise that I wasn't some high level spy they went from excited to angry. Instead of plugging a corporate leak, they looked like fools for allowing me in with such ease under their noses.

When the seriousness of the situation became clear, both for me and the other executives who had supported the project, I had to come clean on everything and insist on taking all the blame to try and save their asses.

It didn't completely work. The executive who'd invited me to the meeting was sacked (and subsequently rehired I'm glad to say, but it can't have been an enjoyable experience for him) while I had to endure an intense period of investigation – which went on for months. I think I finally managed to persuade them of my innocence… Seeing the inner workings of corporate security, complete with shady ex-police on the company's payroll, was definitely not a happy experience for me.

My sponsorship effort had backfired like a nuclear bomb.

Regarding the Volvo race entry, while I had other sponsors lined-up, there was not enough to get the job done properly and we had to abort. To cap it all, Killian Bushe went on to build the winning boat again that year for ABN AMRO and it could just have easily been ours.

Still, it depends on how you look at things. For some people, a failure is the excuse to give up. For others, it's just a learning curve, a bend in the road to be negotiated on your journey to a later and more satisfying success. For the 2008-09 race we took a different approach, which became a major €20 million project when others led by Jamie Boag, John Killeen, Eamon Conneely, Robert Dix, David Beattie and many more who contributed for the 'collective good' joined in – it is a fascinating story which I'll detail in the next chapter.

Chapter two

The Greening of the Dragon

The latest round-the-world adventure started when Jamie Boag was watching the success of the Ryder Cup in Ireland in 2006. Sitting in his armchair on the Isle of Wight he wondered why the equivalent could not be done for the sport in which he was a professional.

At the same time John Killeen was exploring ways to develop the Port of Galway, while Eamon Conneely, fresh from a victory in the World TP52 Championship, was looking for a new challenge.

For my part, I had been searching for an opportunity to get an entry into the Volvo Ocean Race and take up some unfinished business from Ireland's last entry, when it was known as the Whitbread. Also in my own masochistic philanthropic streak, I was either questing for a new challenge or wanting to put my head on the block again...depending on how you view it.

Right then Jamie had the stroke of genius that allowed everyone to combine their goals into something larger. As well as entering a team into the Volvo Ocean Race he also suggested making Galway city a stopover point. By doing this, we had a full package that we could sell to the government.

Together with Jamie, John, Eamon and myself, we also had David Beattie, Robert Dix (a finance specialist and former Olympic sailor) and Gerard Barrett (a downright nice guy who likes, as he says himself 'to stay in the long grass'). Mind you, as some have discovered, to sit in our board meetings, you would have needed the hide of a rhinoceros and a set of brass balls (no sexism intended)!

Without Jamie's drive and early support from John Killeen, plus Eamon to complete the team balance, none of it would have happened. Many more also came in at an early stage, such as Bank of Ireland Governor Richard Burrows, who has both a strong and successful background in business, and those who joined our boat ownership syndicate.

The project has been an extraordinary team effort in entrepreneurship - something I am proud to be part of and, despite some tough calls, we are all still friends and talking to each other!

What we started gives true meaning to the word TEAM – Together Everybody Achieves More.

The starting point was to get an €8 million commitment from the Irish government to host the race in Ireland and seed fund an entry. It took a year of presenting, researching, pushing, pulling, tugging and lobbying with some dedicated partners in order to make this happen.

After we had navigated our joint proposals through a very tough evaluation process at Fáilte Ireland, championed there by tourism professionals John Concannon, Paul Keeley, Keelin O'Rourke and their CEO Shaun Quinn, we then brought it to the government. I met the then Taoiseach Bertie Ahern in Dubai on a trade mission, where his Secretary General Michael Collins steered me towards Gerry Kelly. Gerry was a senior advisor to the government and had been instrumental in getting support for the Special Olympics, and he could see the clear benefits of bringing the Volvo Ocean Race to Ireland. Gerry met with John Killeen and myself and explained that we needed a political champion at cabinet level with other ministers in support.

The turning point came in December 2006 when Richard Burrows offered us the Bank of Ireland boardroom for an evening. By 'facilitating' Richard knew exactly what we were looking for, a breakthrough moment where everybody would agree on the viability and worthiness of the entire project. Bank of Ireland were not underwriting the event, but they allowed us to leverage the venue, which was critical.

At this venue we got a critical mass of personnel together, including executives from Fáilte Ireland and the Volvo Ocean Race. Key movers in Galway such as Ray Rooney, John O'Sullivan, Brian Sheridan and many more who saw the benefits lobbied the Minister for Arts, Sport and Tourism, John O'Donoghue.

Although in favour, before O'Donoghue could authorise the €8 million in seed money the proposal had to make its passage through normal government channels, and this was time-consuming. It wasn't that anything untoward was going on, it was simply the fact that bureaucracies (even in private organizations) tend to be slow and deliberate in their assessments. On top of that, the project was an unprecedented one for the government (the last entry had been funded completely by the private sector) and the civil service were correspondingly cautious with it. It was bold, it was new, and it was a large commitment.

While I respect and understand the need for this deliberation when disbursing taxpayer's money, I personally found the experience quite frustrating, as I'm used to just grabbing the ball and running with it. I was particularly frustrated in this instance, as our window of opportunity was starting to slip away.

Central to our pitch to the government was the quantifiable benefits. The government investment would be earmarked for the development of Galway harbour, similar to any other infrastructure investment, while the boat and the racing team would be funded by the private sector.

On several occasions we understood that the Minister was ready to sign off, but he was always delayed by some new issue or check. For example, the Fáilte Ireland analysis on the benefits of supporting the project was not deemed to be comprehensive enough, so the Minister was advised to get an independent report instead. When the report came back from Deloitte several weeks and tens of thousands of euros later, it showed even greater benefits than the initial proposal had. Principally a €40 million plus return on investment.

It was then decided that, such was the scale and unusual nature of the project, that approval from the Department of Finance was needed. Fortunately both John and Eamon had already met the then Minister for Finance, Brian Cowen, and lobbied for the project. Cowen's initial reaction was noncommittal, but both John and Eamon won him around. It turned out to be something of an anti-climax because Cowen said the Department of Arts, Sport and Tourism already had the money and that there was no need to come to him.

However, the Department of Finance did write a letter supporting the project, which became important later.

It was now approaching the summer of 2007 and we had to apply more political pressure from our side for a conclusion. The Volvo race organisers were looking for final commitment by 24 May. We faced competition from other ports, while at the same time we were falling behind in our schedule to find a boatyard, build a boat and assemble a professional team.

Nor did it help that an election was on the way, as it might mean the project would be left without political backing.

All of these delays meant that by Thursday, 17 May 2007 – one week to the general election and the last day of parliament – the Minister had still not signed off on the seed capital. Thursday was to be Minister O'Donoghue's last day in his office prior to the election, and we knew that if he did not sign it today, it would never happen. O'Donoghue wanted to sign, but did not want to pre-empt the department's evaluation process.

On the morning of 17 May I called Gerry Kelly and told him that the Department of Finance had written in support, and that the independent report from Deloitte was also very positive. Gerry immediately went over to the Dáil and informed the Minister of this.

That afternoon I received a call in my office in Prague. It was O'Donoghue.

'Enda, we're going to do it' he said while explaining that he was off that evening to Kerry to work on the general election.

'Great,' I said, 'can you put that in writing?'

True to his word, I subsequently got a five-paragraph letter from the Department of Arts, Sport and Tourism, committing the government to €8 million for the project. That same evening O'Donoghue issued a press release on the matter, and then went straight off to Kerry to fight for his seat in the election.

In truth, this was the end of the beginning. O'Donoghue had stuck his neck out on behalf of the project. He understood the benefits and showed real leadership when it might have been easier to simply leave it to the next incumbent. We were and are hugely grateful to him for this.

It was just as well, because with the economic crash to come later there is no way we would have gotten it over the line. This is despite the fact that projects like this generate economic activity, and are absolutely vital for the welfare of our island.

Just look at how the economic poles of the planet are shifting. The Europeans, principally Britain, were dominant in the 1800s, before gradually ceding this role to the US in the 1900s. Now there is a shift to the east, with the growth of China becoming paramount to the health of the global economy, followed by India and other countries in the region.

While many jobs and industries have shifted from West to East, this influx of investment into Asia has led to the growth of an affluent middle class with consumer habits similar to ours. China alone is forecast to be the number one consumer of luxury goods by 2015.

Naturally this latent spending power is not something that Irish industry can afford to ignore, and for this reason it is paramount that we grow awareness of our country in these strategically vital markets.

Doing this inside the US and EU was not something that was difficult for the Irish, due to the large Irish community in the former, and our proximity to the latter. However we have neither advantage in Asia, and this means that we will be forced to invest in awareness building campaigns of a much greater scale.

Our participation in the Volvo Ocean Race gives us that scale of awareness at a much greater cost-efficiency than we could achieve alone. I also believe, for all the above reasons, that our involvement should not be a once off for Ireland, but in fact should be a regular commitment. We only stand to win with our involvement. Our pool of knowledge regarding hosting and competing will increase, in turn leading to greater cost-efficiencies from our side. At the same time, the awareness of Ireland will continue to accrue, leading to more desire for Irish goods and services from these markets, plus an increase in tourism followed by direct investment into the country.

If in doubt, consider the following: our Galway festival for the Volvo Ocean Race stopover will be shown by over 100 TV stations and will have an estimated global audience of 1.8 billion people! This is exactly the sort of coverage our island needs, showcasing the country as both host and competitor in a world-class sporting event.

Regarding our use of public funds, we used it exactly as planned. Taxpayer's money was invested in the development of Galway port for the race where it doubled as an infrastructure investment, while private sector sponsorship took the risk for the boat and team.

By now we were juggling a very complex set of responsibilities, and we needed an organisational structure that could undertake it. The result was Let's Do It Global Ltd, a name deliberately chosen to reflect the ethos and attitude of the project. When I initially proposed the name other team members felt it was a bit too unusual, however John Killeen stuck by it, and it was something of a rallying point in the tough times that followed.

Let's Do It Global Ltd is a non-profit company controlling four main entities, each with a specific mission to fulfil. I illustrate it in the following diagram.

Let's Do It Galway Ltd became the special events company for the port, bringing together the interests of the harbour company, the city council and local business.

Let's Do It Green Ltd is responsible for the *Green Dragon* racing team and the Shamrock Challenger Ltd, a syndicate that owns the *Green Dragon* vessel.

Let's Do It Ocean Adventure, a brand, became the final component, linking our schools program and Ocean Youth Trust charity with our global business support network.

The mission of this last company was high on my list of priorities from the very outset of the project. Learning from my last involvement, I was determined that this time our efforts would have an entrepreneurial longevity, or legacy component, that would continue to benefit others even after the race was complete. Overall, while perhaps a little cumbersome at the start, it was an organisational structure built to last.

We also chose to build the organisation purely on experience, ability and merit. In smaller industries such as the marine sector there is a tendency for people to hire their friends rather than the best individual suited for the job. One manager I know and admire called this 'unconscious incompetence' – or not knowing what you don't know. We eliminated this from the beginning (well almost) and attracted an impressive group of professionals to run the project.

Once the organisation and key people were in place, we could properly concentrate on financing and building the boat itself. Shamrock Challenger Ltd was set up under Let's Do It Green Ltd to operate a syndicate whose members would each own a share of the boat. A great deal of work was put into corporate packages to make sponsorship an attractive proposal.

It was a great achievement for us to attract Denis O'Brien as a syndicate member, as he is an entrepreneur I very much admire. His first response was a slightly more colourful version of the words 'the last thing I need is ownership in a boat,' but I persevered and when he came to understand what we wanted to achieve, he joined the syndicate and put his considerable support behind it. He'd set a great example previously with his chairmanship of the Special Olympics.

The same was true of other entrepreneurs such as John Flaherty, Anne Heraty and her husband Paul Carroll of CPL who have made a great contribution to the project, Richard and Cheryl Burrows, Ged Pierce, Mick Cotter, John O'Sullivan and Tom Roche – all extraordinary individuals. Local Galway supporters included my cousin and friend Brian Lynch, John Coyle and Gerry Barrett. Gerard O'Hare, a very successful property developer in Newry, also threw his weight behind the project. Our list started to grow and we are very proud of those who committed.

Naturally we planned that they would get benefit from being involved in the project and team, but many took a philanthropic view that this was a project worth supporting at any rate. It is people like this who make the world a better place.

Back on the island of Ireland Richard Duggan, affectionately know as the 'the digger', came in as our financial director. In a fast moving project such as this with enthusiasts who do not have deep business backgrounds, financial control and management would be critical. Previously Richard had made a success of eTel and Globix Telecom which I refer to later in the book. Another key executive who came in was Fiona Bolger, an extraordinary media professional who took control and responsibility for the communications function.

In Galway we were also fortunate in securing Maria Moynihan, who had been the Chief Executive of the St Patrick's Day Festival in Dublin. We had met on a radio interview when St Patrick's festivities around the world were being discussed. Neil Carney, who worked on the Special Olympics, also joined.

Outside of Ireland Jamie Boag and David Hassett travelled the world to attract global sponsors. This was a tough beat and there was constant pressure but as it turned out, it all came together in the most unexpected way.

When I first became involved in the 1989-90 Whitbread race, the boats used to just stop in the different ports before going on their way. These days, it's much more exciting. The boats are going twice the speed, they create a gala festival at each port, and they are stopping at exotic locations in China and India.

The technology is also correspondingly exciting. The race yachts are built of a light Kevlar and carbon fibre, making them more akin to an aeroplane than a traditional boat. It also means that there are very few places in the world where you can design and build yachts capable of competing at this level.

The opening of new markets in Asia, the timeline we faced, plus the technological complexities we faced in building our boat, all combined to lead us to our ultimate sponsor.

Due to the delays, we were the last team to begin the design and construction of the boat, which put us under real pressure. The Volvo 70 boats are designed to what is called a 'box' rule. This means that the length, weight and other basic parameters are standardised so that the boats are closely matched, while at the same time leaving considerable room for innovation.

As luck would have it, a Dutch team who had reportedly spent €1.8 million on research and development, pulled out of the race and we were able to buy their data for a knock down price. This allowed us to make up considerable time on our opponents. Despite this, with a new route for the race the design challenge was still a tough one. With a limited number of competent designers available for this level of competition, we had to search globally to get the best, and eventually chose Rachel Pugh's design team in San Diego in August 2007.

While we had made some ground on our opponents, we were still behind schedule. Consequently, we took the decision to build the boat in China (which was actually cheaper as well) at Zhuhai, just across the border from Hong Kong, under the supervision of McConaghy's boatyard in Sydney. It was a complex operation, relying on many different components sourced from around the globe. These included a keel from Chicago, a mast from New Zealand, and sails designed in Scandinavia but made in the UK. Ian Walker project managed, ably assisted by Eamon Conneely's construction experience from his world-winning *Patches.*

Building the yacht in China was a high-risk strategy due to the indigenous lack of expertise, but one that paid off. The Western design and Chinese manufacturing, plus the know-how of our Let's Do It team, was a superb combination which delivered our yacht to us on time and on budget. The Russian team, by contrast, chose a UK boat builder that ran over time and over budget, despite starting several weeks before us. Our vessel was in the water at the same time as theirs, even though it took one month to get the boat delivered from China.

Another good outcome was the positive impression that Ian Walker made on the Chinese, both through his Olympic credentials and working relationship.

Several times during the year we had come close to landing a title sponsor for the boat, but each time it fell through. Then, an introduction through the race organisers who were keen to get Chinese companies involved, led us to the Shandong Lingong Group (SDLG), a construction machinery manufacturer. They had been interested in becoming involved in the race when, all of a sudden, we appeared with a world-class skipper and a boat built in China. We won their support based on the strength of the introduction, the relationship and mutual respect Ian and Jamie had built up, plus the work of Tony Helsham and Keith Ellis. Also Lansi Jiang of the Volvo Group in China proved a strong ally and to them we are very appreciative.

Our Chinese sponsor group came to include SDLG, Weichai Power (a diesel engine manufacturer) and the Triangle Group (a tyre manufacturer). These industrial companies are based in the Shandong province located on the East Coast of China, which has an area of 157,000 square miles and a population of ninety-two million people. Qingdao city, a stopover for the race, is also in the province.

To give some idea of the contrast in scale, at a race function in Alicante in Spain, we had the Mayor of Galway, Padraig Conneely, and the deputy Mayor of Qingdao, one Madame Xiang.

'Galway is proud to host the Volvo,' Padraig proudly announced, going on to say that it's 75,000 citizens would lay on a big welcome for the race.

'Yes, we will do the same,' said Madame Xiang, and then talked about her 8.5 million citizens... Could the contrast have been any greater?

While we were thrilled and relieved to have finally found willing title sponsors, it was a matter of some delicacy for the Irish government. We had agreed to call the boat *Green China*, which we felt was a brilliant opportunity to promote Ireland in China, to which most agreed, but it also allowed a minority to raise objections. At the same time, Fáilte Ireland was quite strict regarding how their logo and identity would be presented on the vessel itself. This we respected.

However a degree of paranoia set in, and because of the delays in reaching agreement, we sailed the boat for several weeks around Ireland without any graphics, which was a lost opportunity for all concerned.

Now, by way of showing that such issues aren't confined to Ireland, a massive standoff subsequently happened in China that threatened to derail the entire deal.

The authorities in Beijing staged a major press conference to announce the sponsorship deal and China's involvement, with Ireland, in the Volvo Ocean Race. Over 150 media were lined up for the event, including nineteen TV crews, and both Ian and Jamie flew to China specifically for the event.

Then, just before the announcement, some Party figures in Beijing decided that the name should be *China Green*. If the name China appeared, it should be first. It was almost a disaster. Whatever about the delicacy of *Green China*, there was no way that the Irish government would be usurped in a project that Irish taxpayer's money had launched.

The phone lines burned, millions of euros were at stake as was the success of the entire effort. Neither the SDLG group, who had agreed the name with us, nor the party officials in Beijing would stand down. On reflection, it was not so much the name that mattered as the face-saving that is tremendously important in Chinese culture. At the very last moment somebody suggested *Green Dragon* as an alternative, and since this seemed acceptable to all at that moment, our team grabbed the opportunity. The announcement was made and the show went on, much to everyone's relief...

Maybe it was for the best, because the *Green Dragon* developed a personality and cult all of its own, and the name has more impact and romance to it than either *Green China* or *China Green* would ever have had. Firing the imagination is a huge part of the thrill of these sporting events, and the name *Green Dragon* delivers.

As our team, led by Ian Walker, voyaged around the world we attracted many world-class sailors including Damian Foxhall, Neil MacDonald and Justin Slattery. We also managed to attract Dubliner Johnny Smullen from San Diego where he had worked with Dennis Connors on three America's Cup campaigns and our previous entry into the Whitbread race. Mild-mannered and effective, Johnny played an extraordinary job as shore manager. Many more joined the team (which grew as large as fifty at one stage) in an extraordinary 37,000 mile odyssey that could be the subject of another book. The team spirit, determination, professionalism and ability to punch above our weight against tough opposition has stood out.

As the race progressed I commuted between Prague and Dublin, living on the Internet and telephone and supporting the team in any way I could while also travelling to several of the stopovers.

Keeping the cash flowing and supporting the project has been tough. As a case in point, at one board meeting in Athlone, as we pondered over spreadsheets discussing team finances, a call came through from the team. Our boat had fallen off a fifteen-metre wave near the Philippines, there was a lot of damage and it would need to be fixed... maybe even a €100,000. Where would it all end?

Running parallel to the ocean race was the race to get Galway port ready for the stopover in May 2009.

For many years there had been talk of relocating the famous oil tanks situated along the harbour. However there was nobody to invest in this idea, or lead any entrepreneurial initiative. As well as being an eyesore and a safety threat to residents, because the town had grown up around the harbour, the oil tanks were now causing a serious log jam to the city's development. Because of their presence, you could not even get planning permission for the extension of a fish and chip shop at Eyre Square.

The tanks were owned by Shell, but they were not interested in investing anything further. Being state owned, the local Harbour Company was also not in a position to do anything as they had little resources and no mandate. The closure and removal of the tanks without a replacement, however, would have killed the port.

It was John Killeen who got the ball rolling. At his introduction and with the co-operation of Kilcullen Kapital Partners, we brought an investment group together to build and develop a replacement tank farm on reclaimed harbour property. John's company, Cold Chon Ltd, did a world-class job on the construction management.

Dealing with the oil companies, powerful forces in any economy, and especially on a small island such as Ireland, was a tough challenge and adventure. But we brought in Richard Walsh, an oil industry pro and former director of Shell Ireland, as Managing Director of Enwest Ltd, a company we founded to take over the oil tanks, and squared up to the majors.

However Shell, as the incumbent and the natural future tenant, were slow to move and difficult to negotiate with. Later it became clear that they intended to leave all along when they sold both their retail and commercial oil business in Ireland to the Topaz consortium, promoted by Niall O'Leary's Ion Equity, in 2005.

Not long after this we began our push on bringing the Volvo Ocean Race to Galway. Central to this was the removal of the oil tanks to create a race village. There was a plan B in the event of failure, but nobody wished to go there.

Even though the oil firms would have to relocate the old tanks eventually, the fact that we were anxious to clear the site gave them favourable terms in the negotiations. What should have worked to the advantage of those investing in the new tanks ended up being counter-productive (though since the negotiations Topaz have joined our list of sponsors and we are very happy to have them on board). In the middle of the worst financial downturn since the Great Depression, getting the tanks over the line became an enormous burden. So much so that my cousin, friend and syndicate member Brian Lynch was at one point planning a public demonstration out of sheer frustration. With so many parties involved in the transaction, it was also very complex.

In the end, it was common sense and a bit of give by all that won out and by April 2009 the final agreements were in place that allowed the tanks to come down at the eleventh hour. Key movers were John Killeen, the Galway Harbour Company led by Eamon Bradshaw, and Gerry Barrett's Edward Holdings, a very successful yet low-profile family company which has contributed a great deal to Galway.

The reclamation of the land under the old terminal was a strategic goal in a new vision being nurtured for the port and city of Galway. There is now an enormous opportunity to build a new inner city and harbour. To be successful, it needs scale, imagination, drive and all local interests to pull together for both public and private benefit. But it can be done, and in a way that will leave a positive legacy for many future generations of the city.

If the people of Galway, led by the Harbour Company and Council, can pull together a new harbour can be built, leaving the old harbour to be developed into leisure areas with new residential, commercial and public real estate, integrated with a suitable transport infrastructure. Why not a flagship iconic building suitable for the area? A 'Sydney Opera House of the West' if you will. Or perhaps the tallest building in Ireland – elegantly designed, tasteful and environmentally friendly. A showpiece of Irish construction and design. With real determination, imagination and commitment, all of these things are possible.

Regarding the economics of the plan, the cruise liners and shipping that the new port would attract would fund the property development. It would be a billion euro plus development, but that sort of scale is necessary.

It's in rare moments like this that society can take many steps forward in the creation of jobs, enterprise, opportunities and essentially making the world a better place to live in.

Bringing the Volvo Ocean Race to Galway was a catalyst, and shows what can be achieved. Many other events could also be attracted in the future. Unfortunately a problem with Ireland's development in this regard is the top-heavy nature of our government structures, which are predominantly based in Dublin.

Under this structure of strong central government and weak local government, it's difficult for a local leader to emerge with the necessary political and economic base to drive ambitious new projects that demand strong public and private partnership. This is in contrast to other parts of the world where city mayors can be in office for terms of five years or more. Irish mayors only hold the job for a single year, and the job tends to be part-time. Having this form of leadership backed by a civil service bureaucracy tends not to create dynamism. This is not a reflection on any individuals in that structure, just a comment on a system which I think needs to be changed. Unfortunately for change you need a good crisis and when you get a good crisis it's a pity to waste it – a subject I'll touch on later in the book.

Back on the subject of mayors, when preparing for the Boston to Galway leg of the race, I suggested somewhat cheekily to the Mayor of

Boston that he invite the mayors of Galway (there are two, one for the county and one for the city) to Boston with the Chamber of Commerce President and other dignitaries.

By chance I mentioned this to my sister Pauline and she remembered how almost fifty years ago my father disappeared for a month to Boston as President of the Galway Chamber of Commerce to seek investment for Galway. It's funny how things turn full circle, just like our round-the-world circus, and – *wow* – has our little island in the Atlantic, plus its western capital, changed in fifty years!

Speaking of circuses, there was always a 'bit of the divil' in my ancestral family, the Rabbitts of Galway. One time when a travelling circus was camped at Fair Green, my great-uncle was given the task of minding one of their elephants at his place of business, where he fed it with loaves of bread. Seeing how the massive creature would gobble down each loaf in one go, didn't my great-uncle decide to hollow out one of the loaves of bread and fill it with pepper? All fired up the elephant raced through the town, now the *Green Dragon* route, until it splashed into the ocean at Salthill to cool down...

Chapter three

The Rabbitts of Galway

I don't know if entrepreneurship runs in families, or whether the desire to achieve just occurs randomly in certain people. But there have been entrepreneurs in my family before my time.

My great-grandfather, Cormac O'Coineen, was originally from peasant stock and during the famine times of the 1840s his family travelled to the market in Galway to sell turnips. But times were bad and on the way starving people begged food from them, leaving them with hardly anything to sell.

Cormac left Ireland at a young age, like so many others, with a wake in his honour and ticket on a coffin ship bound for America. He survived the voyage, an achievement in itself given the squalor of the conditions en route, and having landed in the New World made his way northwest to Alaska.

Whether he took the wagon trail across America or sailed around Cape Horn we don't know, either way he endured hardships worse than he had faced in Ireland. Rancid food, harsh climates and hostile conditions. One story passed down in my family even tells of him being attacked by a bald-headed eagle in the Rockies, although I'm sure that's a tale which may have grown somewhat in the telling.

He survived the tough winter storms of 1848 and travelled down into a still-wild California for its Gold Rush, making Cormac a '49er' – one of the tens of thousands of hopefuls who swamped the frontier state in the search for gold. I like to think that the experience of the gold rush taught Cormac everything he ever needed to know about virgin markets. Many of the '49ers' were not hardy folk, but town dwellers who thought that a 'get rich quick' opportunity was in front of them.

Many did get rich quick. For example, Sam Brannan – the man who ran up and down San Francisco with a bottle of gold dust shouting, 'Gold,

gold in the American river!' – made $36,000 in just nine weeks. However, he didn't do it panning for gold. Brannan made his fortune by purchasing every pickaxe, pan and shovel in the region, which he then sold to the gullible newcomers at vulgar profits. A metal pan that once cost only twenty cents in any hardware store, cost $15 from the crafty Brannan.

If you want an example of a recent version of this phenomenon, consider the Internet boom in the 1990s, which Bill Gates described as a modern-day Gold Rush. Huge numbers of e-business ventures were outright flops, but many, ranging from investment bankers to coffee-shop owners, reaped large sums from the commerce that grew up around them.

Unlike most others, Cormac O'Coineen did strike it rich and found – if not an amazing fortune – enough gold nuggets to pay his fare home to Galway in the 1860s, after an absence of sixteen years, and invest in his future. My great-grandfather married, had four children and established a business that included a bakery, grocery store and public house. It was destroyed by fire and he re-established in 1872 in Forster Street, Galway.

One thing that fascinates me is how the local establishment would have received him on his return. Galway would have been a small town, very tightly knit and very class conscious. He had made his money and risen in class, a rare thing in such a stratified society.

However, it's the *riche* that counts and his pub, Rabbitts of Forster Street, still stands and is owned by my cousin John Rabbitt, great-grandson of Cormac O'Coineen.

On Forster Street curiously you also had the Salmons and Foxes Bar – while the Hare and Badger families lived up the road ! To the British civil service at the time, the Gaelic names were tongue twisters and also they wanted English business names. The title deeds still have my illiterate great-grandfather's 'X' and they gave him the name Rabbitt for the business.

As a result, you have several Rabbitt families in Galway and many are not related. Oddly enough names went from Gaelic to the closest English translation, they then went back to different Irish. (e.g., *Coinín* is the Gaelic for Rabbitt – however the English word was used for Cunneen, Cunniam, Coinne, Cooney and so forth – causing further confusion).

While my father grew up with both the Irish and English version of his name, the business was Rabbitt and so this is what stuck. It was only later when I travelled that I felt strong about my Irish roots. If I had an Irish name I should use it – though I am also proud of the Rabbitt family roots...

Although some in my family would rather forget the humble origins from which we have risen, I'm quite proud of my great-grandfather for overcoming adversity. Like ninety-five per cent of the Irish population at that time, he was illiterate but still made his way through a very tough world.

He was a pioneer, an original entrepreneur.

Cormac O'Coineen handed down Rabbitts of Forster Street to my grandfather who passed it on to my own father Charlie. Charlie's real name was Nicholas Cathal O'Coineen (named after St Nicholas' church where he was baptised) but people just seemed to find it easier to call him Charlie, so Charlie he became.

Being the eldest in his family, Charlie was left the pub. However, having grown up there and seen his own father die of lung cancer after exposure to the concentrated tobacco smoke, he was understandably anxious to be rid of it. Having modernised the pub, Charlie handed it over to my uncle Murtagh, whilst he devoted himself to his many and varied interests.

My father was a man ahead of his time. Despite suffering from the inhibition of a very bad stutter, he became president of the Galway Chamber of Commerce and national president of the Construction Industry Federation. He started a fish farm, a boat-building company called Hickey Boats that used progressive designs from the United States and was the founder of the Galway Oyster Festival – amongst other things.

He also worked hard to improve the lives of others. He was constantly on delegations to Dublin to persuade the government to designate Galway as an industrial centre and in his capacity as CIF president he introduced the first pension for construction workers in Ireland, from which many still benefit today.

He was also a devout Catholic. Our house was full of religious books and every evening he would have his eight children kneeling down to say the rosary together.

His full time occupation was running a construction firm called Malachy Bourkes, now called Moy Construction. In the 1950s, the company had one very big government contract for a hydroelectric programme which employed 2,000 men.

For political reasons the government held back a cash payment for a year and a half and the firm was almost bankrupted. It was a typical scenario of 1950s Ireland, big business was political and the country was held back over disputes which had nothing to do with economic or commercial reason.

Despite being ahead of his time, the environment was such that Charlie was never rewarded financially in the way a man of his calibre would be today. Ireland was a different country back then and even if you reinvested all your money, as my father did, there was limited potential. But his workaholic lifestyle did give him incredibly high blood pressure. He suffered a stroke and died young.

I never really knew Charlie that well. Between his enterprises and his eight children there wasn't much time for bonding, so to speak, and the concept of quality time didn't exist. But Charlie was without doubt an entrepreneur.

Because of my father's various dealings, we didn't actually have much money in the 1960s and 1970s when I grew up. While we didn't go to school barefoot like others did, the size of our family and my father's tendency to reinvest meant that there was very little cash in the household. In addition, the values prized in our household were education and religious devotion rather than material gain. I prefer not to categorise our socio-economic status as either 'working' or 'middle' class as I think these are terrible labels that people tend to get hung up on. I would say we generally got by financially and we didn't complain.

Except for me, perhaps. I was, and remain, terribly stubborn and I quickly received a degree of notoriety for it. I am what's known as a 'contrarian', if someone said black was white, I'd say white was black. I was a horror of a child when I was growing up. My snowballs had stones in them, I pulled stunts and played dangerous games that often ended with someone other than me being hurt.

When I was about twelve, I decided that I wanted to be able to beat up anyone I wanted. So I took up judo and became quite good, reaching the brown belt after a couple of years. By the time I was fourteen, I began to hang out with the tough guys and pick fights, believing that I would be able to throw anyone over my shoulder and beat the crap out of them. With that sort of attitude, my first street fight was not far away. Going into the classic judo poise I squared up against another guy, readying myself to throw him over my shoulder.

Flick. Bang!

By the time I had worked out my great throwing moves the other guy had punched me in the face, knocked me on my arse and was stamping my head into the ground.

So you can see, I learned the hard way what he knew from common sense. In a street fight, you move first and you take the initiative. You just don't go up to some person and start bullshitting to them like I did, saying the I'm-going-to-beat-you-up type of thing. I learned that you strike first, hardest and quick, and then you get out. My judo skills were a load of gobbledegook. Great for exercise and fights in the dojo maybe, but useless on the street. That said, the experience toughened me up, and I gained something of a reputation from it.

As a teen, I hung around with a lot of different people most of whom were older, bigger and tougher than I was, so I had to develop my senses and sensitivities accordingly. When you're smaller than everyone else you have to be a lot more astute, a lot more agile and be able to respond to the other guy's actions quickly. Later in my life I had to do this in a different fashion when I took on established businesses in difficult markets. Going against the grain was an early hallmark.

In my early teens, there was a period when I simply got a big kick out of making loud bangs. Our secret gang started the bomb season in the neighbourhood about two months before Hallowe'en and kept going until well into the New Year. At first we were not so good at it but with practice our standards and bang-quality improved immensely until they became so loud that we had to explode the devices underwater. An odd time a dead salmon or trout might float to the surface, killed by the concussion of the blast.

Getting drunk or high was another source of fascination, probably because it was again strictly prohibited. It was a blessing that no recreational drugs of any description were available at the time (though this was something I experimented with later) but we did try other things. Word had it that aspirins mixed with Coke would give you a high of some description, so I went down a back laneway to gobble down half a bottle of aspirin with a load of Coca Cola. I didn't get drunk or high, but I was extremely sick for a week.

We then procured some cider. Local travellers told us to line our stomachs with dry bread to soak up the alcohol and keep it in our systems for longer, which we did and subsequently enjoyed mad drunkenness. Using our *Fortunes in Formulas* book we attempted to make our own cider with apples stolen from the local Franciscan monastery. We squeezed them and fermented the juice, but unfortunately although the end result was alcoholic, it was also poisonous, and made us all sick.

However, as a lad, the only thing that retained my passion was the sea. Talk of ships and oceans always fascinated me and water lay in every direction around our home. The River Corrib, which flows from Lough Corrib and the Connemara Mountains, meandered its way past our house on its way to the sea. Two miles over the hill were Galway Bay, the Aran islands and then nothing else but the wild Atlantic until the shores of America.

Sailing beat school any day and I wanted to run away to sea. One story that had a deep influence on me was Joshua Slocum's solo circumnavigation of the globe between 1895 and 1898, beautifully told in his book *Sailing Alone around the World*.

Slocum's fascinating account of his voyage in a relatively old and inexpensive boat really fired my imagination. Although I was generally contemptuous of books (excluding *Fortunes in Formulas*, they were only for swats, squares and grade hunters), I made an exception for maritime tales and read all of the old classics. My interest in everything that floated was more than just the physical aspect of being on the water, it represented freedom, adventure and travel to faraway places. I thought the sea was an education; my parents thought the Jesuit fathers were a better choice. Unfortunately school brought out the worst in me. I hated it.

I went first to Scoile Fhursa and then later the Jesuit-run Coláiste Iognáid, both Irish-speaking schools. The language was not a problem for me, but the system and the attempts at discipline were. I was the classic contrarian for the entire time that I was there. While most children are excited by the prospect of learning or school, after my first exposure to blackboards and lessons my reaction was the very opposite.

At Coláiste Iognáid, I joined the rowing club and was coxswain for many schoolboy crews. I once again found myself with lads three and four years older, and because I was smaller and lighter, was the perfect person to call time and steer as they rowed.

In 1971 word got out that a group was coming together to form a sailing club. The first meeting took place in Corinthians Rugby Football Club. I went along and was somewhat nervous among the strangers and older men, but somebody bought me a pint and I knew that I had really grown up. This was my first experience of being around what was known as 'real men', a customary term that was used to describe traditional people and was not intended in any sexist way.

These men agreed that two Mirror sailing dinghy kits – which we would build ourselves – were necessary to start the club, and made the decision that night to purchase them. Following in the footsteps of these men, I later built my own Mirror dinghy from a kit and gave it the ignominious name of *Crubeen*, being a pig's trotter (deep fried crubeens were once a popular dish in Irish chippers but are now, perhaps mercifully, less available).

This rowing club was pretty much the limit of what I was interested in at school as the rest of my time was a constant battle against the rules. Since Coláiste Iognáid was an Irish-speaking school, rugby was banned and we were supposed to devote ourselves to Gaelic games only. For that reason I set up a rugby team with some others and got people from clubs outside the school to provide us with coaching. Just to spite our headmaster we entered, and actually won, the school's cup in rugby – it was one of the great victories for us.

However, once again I was punching above my weight. Even though I was smaller I wasn't scared of a fight and that was important in schools' rugby. It was always a help going into a game if the guys were afraid of you.

Of course, had the school banned hurling and enforced rugby, we would have been super hurlers instead. It was just the psychology of it that spurred us on, the doing of what one was not supposed to do.

'A trouble maker, a biteen daft,' was how one of the priests described me. 'A fly in the ointment,' he added.

In retrospect, I was really bucking against authority of any description. On several occasions I was expelled, though each time ways were found to get me taken back. It was a real hallmark of liberalism on the part of the school that they put up with me for all those years. Even so, I wouldn't describe myself as being a rebel. I just was what I was.

Stubborn? Definitely. Wrong-minded? Perhaps. A rebel? Not really. Rebels usually have a cause to fight for. I didn't, I was just very, very obstinate. Punishments were no deterrent, no matter how rigorously they were enforced, until the headmaster got wise and realised how much I liked the school's rowing club. He banned me from the club and for a while succeeded in disciplining me, a bit.

Eventually I went too far. I played a low trick on a teacher I didn't like, and the headmaster insisted that I apologise to her. Being the stubborn one I refused point blank. I was expelled and told that the school would not entertain me again until I gave an apology.

I refused, and that was the start of a deadlock. There was no physical punishment, no loud lectures, no excommunication. I was not going to be allowed to finish my education until I said sorry. To keep up appearances to my parents, I left the house every morning and instead of going to school I headed off to the rowing club or the docks instead, and was quite happy. After three months, however, I was found out and was put under pressure from all sides to go back and give an apology.

It was the most difficult thing I had ever done in all my life, but I went back and apologised to the teacher. To this day I regard it as the best lesson I learned during my school days. It is the simplest thing in the world to say 'I'm sorry', and when you are wrong you must recognise that you are wrong, you cannot be stubborn. When I apologised it was like a burden had been lifted. I never admitted it at the time, not to anybody, but deep down I knew I had been at fault and accepting that fact was the only right thing to do. But it took several months to force me into that situation, and even then it didn't come to me naturally.

However, things didn't change. Because of my months of truancy, I did very badly in my Intermediate Cert and in the last year and a half of school realised that, unless I studied very hard, I'd have to go out and work when all my peer group were going to college. I'd have to enter the real world and take probably the first job that came along, which was not a comfortable thought. I felt that without further education I would be nothing. Seventeen-year-old kids don't necessarily want to confront this type of situation, but I could see a dead-end job in store for me and I dreaded it. So for the eighteen months before my Leaving Cert I studied as hard as I possibly could.

Although my schoolwork up to that point had been atrocious, I had never considered myself to be stupid. Unsurprisingly though, the headmaster did. Working out what I needed for college, I decided to take the honours level Mathematics course because it was worth twice as many points as other subjects. When I presented myself in the class, the headmaster had a fit. 'Get out of the room!' he told me, 'You don't have the intelligence, you'll hold the other boys back!'

Contrary as ever, I was determined to prove him wrong. I caught up and finished at the top of my class.

However, I was still willing to cause myself problems and in the last few weeks of term I brought a cow in from the fields and put it in the teachers' toilet where it promptly shat everywhere. I was expelled yet again and started a school strike.

A group of other lads and I were all standing outside the railings when the headmaster strode out to us. Through the railings he fixed me with a steely eye. 'Report to my office right away, young man,' he said with a barely concealed rage.

'I will not,' I replied.

The headmaster turned so red I thought a seizure was imminent. 'Why not?' he managed to get through gritted teeth.

'You've expelled me. I'm outside the school grounds and outside your jurisdiction.'

And outside the school I remained, because there was only a short time before the Leaving Cert examinations. The Jesuits and my teachers were very tolerant though, and I was allowed to return to school to sit the exams.

Despite all of my shenanigans during those years, I still managed to get all the points I needed for college.

This happened because I'm lucky enough to have a good grasp of abstract concepts. For instance, while I wasn't good at ordinary level mathematics, I was good at the honours level because it was more theoretical. I was never a big detail person. Not that I couldn't do detail, but what I really enjoyed was the big picture, or the more strategic-type stuff. Pretty much what I practise in business now.

Irrespective of all the unruly activity myself and the other kids got up to, I never felt like I belonged. I didn't feel a strong comradeship at all and I used to think that I was the odd man out – that I was not destined to have any friends or be with people of a like mind. It was only later when I ventured out into the bigger world that I realised that there were other people like me. As a teenager, however, it isn't always possible to see these things clearly, which is why life can sometimes be so tough at that age. When I was an adolescent, life looked strange to me, and I still think of it as a never-ending tightrope walk.

I was accepted into college, and while my family couldn't afford to pay the fees because of my father's illness, I did well enough in my grades to receive a grant.

Therefore, in September 1972, I started a degree course in Engineering at University College Galway.

Chapter four

Alcohol, the Army and Academics

I chose engineering purely because that's what my father had done. In truth I really didn't know what I wanted to do with my life, professionally or otherwise. Although I always had a mechanical bent (I did enjoy breaking things apart to see how they worked), I quickly found engineering too narrow an area for my liking. Scientific and technical modules didn't do it for me and halfway through first term I switched to a Bachelor of Commerce degree, mostly because I had fallen for a girl doing the course.

It was a good choice for me because the arts subjects were far more liberal than engineering, and I enjoyed it much more – just don't ask me about the girl!

Unlike school, I thrived in the liberal academic world of college. There was no discipline to rebel against, and as a long-haired freaky student I was free to indulge all of my pursuits. Within months, I had formed a sailing club, complete with a grant from the college authorities, so I got to continue with my first passion.

But I kept up with many things other than sailing. In fact there was little that I was not involved in, ranging all the way from chess to student politics. I joined the mountaineering club and on Sundays went off climbing in beautiful Connemara. I was accused of being lucky – with raffles, exams and such things – but this was because I would try or chance anything.

You can't expect good luck if you never take chances. To be lucky you've got to put yourself in a position where you can be lucky in the first place. If you're not in you can't win, and you'll never find out unless you try – that's my simple philosophy.

However, in other ways I was a loner, combining a massively extrovert personality with a very introverted side that was only happy out on the sea.

Whether it was climbing or swimming or running, I always took a somewhat perverted delight in pushing myself to the limits of physical endurance. Sometimes this took unusual forms – one of my lesser claims to fame at that time was coming third in the annual pub crawl competition. Held during Rag Week for charity, it was regarded by many as a prestigious event and the winners were pointed out to strangers with awe. 'That's the fella. He must have a stomach like a mop and a helluva plumbing system.'

The pub crawl was three miles around the heart of Galway, with a full pint being drunk in each of the seven pubs. Each team carried its drinker (yours truly in the case of my team) on a stretcher and the individual could neither run nor puke, under pain of disqualification. Whether the tradition is still being honoured today I don't know, but for all the crowds and tension back then it might as well have been the Olympics. Though the only really Olympian thing about the pub crawl was the training. It was the culmination of days and hours of preparation, first with water and then with beer, to extend stomach capacity. I practised by knocking back pints of the old H2O as an economy measure. Beer cost money.

I also tried to be innovative regarding the transport. (Not surprisingly, given the way students think, everyone cheated as much as they could get away with.) Cute as bedamned, I arranged to have an airbed on my stretcher. It was the bumping that upset the stomach, and I felt that a good suspension system would absorb the shocks.

Perhaps I should have stayed with engineering.

On the day of the pub crawl, we hungrily awaited the signal to go, and with it we raced off with the cheers following us. After a short cut, unnoticed by officials, we were in the lead, roaring and shouting and urging the stretcher-bearers on like Egyptian overseers at their slaves. In a very short space of time I was rapidly losing count of those great pints, lined up ready for us at each bar and looking bigger and bigger with each stop. In the end the bouncing took effect and I threw up discreetly in a telephone box so that the judges wouldn't see, and roared home to glory to take third place.

Maybe it was better that we didn't win. Cruelly the first prize was a barrel of beer, which the drinker was incapable of enjoying because of his condition.

I did better in another Rag Week competition, the boatless boat race, which took place on the old canal. Having established an early reputation as an expert in boating affairs, I felt my pride was very much at stake. My secret weapon consisted of two plastic drainpipes with a car seat lashed on top, driven by a one-manpower engine, dressed in pyjamas for a streamlined effect and using canoe paddles. The competition included a Mini car tied to big barrels and a man desperately keeping above water by means of 150 balloons that burst one by one as the race progressed.

My fiercely competitive nature combined with my knowledge of maritime affairs meant that it's safe to say I kicked their asses.

Because of the financial situation at home, it was necessary for me to work my way through college. I took any job I could in Galway, and during the summers, worked in London in pubs or whatever else. Odds and sods really.

It was in London at the age of seventeen that I first heard of getting a 'start'. Brian Lynch, a friend of mine and now an eminent west of Ireland solicitor, told me a story and I immediately filed it away under the valuable lessons section of my brain.

We had all heard that if you got to London's Cricklewood Corner by six in the morning, and if you looked big and tough you could get a 'start' from a 'ganger' (a foreman). If they liked the look of you, you were invited up onto the back of a truck and driven to a building site where you would work for twelve hours. It was a very tough job but you could make £100 a day – a fortune to us at that time.

Brian dressed the part as a hardened site labourer, big boots and dirty clothes, and got there by six. There were lots of men, tough looking tobacco-chewing types, all standing around. Trucks came quickly, filled up with labourers and disappeared off to the sites.

In the midst of all this commotion, Brian went around asking, 'Do you want a start?'

He got a series of grunts in return.

'How much?' some asked.

'£100 a day.'

'Fine.' The deal was sealed.

The trucks came and went until they didn't come anymore. The men who had said 'fine' to Brian stood around him.

Then the penny dropped. Brian realised that a 'start' was an *offer* of work, not the person looking for work, and he should have been asking, 'Have you got a start?'

A small, subtle but critical difference. It was a very dangerous situation. When all concerned worked out what had happened, Brian was lucky to get away with his life, or at the very least without a severe beating. He had ruined employment chances for those labourers and he got away from Cricklewood Corner as quickly as he could.

I had always opted for less dangerous ways of making money. While still in secondary school I joined the Army Reserve, known then as

Forsa Cosanta Aitiuil or FCA, at age fifteen (you were supposed to be seventeen, but I lied). The £100 for the two weeks of annual camp was big money for us then, relatively speaking. The pay was the only reason I joined, that and the uniform (the FCA was also derogatorily known as the 'Free Clothes Association').

As teenagers we really hadn't the slightest clue as to what it was all about. You needed a great imagination to be in the FCA at that particular time. One moment you were walking along a field, the next the sergeant shouted out 'the enemy', and you ducked and you hid and you pretended that you were under fire.

Like I said, we did it for the money. I'd be lying if I said it was motivated by a sense of national duty.

Ironically, I was made a corporal in my third year of college. I'd had plenty of practice shouting commands when I was a coxswain, so it really wasn't that unusual from one point of view. I had to shout very loudly because there were no megaphones or electronic devices to assist and this developed my voice quite a bit.

But I never really wanted to lead for the sake of it – it was just something that came with the job. I also agreed to be a corporal to get more money, basically, as the higher the rank the more you got.

However, I did do a competent job. At the end of one annual camp, my team was clearly out-performing the others in the military skills competition. Thinking things were fine, I got permission to go early and my team fell apart – without my leadership, they were lost. I felt guilty about it later, but not too much.

I can honestly say that I never connected with the military culture in the slightest and regarded the army as idiotic. To my mind, it was an extreme waste of resources and a waste of energy. Whatever the justification for war, I still consider the military culture to be quite a self-defeating and pointless way of thinking. I have no ideals about military service and no macho attitudes. I never saw it as serving my country.

However, it did teach me how to march and they knocked a little bit of contrariness out of me, which I suppose was a good thing.

The highlight of my military career happened on guard duty in a field in Cleggan in Connemara. I was on twenty-four hour duty with all the fellows in C Company, which was the Irish-speaking unit.

Straight out of a Spike Milligan script, these defenders of Ireland decided to have a farting competition. They all got cranked up by eating onions and turnips and everything else and then there was a big competition between a Sergeant Hanly and a Corporal Joyce. Hanly trained his arse to whistle and he had the loudest and sharpest fart, while Joyce had a long slow gurgling one, so he could fart longer.

I can't actually remember who won. To cap it all, in December of my first year in college I was offered a cadetship. That probably sounds crazy in the light of everything I have just said, but I wanted to go to sea and at the time the army and naval service were combined.

I felt lucky to have been selected because it was an incredibly competitive process, and I thrived on anything that was competitive. But I handled the interview well because I immediately picked out the psychologist on the panel, decided what they were looking for and fed them the sort of clichéd answers they wanted to hear. Having come through the mind-crushing experience of school, I knew all there was to know about how the system worked. I had the military selection procedure figured out and exploited it to the hilt.

However, by the time the naval service got back to me to say that I had been successful, I was already settled into a relatively carefree life in university. Being in the laid-back environment of university and faced with the choice of going into a strict hierarchy, which values obedience above anything else, and staying put, I had to think seriously about whether or not I wanted to take it up. I turned it down, which in retrospect may have been a mistake because of the great education you receive in the naval service. I later regretted the decision because I would have been paid a salary going to university, though I would have had to leave for a year before going back, and I would have returned to University College Galway because that is where the cadets take their academic courses.

It still remains a regret, but sometimes that's the way life is.

Whether I actually would have undertaken a military life, having been commissioned, is another question. To be honest, I imagine that I would have done my stint, even if I could have resigned on finishing the degree. But there is no doubt that the military life would have grated on me. I didn't like the distinction between 'them' and 'us' regarding officers and enlisted personnel. That's part of the army psychology and is different to running a good organisation.

In the army, you need a lot of stupid people and a few smart people to lead them. When the smart people tell them what to do, the stupid people do it without thinking. Fine if you want to send people to their deaths perhaps, but I don't think it's a way you can or should run a modern organisation. It's demeaning to those receiving the orders and it also doesn't work – particularly in the service-type businesses that I'm involved with.

The entrepreneur is often more of a coach than a big chief. For starters, you're trying to attract people better than you in particular areas, and therefore it can't be a direct command structure, as in 'I speak, you do'. That's why organisations have many specialised executive posts in marketing, finance, human resources, administration, and so on. As the chief executive you cannot start issuing orders to specialists when you aren't as qualified as they are.

In reality, you've got to give your executives the freedom to make decisions and develop themselves. Of course, you can never run things entirely by committee either, someone has to give the order at the end of the day. But having given a general directive, there is a world of difference between allowing others to decide how to achieve that target and adopting a military-style approach based on absolute domination and absolute submission. The first approach, which is my own style, allows others to develop themselves as professionals and human beings.

Probably the most pertinent job I had in my college days was that of a photographer. I invested in a Polaroid camera when they were new on the market and I used it to take snapshots of tourists and then sell the photos to them.

I had a great trade at Christmas when I set myself up with Santa Claus. All the kids would come along to see Santa and sit on his lap. Then all the mothers would come along to see their kid on Santa's lap. Then I would come along and take a snap of the kid with Santa and sell it to the mother.

Although photography was not going to be how I made my livelihood, the whole experience with the Polaroid still followed the same principles of business. You see a market for a service and you provide that service in return for cash. In this case, I had to invest in equipment before I could exploit the opportunity, but the camera and film quickly paid for themselves.

Thankfully, however, my college costs were lower because I lived at home.

So when all the boozing, the socialising, the competitions, the societies and the part-time jobs were done with, there was only thing left to do. Study.

In the commerce degree we had a broad range of subjects – and we also had a broad range of lecturing styles. The greatest memory I have of any academic I heard in UCG was sociology lecturer Michael D. Higgins, now a serving politician.

It was my first encounter with a lecturer who had a real personality. He always arrived late for the lecture, but he arrived unusually late one morning at thirty minutes past the hour instead of the usual fifteen. We were sick of waiting by then so we were all just leaving the building when he came racing along.

He was hanging out of the back of a car, looking as if he was still recovering from a night on the town. But, despite appearances, he still found the energy to whisk us all back into class and give us the most brilliant lecture we ever had, especially since we found sociology so difficult to grasp.

The quality of the lecturing in the university varied greatly. Michael D. knew what he was talking about because he was an active politician and could relate his theoretical knowledge with what was happening in society. Along with Michael D., we had an expert in commercial law whose lectures were just as informative, probably because he was also a practising lawyer. It was the same with psychology, we had a particularly good lady who had also worked professionally.

It was the full-time academics who were disconnected from reality. Some of the courses in college were awful, because those who were teaching them didn't know or care about the subject. These were professors of business who knew shag-all about industry. We didn't know it at the time, but their courses were just a load of academic crock, spouted by people who had never worked in the real world, or had any intention of ever doing so.

If you want any proof of this mentality, go to the ex-communist bloc. In central Europe the same professors who were teaching the marvels and ideals of the communist world are now teaching the marvels and ideals of the capitalist world.

The very same guys!

As it turned out, I didn't have much difficulty in passing my finals. It was in fact much easier than the Leaving Cert.

A lot of students had, and still do have, a problem adjusting to all the freedom of college, but I thrived in the campus environment because of my self-discipline. University was an out-of-the-box-type of thing. Your work had to conform to what the lecturers were saying and they passed you. They had no choice, because what I gave them in my exam papers was only what they had told me in the lecture hall. This wasn't the most scholarly attitude I'm afraid, but it sufficed for what I wanted. I wasn't interested in academic excellence, I wanted to get my piece of paper and then make it in the real world.

In the business approach, you've got to understand that things are target oriented. You must get the job done. Of course academic discipline is necessary to stand back and look at processes, but I still think that a lot of the academic world is not embedded in commercial reality. As the saying goes, those who can't do, teach.

Universities are decentralised organisations that operate within a chaotic environment. Beyond basic methodology there are few standards that can be applied to academic excellence, no one can say what will work or not. You simply have to formulate the theory and then check it out. This chaos leads to harsh self-selection within the disciplines (academics spend all of their time attempting to disprove each other's work) and ultimately the production of sound academic theory.

When I decided to write this book, I got some academic textbooks on entrepreneurship, and found one book in particular that was so convoluted, so analytical, that I just gave up. At that stage, I realised that entrepreneurship is a thing that's virtually impossible to teach because there is an inescapable human element at the heart of it which cannot be manufactured – and that's the desire to excel.

You cannot recreate the hunger, the passion, the need to succeed. No amount of theoretical abstraction or analysis can transfer that to a student. An awful lot of business teaching is looking at something in hindsight, handing out case studies that analyse the activities of the entrepreneur after the events are long since concluded. But you cannot simply copy all the time. It is not a paint-by-numbers profession. Sure, you can see a good business idea in one country and try it out in another, but the way that you execute your business model will be entirely dependent on your style, your approach and your attitude. And that's only to begin with. Different countries will have different cultures, legislation and tastes. The true entrepreneur has to do a lot more than copy.

If you compare entrepreneurs, very few are the same. There are common traits that have been isolated, certain characteristics that are common across the board. These are usually features of a strong personal character – willpower, determination, competitiveness, charisma, and so on. Academics have identified these qualities, but they cannot create a textbook that teaches a student how to have them, to make that student a successful entrepreneur. I mean how can you create a Picasso? By going to art school? No amount of technical instruction will give you that spark, or can bring out what is not there to begin with.

I understand that entrepreneurship is currently a fashionable subject in the academic world, and that some third-level institutions claim that it is something they can teach to their students. Like many things academic, it probably makes a good theoretical subject, but I'm very sceptical of the success of these courses. I'm not saying that they are entirely unnecessary, because the alternative is do nothing. All you can do is lay the foundations, communicate the essentials and reduce the risk of something going wrong. Without doubt it would be better to have one student out of a hundred prevail with the help of what she or he learned in class than to have them not bother to do it at all. Especially when that one student may go on to employ thousands of others.

But it's not a science, and there are no dictums that can be learned off by heart and then applied to all situations.

Consider the following.

Heat water to 100° Celsius and it boils and produces steam, a pure and simple scientific fact. One follows the other.

Release *Playboy* magazine in every country in the world and it will enjoy exactly the same market share. Not true. One does not follow the other, even if you copied all of your procedures perfectly from country to country. In fact if you did that, you'd definitely fail.

In business, the creative art has to be recognised. The societies where it is recognised, respect and understand that they will produce great entrepreneurs, because those entrepreneurs will be able to devote themselves more fully to setting up businesses. If the society is disrespectful or derogatory towards entrepreneurs, then the entrepreneur has to devote a good part of his or her energy negotiating with one needless obstacle after another, usually in the form of negative attitude – either of an individual or organisation.

In Ireland, entrepreneurship was traditionally looked down upon. When I started in University College Galway, it was the ones that did the BComm who were no good, while the people who did languages and arts were respected.

It's only when a society understands the dynamics of success and begins to respect it that a transformation can take place, and that's been happening in Ireland only since the mid-1990s.

Entrepreneurship is not for everyone, so it can't be institutionalised. But it is possible to avoid a society that crushes it before it can be developed. The basics can be laid down and individuals allowed to develop them.

Personally, I have to admit that I really didn't care about my studying. It wasn't all useless of course, the BComm was a good balanced degree, and parts of it kept coming back later in my business life, so I suppose it gave me some foundation. But most of what I needed to know was just common sense, and you don't have to go to university for that. Many successful businessmen haven't gone to college at all, and they don't need to either. They already understand the fundamental human relations that enable us to be manipulated as consumers. They know what we want and they give it to us – at a price.

They know what the hot buttons are that will make us want their services or products, and they know just when to launch them or withdraw them from the market. They make all of these decisions based upon their understanding of human behaviour, focusing on what we want, so that they can make a profit. You can't sell something that isn't in demand, though good salespeople can make you want a product that you didn't even know existed ten minutes before. They do this by finding out what you want, and then convincing you that you can have it by buying their product. Great business people just make this happen on the larger scale.

For me, the days in UCG were important for the social life and the liberal atmosphere. The studying was mostly a load of gobbledegook, it didn't really have a lot of relevance but I did it anyway to get my degree. In no time the unreal student days were gone and, once again, it was time to face the real world.

Maybe later.

To follow the route of my friends into accountancy or commercial offices offered no charms at all. Travel and escape were what I wanted. There were few opportunities and less money for such luxuries but somehow I had to avoid the fur-lined mousetrap. Only in insecurity and travel could I find the stimulation I wanted. Westward, chasing the sun as it set beyond the sea horizon, I went to across those Atlantic waves as my ancestors had done – and landed in a neighbouring continent.

Chapter five

Across the Atlantic...

The sea knows no nationality, despite what you might think. With two-thirds of the planet covered in ocean, there are few boundaries or frontiers other than natural ones. However, when you take a detached look at the maritime industry, it is incredibly conservative. There have been few major technological breakthroughs in the shipping or sailing world and due to the unpredictability of the ocean, which is part of its savage beauty, you never know what it will throw at you. This combination leads to a type of 'go with what you know' mentality amongst seafarers and a desire to work with the proven technologies at hand.

Despite this I believe that the sport of sailboat racing can be enjoyed by everyone. It's a sport that uses natural wind energy, deals with nature and the elements and is environmentally friendly. In spite of the tag of exclusivity, money is not a barrier to entry. Racing yachts are certainly expensive, but the average vessel will need a crew of five or more. While the person who owns the yacht pays the bills, he cannot put to sea without the rest of the crew, most of whom are just ordinary people.

A lot of what I've applied or used in business I learned whilst sailing. To win in the bigger yacht races, it is necessary to combine management skills, design, logistics, sailing ability and teamwork. It's been a gradual process, and when I started out I never considered that one might complement the other.

For the first few decades of my life sailing was an exclusive passion that I wrapped my life around, sacrificing steady jobs and a conventional career path to do so, until it became untenable. In fact, before I left Canada in my little dinghy, I tore my last dollar bill into pieces and let the breeze carry it away. It was a potent symbol of the way I would live my life for years to come.

That was in 1976 and my first solo transatlantic voyage had come about as part of a bet.

It was a cloudless, starlit night and I was crewing on a fifty-footer somewhere off Bermuda. We were going from the US to the Caribbean and I was on watch with a Mississippian called Al. We were talking about survival at sea and whether it would be possible to cross an ocean like the Atlantic in a dinghy.

I was of the opinion it could be done and was expounding my own theory. 'I'll bet you'd never have the guts to do anything like that,' Al said abruptly in his southern twang. 'You're just talking.'

Al didn't know but that was exactly the wrong thing to say to a contrarian like me. Being told that I could not to do something was often challenge enough to make me give it a try. We struck a deal right there and then on that yacht. If I succeeded I would get a bottle of whiskey.

Of course, there was more to it than that. If someone told me to step out in front of a speeding lorry, I wouldn't oblige (not unless there was something in it for me anyway). But in this case it just so happened that the idea of undertaking a maritime adventure struck a chord in me. I could be a modern-day Joshua Slocum!

Well, not quite. Slocum's voyage had a certain venerable dignity to it that mine may have lacked, but a dinghy on the Atlantic was good enough for me...

If I hadn't had the belief, the gut feeling that this could be pulled off, I would not have set out in the first place. Even so, the gut feeling has to be complemented by good research. Between part-time jobs in the US, I researched the experiences of other people who had undertaken similar sailing ventures. There's still the element of chance, the pure luck that's either good or bad, which can deflect even the best preparations, but if you research well, you will sleep better at night – believe me.

Think of an untried venture as walking the plank.

Walking the plank is so much easier if you check the water depth. Are there sharks? If so, are they man-eating? How far is it to swim ashore? Will the water be cold or warm?

For instance the popular image of Christopher Columbus is that he bravely sailed over the horizon in a valiant quest to find a new world. The truth is a little more prosaic.

For almost ten years before setting out on his first voyage of discovery, Columbus did very detailed research, much of which was gathered during sojourns along the west of Ireland. He learned the lore of the local fishermen and visited the monks, maybe to read the *Navigatio Santi Brendani Abatis (Voyage of Saint Brendan the Abbot).*

Noted on a sidebar to one of the logs Columbus kept is the story of 'mummified bodies in a dug-out Indian canoe' which arrived in Galway Bay one time, perhaps courtesy of the prevailing winds from America. The Galwegians even joke that Columbus got a road map of America before setting out.

For my own trip, I did my research and prepared my fifth-hand rubber dinghy (it had been used by MGM studios in the filming of *King Kong* and *Airport 77*) while working as a waiter in Annapolis, Maryland. Eventually, I drove with the inflatable and all my other gear loaded in the back of an old Plymouth station wagon. I might have been better researching which car to buy. It went all right, but it rattled a lot and had tyres as bald as Patrick Stewart.

The most memorable and terrifying part of the journey, in particular for the hitchhiker I picked up, was having to maintain a speed of over fifty miles an hour navigating through the very complex multi-lane highways circumnavigating Manhattan.

Eventually, I made Marblehead in Boston, and was determined to repay the banjaxed vehicle with a grand funeral at sea.

I placed a good, heavy brick on the accelerator, kicked the gearshift and watched it fart and splutter down the pier before diving into the waters where it vomited oil and gas like some decrepit drunk... Well, that was the mental image at least. An O'Coineen production through and through, it also included a dramatic gunfight, a beautiful woman and lots of corpses – none of them mine. As it turned out someone paid me $200 for the car (fool!) and Marblehead was saved from an *Exxon Valdez* -type disaster.

The last thing I did was spook the local clergyman. I asked him to bless my boat, more to see the expression on his face than for the holy protection. 'Will you bless my boat, Father? I'm setting sail for Europe...'

He kindly agreed and brought his prayer book along for a suitable benediction.

Expecting a pert yacht with well-trimmed sails, he almost fell over when he saw the rubbery thing that was waiting for him.

Thank God for religious ceremony. The priest mustered his dignity and began with a 'Bless this craft and all who sail in her...' while the rest of us stood there solemnly, biting our tongues to hold back the guffaws.

When I sailed out of Marblehead, Boston, I was certain that I would make it. Nobody else was sure, but I didn't let that stop me. To avoid being stopped by the coast guard, I chose a low-key departure that attracted no attention or publicity. It wasn't so much that the coast guard would have cared about me drowning, they just wouldn't want the expense of looking for me. Anyway, I was naive and innocent, and even if I'd wanted to generate publicity, perhaps for sponsorship and the like, I wouldn't have known how.

The one notable effort I made to drum up commercial support involved the Heinz Corporation. At the time Tony O'Reilly was the CEO of the company and the highest paid executive in the United States. I rang them up and by chance was put directly through to O'Reilly himself. Tony, hearing a few words, promptly put me through to a PR guy who, not really understanding what kind of trip I was planning, organised a supply of tinned beans for the voyage. Although the beans were probably offered in an attempt to get rid of me, I was nevertheless grateful for them.

There was a second offer of support made to me from another quarter, but I ultimately turned it down. When I stopped in Canada I met a guy who knew a guy who owned a sex shop. The sex shop guy thought that my rubber boat would make the perfect advertising vehicle for his enterprise and offered to pay me to carry the name of his establishment.

The costs of my voyage were minimal, so I didn't really need the money. Furthermore when you are doing something for sponsorship there has to be some rationale to the relationship. Racing sponsorship is all about benefit, what's in it for the other person. When I was young and inexperienced my attitude was 'give me, give me, give me', but the response was, 'Well, fine, but what do I get, what do I get, what do I get?' I learned then it was a transaction, if you can identify what you can give, then you will get.

For someone to sponsor you going off on your own across the Atlantic in a small inflatable really makes no sense. In fact it might even be considered irresponsible due to the high risk involved. However, the sex shop owner was not concerned about my failure. In fact, he was counting on it. He wanted to pay me to carry his advertising on the bottom of my craft because he was convinced that when I capsized the name of his shop would be beamed all over the world during the rescue...

Enter noise of helicopter rotors. Excited journalist shouts into television camera to be heard above the din:

'We are now hovering over the mid-Atlantic where rescue vessels are desperately trying to haul twenty-one year old Irishman Enda O'Coineen from the freezing waters. I think we can see him now. Yes. Yes. There he is. Clinging to what looks like the bottom of his dinghy. And wait, there's something written on the boat. We're zooming in now. Wait for it. It's, it looks like, I think... *Joe's Sex Shop.*'

I didn't take the sponsorship. I could have done with the money but there were certain levels that even I wasn't desperate enough for, including portraying myself as the best customer of a sleazy haunt. But it was a good example of opportunism on the owner's part.

When I departed Canada, I launched myself into the Atlantic. The ordeal that followed was a moving human experience which pushed every aspect of my simple existence to the edge, mentally and physically. Much of it had to do with the complete isolation of the voyage, and while I wasn't lonely as such, the absence of human contact did have an effect. It's a thing that's difficult to explain.

For instance I'll never forget arriving in New York City on my own for the first time. Above in the skyscrapers, below in the underground, in cars and on the pavements, I was surrounded by thousands of people and yet I felt totally on my own. In fact I had never felt lonelier in my life and yet I was in the middle of all that humanity.

In my dinghy, by contrast, I was completely cut off for almost three months. I was hundreds of miles from the nearest land with nothing but the ocean on every horizon. Yet I was not lonely. It was necessary to prepare food, navigate, set sails, steer, and so on. The psychological aspect was the most challenging, just becoming used to my own company for so long.

The massive failure came almost two months later, some 300 miles off the south-west corner of Ireland. Having been at sea alone for forty-six days and almost home, I was overconfident. I relaxed my guard and was capsized.

To this day I can still hear the sound of that massive, rolling wave which flipped me into the night-time waters and trapped me in darkness. But my survival instincts and will to live are strong. I couldn't get my dinghy right-side up again, but I was able to climb up on its belly and turn on a compact Emergency Position Indicator Beacon.

The EPIB, new to the market and given to me by a friend, saved my life. A transatlantic flight picked up the signal and a Nimrod Jet took off from Scotland to find me. I was picked up by a ship belonging to the NATO war fleet that, when not protecting the free-market world from the communists, also fished crazy Irishmen and their MGM dinghies out of the drink.

I later found myself sipping tea in the wardroom of a British warship where I was treated like an officer and gentleman. Even if my vessel was only sixteen feet in length, and it had to be inflated even for that, I was the captain and naval etiquette demanded that I be treated as such. I was accommodated in an officer's cabin and spent a week at sea on naval exercises. It was a glimpse of what my life might have been like had I taken the cadetship with the Irish navy years before.

The royal navy picked up my dinghy as well and, once it was recovered, I cheekily asked that they let me re-inflate it and put me back into the sea. I was very persuasive and the Dutch commodore of the fleet flew over from his ship to consider my request. It then went back to the HQ in London, who answered with an emphatic 'No'. They believed that they would look like idiots if they were subsequently forced to re-rescue me.

My great failure made newspaper headlines around the world. I suppose when I think about it the story was a little bizarre...

There were many, many things that flowed from that failure. In fact failure can sometimes be more successful than success itself. I remain convinced that had I completed that additional 300 miles and made the landfall at Kilronan in the Aran Islands, hardly anyone would have noticed.

That would have been just fine too. I would have been more than delighted to complete the master plan of landing on the beach, pulling the dinghy ashore and going up to *Tí Dalaigh* (House of Daly, as it was then) for a pint of Guinness and ringing my mother to say I was almost home.

After my attempt on the Atlantic, I was something of a celebrity, a non-hit-wonder more than a one-hit-wonder, so to speak. My name was in the papers and I was on television a few times, but it was over and done with in a flash and I was glad. Readjustment back to normal life was a difficult process and I learned that, while your name might be in the media, all that matters is what you achieve within your own spirit.

In cash terms, I ended with £1,000 from the proceeds of newspaper articles. To my simplistic understanding of money at the time, this was a fortune. I could now indulge my only materialistic ambitions in life – to own a grandfather clock, a tandem bicycle and a Morris Minor.

I bought the latter and hoped to get back into the swing of things by doing the ordinary stuff that other twenty-two-year old guys were doing. Having a girlfriend for instance... I was at a ceilí in Connemara when I found *the* girl. She was dancing away in a light dress, nineteen years old and beautiful. She had a chirpy personality and I was smitten.

She must have liked me too because we danced together to the 'Walls of Limerick', 'The Siege of Ennis', and other jigs, reels and hornpipes. I asked if I could walk her home. Siobhan (I think that was her name) said yes.

I'll never forget walking that country road. It was crisp and cool, but not cold. The dew was out, the air was pure, sounds were gentle and everything was silver from the half-moon above. We held hands and talked about each other's families, our interests and all the other innocent chatter that comes before an intimate episode.

Then a youngster – I'm not sure if it was male or female – called from behind a stone wall.

'*Sin é, sin é...*' ('There he is, there he is...')

I wanted to wring the kid's neck. He or she had a piercing tone that would have sliced granite and it was ruining our moment.

'*Sin é an fearr, sin é an 'lunatic' a chuaigh trasna on 'tAtlantic' san báidín rubbair!*' (' That's the man, that's the lunatic, who went across the Atlantic in a little rubber boat!')

With that, my fragile young love left me as fast as Shergar, never to be seen or heard from again. The little git who had pointed me out ran off laughing and I was left there on my own on an empty Connemara road that no longer felt gentle, pure or romantic.

Perception is everything. Some had considered my crossing as a great adventure. Others a contribution to the research of safety at sea. (Yes, that's right, safety at sea. Read the back of *The Unsinkable Kilcullen*, the book I wrote on my adventure.) To the denizens of Connemara it was utter lunacy.

There and then I realised that I was not headed for normality. Where I grew up, the average person who did strange things was called a lunatic. Of course if the person were wealthy and did the same thing, they were called an eccentric. I was going to have to endure the lunacy label until I could make some money.

Now if you're an entrepreneur a more positive way to view things is this: You're in place. But nobody else is ...

In society we need rules to govern ourselves, to keep balance and a minimum of civility. But rules should not be there to trap us, or to repress us or to make us conform. Of course we are self-censuring as well, we often subscribe to fashions and norms just because it's easier. One side-effect of our increased communication and globalisation is that the scope to depart from the norm is decreasing. Global branding and the domination of the media by wealthier countries is all part of that.

Entrepreneurs are change makers. We are creators, we are catalysts. We question the *status quo* and we make new things born of our imaginations a reality. We are unpopular. We are hard to understand. We are irritating.

I for one have definitely found myself under suspicion on more than one occasion. Those who distrust you may not even realise they do, but unconsciously or otherwise their actions towards you are negative.

Sooner or later, entrepreneurs find themselves having to deal with things by themselves.

If you can get somebody to come with you, great. But in my case there were not a lot of people interested in joining me at the age of twenty-one for a crazy voyage from Boston to Galway in a rubber dinghy.

Even though I'd sailed nearly 3,000 miles, the reputation that was attached to me was one of failure. 'And now we have the man who nearly made it across the Atlantic!'

These were the words of a yacht club commodore introducing me before to a lecture I was about to give. Polite laughter followed from the audience, but inside I was burning. The words were a red rag to my pride and bullish sentiments, especially since I had crossed the Atlantic on small boats several times since then, including a twenty-one-footer in the 1979 single-handed transatlantic race, or mini-transat as it's known.

For that competition, it had been a struggle even to get as far as the start line. I had sold everything I owned, sailed my boat 2,000 miles to qualify just to stand in a mixed group of loners to meet Penzance officials. Days later, I was alone in the middle of the ocean, thinking what a daft competition it was. 'Here I am, all alone, racing against competitors I cannot see. The real competition will be with myself and the elements'.

Then my mast broke and to get back into the next leg of the race from the Canaries to the Caribbean in two days I had to network and lobby like never before. The only way to get the new mast to me was to approach the vice-president of the Spanish airline Iberia.

Although I looked like crap, I was introduced to him at a reception in the plush Club Rio Nautico de Tenerife and I persuaded him to use his influence to speed the mast from Heathrow to Tenerife.

When I got the mast, I flagged down a small truck in the middle of the street, convinced the driver – a complete stranger – to help me transport it. I also got help from customs officials and the Irish consul to get the mast into the country legally, before having a run-in with the Spanish cops which needed further diplomatic assistance.

When the yacht club commodore made his witty introduction, I realised that unless I had another go in a similar dinghy, I would be stuck with the stigma of failure for the rest of my life. Enda O'Coineen – the great failure of the Atlantic. Or if you were speaking to a Connemara person, 'an lunatic mór...'

It was not a label I was prepared to endure so I knuckled down to organising my next transatlantic attempt.

My approach to the bank would have to be subtle if I was to get a loan to cover the cost of the new dinghy. I'm uncomfortable with lies, so if the bank manager asked me what I needed it for I'd just have to give it straight.

I had the new boat on the back of a trailer outside the bank when the manager came to inspect it. 'It's a grand boat,' I said to him. 'You could even cross the Atlantic in it and I might give it a try.' He nodded away absently, taking it as a joke.

My conscience was satisfied.

Again there were the usual preparations and my second attempt, in 1985, had its fair share of scares. Now people might think that when you undertake hazardous ventures that you have no fear to start with but I can say that, in my case at least, that's totally untrue.

Wherever there's risk there has to be fear. We fear for good reasons most of the time and we should heed the feeling. The moment you become over-confident and lose your fear is the moment you take a fall. Fear is healthy when channelled in the right way, and fear and nervousness even in a business situation is good because it makes you sharper. Anybody who says they aren't afraid or aren't nervous in any situation won't survive. Fear is part of human nature and a survival instinct in itself.

This time, I made it.

I capsized along the way, but there was no rescue required because I had a self-righting device on the boat. As for the other hardships, it all came down to single-minded stubbornness. Never give up.

I had achieved the first west–east crossing by inflatable, but in many respects being the first mattered the least of all. When I crawled back up on land and fell asleep in a real bed for the first time in months, I was putting more than my physical body to rest. I was letting go of a decade of inner conflict and a burden of failure. When I awoke the next day, I could make a new start with new plans.

I never did get that bottle of whiskey from Mississippi Al either, but I'm still hopeful. The bottle is now over twenty-five years old, and it should taste pretty sweet – sweeter even than the look on his face should he hand it over.

As I suspected, my successful voyage did receive far less attention than my failure a few years before. But the international media had far bigger fish to fry that year when Richard Branson's *Virgin I* went down off the Scilly Isles near Cornwall in a failed attempt to win the Blue Riband trophy.

I happened to have personal contact with the *Virgin I* navigator, a man called Dag Pyke, because he wrote for a boating magazine which I owned at the time (I'll describe later how I came to own it). Because of the contact, it seemed like a good idea to me to get some Irish involvement in Branson's next trans-Atlantic attempt.

The big challenge was getting a clean and quick fuel supply – several hundred gallons of it – some 500 miles off the coast in the rolling Atlantic swells. To do that required a suitable vessel to be on station for over six weeks while the *Virgin II* team waited in New York for the proper weather window.

The Irish naval service seemed perfect for the job, so I asked Defence Minister Paddy Cooney to join me for lunch. It was questionable whether he'd make time for someone of my credentials, so I also invited the adventurer and author Tim Severin to join us. That made it an attractive offer and Paddy accepted.

Over lunch, I outlined how the Irish could gain in promotional terms by assisting *Virgin II*. I had already researched the details with some naval operations people to see if it could be done, so my suggestions were not just empty waffling.

The minister heard me out. 'Sure,' he said, 'the naval service will be happy to help.' Having received his permission, I still had to get the whole plan through formal channels and other civil servants before it could be properly stamped and signed by him. However, had I started with proper channels it would never have gone anywhere. To seal the refuelling deal, I met Branson himself at the Southampton Boat Show, which we had jointly been invited to officially open. I was the man who had just made it across the Atlantic in a dinghy, while Branson had tried in his big motorboat and sank. After the show, I was invited back to the barge where he lived – before it too sprung a leak and went down.

Virgin I made great news while nobody much cared about my story. However, seeing just how popular Richard Branson had become reminded me of the paradox of failure and success.

He had failed, but he had failed spectacularly, glamorously and valiantly – and that made him a hero.

The next thing to do was to get Branson to Dublin to nail down the details for the refuelling, not yet public, and open the Dublin Boat Show. The same evening I had been invited to appear as a guest on the *Late Late Show* where the whole idea was that I had succeeded where Branson had failed.

However, when I mentioned that I could get Richard Branson for them, RTÉ nobly gave me the flick and Branson was invited in my place – Failure 1, Success 0.

In truth he made great television and was better than I would have been, most notably for his wild card market research. In the middle of the show he made a declaration.

'I'll fly people Dublin to London at £50 a head – provided Aer Lingus do not screw me up on the landing charges.'

'But Mr Branson, it's Aer Rianta who run the airport.'

'Oh, right.'

'Would that be Irish pounds or sterling?'

'Irish pounds,' Branson replied, clearly not realising there was a difference.

So the rate became £55 from Dublin to London, making the headlines in all the newspapers the following morning. The duopoly of British Airways and Aer Lingus had the market in such a way that they could charge four times the amount. To the Irish public, who were leaving the country in droves for work abroad, Branson was no less than a saviour.

Walking down O'Connell Street, the English entrepreneur was also struck by the large number of young people in the capital. On the basis of this, he made two decisions, to provide a budget airline service and a Virgin store for the Irish market. In that twenty-four-hour visit in winter of 1985, Branson committed to launching two major enterprises that otherwise would not have happened. That's one hell of a gut feeling to have in such a short time.

The point is that he went with his instincts. There is a market – let's do it. To be properly financed, his business plan would, of course, require detailed analysis and preparation, but it was his exposure to Ireland that acted as a catalyst. Expanding into Ireland is a common enough strategy for British enterprises, but had the company based its decision on market research alone two things would have happened.

- First they never would have got a real feeling of the market.
- Second every company would have moved at the same time.

If you don't grab, you don't get, and when you see an opportunity and that opportunity speaks to you – really speaks to you – you've got to go with it. This mightn't appear like rational argument, but isn't life a lot more fun when you do what you like? It's the same as a relationship. Nobody can account for taste, no one can say why one person is attractive to another person and simultaneously unattractive to someone else again. But you still go for the one you find attractive. Kissing the unattractive person is just no fun at all!

Business is the same, go for what you like.

Getting involved with the *Virgin II* challenge must have had some kind of subconscious effect on me because in 1992 I decided to attempt my own speedboat record. Not an attempt on the Blue Riband record, that was just a teensy weensy bit beyond my resources, but a record for the fastest time around Ireland in a powerboat.

I needed partners and hooked up Dag Pyke again and then with Trevor McClintock and Wesley Armstrong. Both are from Northern Ireland, McClintock was the distributor of Smirnoff Vodka and Armstrong was one of the largest marine operators on the island. I persuaded McClintock that he could be Ireland's answer to Richard Branson. It must have struck a chord because he sponsored the boat, called the *Smirnoff Flyer*, and all three of us left from Carrickfergus.

We had four refuelling depots around the coast, including the Aran islands, organised by the secretary of the Royal National Lifeboat Institution, and the plan was to spend only fifteen minutes at each one.

VROOOOMMMMSSSSHHHH! Engines revving we raced into Kilronan, adrenaline pumping, crash helmets on and under extreme pressure to fill this sexy mother of a boat and get her going around Ireland again.

Then in true Father Ted style, the quite life of the island began to take over. Our diesel tanker was there but it was ten yards away, so we had to start the tractor to drag it down.

Chug Chug Chug...

Waiting on the pier was the island doctor, Marian Broderick (now part of the island establishment but known to me as a once-wild UCG student), the post office guy, Cauley from the lifeboats and, of course, the priest. We chatted away as Gaeilge while the tanker was being put in position.

I started writing a cheque for the diesel. 'Arrah, the ESB won't miss a few gallons,' someone said, making the electricity company one of our unknown sponsors.

Not being able to speak Irish, Pyke, McClintock and Armstrong couldn't follow any of this.

Our tank was filled and we were ready to go, but they insisted on bringing us to the best house on the island, which was the priest's house, and giving us a five-course meal. Right in the middle of our record attempt, they wanted to give us dinner.

Well it would have been impolite to refuse so we stayed for that as well. Then at the end of the meal the priest comes out and says, 'Will you have a drop of the holy water on the boat?' making my Belfast companions recoil because they thought the priest was about to bless the boat when in fact he was slipping us some poitín. That priest was quite a character and he subsequently eloped with his housekeeper.

Eventually, the islanders let us go and we finished our record, doing it in a respectable time despite having a five-course meal in Kilronan.

A few days after the event, I was with the boat in Howth and I came in alongside the marina. An Taoiseach Charlie Haughey was there on his yacht *Celtic Mist*, and he recognised the boat from the newspapers. He had been having dinner on his yacht with some of his associates, including Dublin undertaker Tom 'the last man to let you down' Stafford and election agent Pat 'vote early and often' O'Connor. Dinner was finished, but they had a few bottles of wine and invited me aboard to join them.

We talked about the trip and boats in general, a subject in which Haughey was quite interested, and then we got on to the subject of Dún Laoghaire where there was a big controversy over the construction of a marina. The smoked salmon socialists and environmentalists were all against it, while the boat people, myself included, were all for it.

Then Haughey waded in with his gravely voice. There was two things he associated with Dún Laoghaire – local TD David Andrews, and more curiously, elderly ladies.

'Andrews, that fellow Andrews... thick as two planks, I would never have him in any government of mine,' said Haughey.

Personally I admired Andrews as he was one of the few people to stand up Haughey. He is also related to me through marriage to my cousin Clare Cusack. Clare is sister of Paddy Cusack of Boomtown Rats fame. Paddy went around calling himself Pete Briquette, after the turf products, and the English consequently thought he came from France.

Anyway, Haughey rounded up on the south Dublin port with, 'Dún Laoghaire, that fucking place Dún Laoghaire never did me any good. Fucking garrison town, full of those little old ladies with their poodles walking those fucking piers, pissing on those lampposts.'

The conversation went on after a few coarse laughs but I found myself stumped by Charlie's remarks. The stuff about it being a Fine Gael stronghold I could follow, but poodles and lampposts? That made no sense.

Sometime later I was walking up the pier in Dún Laoghaire when I noticed the very many old ladies and small dogs that were about. Intrigued, I stooped down to inspect the lampposts and discovered that Haughey had been right.

*The **Green Dragon**, our iconic Irish Chinese entry in the Volvo Ocean Race.*

The unthinkable bodhrán player... With the 'Green Dragon Ceili Band' led by Micheal O'hAmhlain and sons Cormac and Angus from Innisoir of the Aran Islands. In a session on the spectator boat with Mayor Padraig Conneely of Galway, at the Volvo Ocean Race start in Alicante.

The full Let's Do it Green Dragon Racing Crew and Shore team, lined up and ready to go with Skipper Ian Walker in Alicante. From left to right: Scott Millar, Matt Gottard, Peter Tans, Lucy Harwood, Clayton Jackson, Tom Goddard, Warwick Kerr, James Carroll, Johnny Smullen, Ben Clifford, Henry Foster, Kim den Boon, Katie Watts, Jamie Boag, Johnny Mordaunt, Ann Other, Justin Slattery, Phil Harmer, Marcus Ashley Jones, Freddy Shanks, Tom Braidwood, Anthony Merrington, Andrew McLean, Guo Chuan, Damian Foxall, Ian Walker, Neal McDonald. Photo: David Branigan/Oceansport.

With Mayor Menino of Boston, Joe Fallon, Boston Volvo Host and Jamie Boag, Team CEO on a satellite link to the Green Dragon, powering through the South Pacific, we sang Happy Birthday to Skipper Ian Walker. Photo by Bill Brett.

The Lets Do It Galway organisation team, during a visit of An Taoiseach and dignitaries. Front row from left - Eamon Conneely, John Killeen, Taoiseach Brian Cowen, Enda O'Coineen, Maria Moynihan Lee, Shane Moran and Mark Lydon. Next row up from left - John Murphy, Lisa Hallinan, Garret O'Beirne, Frank Fahey TD, Eamon Bradshaw (CEO Galway Port), Neil Carney, Cienna Smyth, Craig Flaherty, Zoe O'Connell. Next row up from left - Michelle Cheeseman, Fiona Bolger, Gwen O'Sullivan, Eamon O'Cuiv TD (Minister for Community Rural and Gaeltacht Affairs) and Patrick Sweeney. Back row from left - John Concannon (Director of Regional Development Fáilte Ireland), Joe McGrath (City Manager, Galway City Council), Fiona Monaghan (General Manager, Fáilte Ireland West).

At the Galway Docks round-the-world send-off party, David Beattie, Brian Lynch and Bertie Ahern.

'Tanks? No thanks!' The infamous tanks being demolished just in time for the Volvo Ocean Race, much to everyone's relief. Photo courtesy of Connaught Tribune.

Early photographs of myself. Below in fancy dress as the 'Nutty Professor'. Real science came later with bomb-making and home made cider.

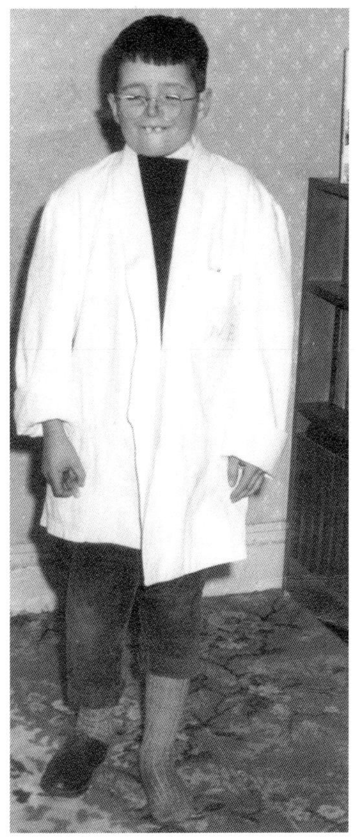

My Grandmother, Sarah Kilcullen (1883-1955) from Enniscrone, on her wedding day to my grandfather, Peter (1878-1943). His father, Cormac, left East Galway, found gold in California and was one of the few to return to Galway. The pub he founded remains in the family until recently.

Conan and John Rabbitt, in front of Tígh Chormaic - the House of Cormac - now in the family for the fifth generation. It was signed for with an 'X' by my great grandfather who bought it with a 'little gold' he found in America.

Racing my first 'yacht' on Loch Corrib, a Mirror dinghy called Crubeen.

Winning the 'Boatless Boatrace' (a car seat strapped to two Wavin pipes) during College Rage Week for charity.

A substitute for my formal university degree graduation ceremony, which took place in Cape Cod with cousin Brian Lynch.

At age 21, departing Marblehead, Boston for Ireland in my dinghy on the adventure of a lifetime as the result of a bet – and an interest in survival at sea! Guinness had supplied some of the beverage for the send-off, and the unusual haircut was the result of a bowl and scissors over my head the night before.

Having almost made it I got into difficulties off the west coast of Ireland. The RAF dropped a liferaft and a supply ship picked me up. A few years later I set out again in a similar sized inflatable and completed the voyage in under a month. Photographs courtesy of the RAF.

The metal poles really were being corroded by dog piss. So much so in fact that they had to be reinforced.

Affairs of the nation indeed.

Meeting people like Charlie Haughey, and indeed Richard Branson, Dag Pyke, Trevor McClintock, Wesley Armstrong and so many other interesting people has been a hugely enjoyable part of sailing. However I know that there will be plenty of people who will say that the only reason I made money was because I knew people in sailing circles.

To an extent these people would be right. I made tremendous contacts in the sailing network, met many people who helped along the way and made many friendships. But I never started sailing for those things specifically. I sailed because that was my passion, and all other things came from it.

However, it does underscore the importance of networking. Networking is often considered a bad word. For some it has a ring of deviousness, suggesting perhaps that you are trying to use people. For others it's cliquey and exclusive, a wall that can't be breached unless you're 'in the know' – and there's definitely some grounds for such negative connotations.

Certainly when I was younger, I used to resent very strongly the fact that people who had connections got jobs and positions while those who didn't were left on the outside. Now I understand it. Open networking is nothing more than minimising risk by bringing together people that you're comfortable dealing with.

Standardised interviews and other selection criteria, when properly and expensively done, can yield relatively significant information about potential candidates. But personal reputation is far better than this. Even if you've had a few bad experiences, and a few positions which didn't go right for whatever reason, your general abilities will be known in the communities you're active in. Particularly in this electronic age of easy, instant communication, you stand and fall by what you do.

What doesn't work is networking which is narrowly conceived and below board. If you give a job, task or business to someone as a favour, or because they're a family member or social contact, or for a backhander, then you're simply being corrupt. Nepotism and the like are ultimately unsustainable because you'll have substandard staff, substandard production and a substandard performance.

Instead you should get involved with social groups because you have a passion for whatever it is that brings those people together, not because you want to network with a lot of wealthy or connected people.

In fact the skill of the entrepreneur is being able to bring together many different elements, including different people and different types of people. And I would add, to have a whole lot of fun doing it!

Chapter six

My First Business

After my first transatlantic effort I returned to Ireland in 1980 with no money, no employment and no career. In typical style I had come back to Ireland with no plans or direction at a time when everyone else was leaving. While more exciting things were ahead of me, they were only made possible by developing my own business.

I was desperate for work, but there was just nothing out there. I had assiduously avoided career employment all my life and truth be known I was pretty much unemployable. But now I was living on social welfare with bugger all money and I would have done absolutely anything.

About that time, McDonalds was starting to build its franchise network. I decided that I wanted to get into management, and because McDonalds were an American company with good management systems, I applied for a job as a trainee manager, thinking that I could perhaps advance with them.

I was turned down, probably for being too honest about my recent background and education, my university degree having made me overqualified.

But I soon discovered that people wanted to pay me for writing about my adventures at sea, when previously I'd talked about my experiences for nothing. What little employment I had came from freelance articles sold to a wonderful chap called Norman Barry. Norman was the publisher of the boating magazine *Irish Boats and Yachting*, which was a very successful publication when it first started.

Barry was a very good guy who gave me a break, a 'start' if you like, and he later helped me kit out a boat to compete in the mini-transat race.

Although I have great respect for Norman Barry, he was journalist and PR man who had not made the transition to thinking like a businessman. For example, for the transat race, he presented me with a big sponsorship cheque, and he made sure that there was a fine photograph of it in his magazine.

What the readers didn't know was that the cheque bounced.

Traditionally many boating people in Ireland simply bought imported UK magazines. Then Barry's *Irish Boats and Yachting* entered the scene at a time when there was a booming market. However, its publisher came to be seen as somewhat arrogant and monopolistic by the marine traders, a view which I'm inclined to agree with when I consider some of the amateurism and poor business practice of the publication.

The *Irish Boats and Yachting* team made a lot of mistakes, the principal one being a failure to print the magazine's advertisements properly. This meant that their primary customers, the advertisers, were not getting what they paid for. For a magazine, especially in Ireland where low circulation makes it almost impossible to garner a profit from the sales price, alienating your advertisers is the worst thing you can allow to happen.

If the customer base of *Irish Boats and Yachting* had been nurtured and if the magazine's staff had not got carried away with their initial success, they wouldn't have left a gap in the market for a new competitor.

The next competitor was *Sail and Power* magazine, which was produced by a very hard working and friendly man called Eric Parks who also published *Angling and Shooting*.

The *Irish Boats and Yachting* team reacted in a very immature way to the new competition. They acted as if they had a right to a monopoly position, and criticised the new competitor.

This is something you can never do in a free market. You have got to respect your competitor, and if you want to survive, you must deliver the service or product in better fashion than they do. In this case *Irish Boats and Yachting* should have consolidated their relationship with their customers and delivered a superior service to their advertisers. The fact that they exploited their monopoly position with bad service and bad attitude wedged the door open for *Sail and Power*.

For their part, *Sail and Power* were good people but they had no real understanding of the marine market. They were just diversifying into what must have looked like a related subject to the same market that enjoyed hunting and fishing, but they didn't have a real feeling for the industry.

I was on the dole, writing a few articles here and there for Norman Barry, when I decided that I would start up my own boating magazine. I really knew very little about publishing but it seemed like a good idea to try as I knew about boats and I knew a bit about writing.

From a business perspective, my whole idea was stupid. There was no logic to it whatsoever. There was no spare customer base left in a marketplace that already supported two magazines. And the reality of it was that there could only be ever room for one magazine, and even one magazine was barely viable.

Now there is only one condition where you should enter a market like this, and that is when you are prepared to deliver your product cheaper and better than your competitors.

I decided that I could produce a magazine that would cater for what people wanted. I didn't follow a business plan, I just looked at similar magazines in England and America, decided to copy those, style it for the Irish market and do it better than the others. I didn't do any market research, but I did know my subject.

To set up that magazine I needed two things: money and a good journalist. How do you start a business with no money? The concept of venture capital didn't exist, or at least not for me or for my type of venture, the concept of seed funding didn't exist and certainly the concept of a bank lending poor people money for businesses didn't exist.

However, as I hadn't bothered myself with any of the other difficulties ahead, there was no point getting discouraged over money either.

Nobody I knew had, or would, invest cash in the business and I had no funding of my own.

Then I learned that magazines were paid for by advertising and so I created a rate card listing the cost of advertising in the magazine I was going to produce. Using the existing magazines and the telephone book as a source, I began to 'cold call' potential advertisers. I began the effort in the early months of 1981, planning to have the magazine up and running for the annual boat show in March of that year. For consumer publications, you usually start in winter to cash in on the big spend for Christmas, but the boating sector's push for exposure to potential customers was at the start of summer, and that was why the boat show was in March.

The cold calling was tough. I wasn't a natural salesperson and, even though I didn't like doing it, I had no choice.

It was the rejection I disliked. The life of the salesperson is one of rejection, and none of us like to be rejected. When I lifted the phone, nine times out of ten the message was 'fuck off', if not exactly in those words.

This experience has led me to develop a huge respect for the sales function in business, but back then I didn't have any respect for it, because my culture didn't have any respect for it. Though my father had been in business before me, it was at a different level. I had grown up with a more civil service, production-led mentality, and my early training as journalist had not helped either.

However, the cold calling had to be done, so I rolled up my sleeves and became one of the most despised of all creatures, the foot-in-the-door salesman.

Selling advertising was for me the psychological jump from being a writer to being a real businessman. Journalists know a little bit about a lot of things, and they tend to have a very aloof attitude towards anything that is commercial because they think it will pollute the quality of their writing.

This can be true on a lower level of journalism, and you can see it a lot in central Europe where people are still paid to write favourable articles, but a good journalist will respect both the need for impartiality and market forces. Although they often work against each other, they can also work in unison. At the end of the day, most readers aren't stupid and they can see when an article has been bought as opposed to written from an objective viewpoint.

I had my techniques for increasing my success rate. A lot of the time, I was selling advertisements to large multinationals who had separate sales and advertising agents. I'd call the advertising agent and mention in the passing that I was talking to the manufacturer. Then I'd call the manufacturer and drop in to the conversation the fact that I was talking to the advertising agent. It wasn't a lie, because I had been talking to both, but it was a manipulation of sorts that was necessary for the process of the sale.

So with my call the manufacturer might think, 'Oh, the advertising agent is interested. I better listen to this.'

Whereas the advertising agent might think, 'Well, if the manufacturer is interested. I better listen to this.'

I never advocate telling an outright lie. Morally it's wrong, and practically you destroy your chances of building trust with your clients or partners. So don't do it. But there are other ways to persuade, and I just happened to use that method. Selling is an essential function and I was selling something that I liked and was happy with.

To get my publication launched, I had to get £11,000 worth of advertising orders. I knew the printing would cost £9,000 and the bank needed a certain percentage more to cover interest repayments – hence the magical figure of £11,000 to get £9,000 from the bank. That was a lot of money at that time, probably the equivalent of €35,000–40,000 at today's advertising rates per page. I hoped that selling advertising would cover the bank's overdraft.

With the money end sorted, I now needed a good journalist. For content, I secured the services of 'Winkie' Nixon (or William as his charming wife Georgina would have us call him). Winkie was a great writing talent who I believe was wasted in Ireland to a certain extent. He had grown up in a very respectable and conservative family in Northern Ireland but was banished to the south at an early age for sowing some of his wild oats.

Winkie was a wonderful man with a heart of gold and I made him a partner by giving him twenty per cent of the business. He had been treated very badly by his previous publication so he had nothing to lose. Though he had no aspirations to be a businessman he deserved to be cut in on the venture because of the value he brought to it. Without him, launching the magazine would have been much more difficult. My time was much better spent selling advertising space.

Winkie was also pragmatic about the ideals I had aspired to as a journalist. I was told, get the facts and follow the five Ws and the H – the Who, What, Where, When, Why and How of the story, to speak in the journalism lingo.

It was all lost on Winkie though.

'Get out of that,' he said. 'You're in the entertainment business!'

He had me there. Boats are grown men's toys, and that was our market.

By February, I could show written advertising orders to the tune of £11,000 to the bank. It was virtual money because I couldn't receive it until the magazine was delivered with the advertisements in print, but, to my eternal gratitude, the bank manager gave me an overdraft. To get it all together in the final four weeks I rented an office in Dún Laoghaire for £40 a week and had Biddy Clarke working for me part-time.

Biddy was a great asset, but threatened to walk out during the start-up just because I put my bare feet up on the office desk to pick at my toenails. I put my socks back on.

To save money I outsourced anything I could. The concept is quite well known and used now, but it was less so then. But because I started with a clean slate and with a very tight financial situation certain ways of doing things were just obvious. That was facilitated in the publishing industry because you traditionally had to bring many different elements together.

I went for quality, getting a very good graphic designer and using the best photographs I could find. I got another person to do the plates for the magazine, and then a distributor and the best printer.

The major expense I now faced was getting the first few thousand copies in print. With all the rigging up necessary for the printer the first copies incur a crippling cost, while the additional expense for the next few thousand copies are marginal. Trade magazines therefore get whacked with almost the same production costs as higher circulation publications.

Unsurprisingly, the printer would not deliver the magazine until his £9,000 print bill was paid. I really didn't expect him to take a chance on me either. The Irish economy in the 1980s had very little money and very little employment, so the printer wouldn't have been in business if he took risks like that. But the result of this was that the magazine became a pure cash-flow operation.

Six thousand copies of the magazine, called *Afloat*, were rolled off the presses in time for the boat show in March. We launched it there and gave it out free to everybody, getting an instant circulation to both advertisers and readers.

The magazine was both subscription and sold off the shelves on a sale or return basis. We put copies in shops all around the country and the shops got a fifty per cent mark-up so they were given a huge incentive to stock it.

But really ninety per cent of the revenue came from advertising. Subscription and shop sales were just jam as the edition was paid for even if no one bought a single copy. This could be somewhat tricky for advertisers, because they could fall victim to vanity publishing, a stunt which was pulled in Ireland in the 1970s and then again in eastern Europe in the 1990s. Somebody would sell advertising space to twenty companies or people, print a hundred copies of a publication and send five copies – bearing the advertiser's photograph – to each advertiser. There would be no public circulation whatsoever, but the advertiser would be so enamoured by their photograph in the magazine that they'd never think to ask.

Getting printed, however, was only the first hurdle. I now had two established competitors to take on. To beat them we had to match, and better, their standard to claw into their market share. This was tough, because the Afloat market share was low, and so were my resources.

In September 1981, I also married Suzanna and got a mortgage on a house. I wanted to live on a barge but my bank manager's advice prevailed (it had to, he was the one with the purse strings). He didn't want me, and rightly so, putting money into something that would only depreciate. These new responsibilities all added to the stress and desperation.

Running *Afloat* was a dog-eat-dog operation. It was the toughest business period of my life, and I say that including everything that I have tried since. Twenty-hour days were not uncommon, although twelve hours a day, six days a week was the norm. The tiny marine industries were terrible bill payers and we also had to contend with a deep recession. But I was a driven person and obsessed with succeeding. The challenge sparked a fiercely competitive blaze in me and I let it take over.

And it worked.

In the end, my work rate and low cost base was so well worked out that it became impossible for *Irish Boats and Yachting* and *Sail and Power* to compete – so they dropped out of the marketplace leaving it entirely to *Afloat*. I will say that it was useful to learn from the mistakes of others, but beyond that it was a total disadvantage for me to come late to the market. What made it work was the fact that I was prepared to work inhumane hours, and no ordinary Irish business could compete with that. You can't succeed against someone who's producing a better product and is doing it at a lower cost.

There were other factors as well of course, the boom periods that had seen *Irish Boats and Yachting* debut on the market were long gone, and in my three years of effort I had made a monopoly of a tiny market in recession.

But like the salesman, I had got my foot in the door.

Successful early entrepreneurship is about leverage and cash flow. You leverage the knowledge you have, you leverage the knowledge you can get and then you leverage your assets.

I had leveraged my knowledge of sailing, my lesser knowledge of publication and writing and to another degree my own reputation. I then leveraged the knowledge I could get by bringing in the best quality people I could find, starting with Winkie Nixon and working down.

Leveraging my assets was to come some time later, but I did that too. Once the bank had given me an overdraft I had cash flow, and between the cash flow and the leverage I had a business with a good product and advertisers.

The magazine looked good, it was launched at the right time and the advertisers were happy with it. I didn't make the same mistake as *Irish Boats and Yachting* and I worked on my relationship with the marine traders enough so that they formed a solid client base for the subsequent issues. Soon it was turning over £100,000 a year.

I learned then that no matter how small the market, or how small the customer base, you really have to look after them. In fact if your customers are few in number you better be damn sure that you do.

And then it was just a matter of work, work, work to make it continue. It was like a dog chasing its own tail to get the magazine out again and again. It was tough and it didn't really get that much easier. Fundamentally the market was small and it wasn't growing. In fact the reverse was true as it actually contracted for all of the 1980s, leaving it in the doldrums.

The content of *Afloat* was quite conservative. It was monthly and low circulation – not much room for sensationalism. Not that I didn't try. It was about the third or fourth edition of *Afloat*. Invariably we'd work all night to get it ready for the printer on time, with a deadline of 8.00 a.m. to get the plates ready and get the machines going.

Now in publication design, you often have to make sure that your 'plugs' are correctly positioned on the front cover. Plugs are those little paragraphs telling you about the wonders of this month's edition ('New keel design gives ten per cent less drag!' etc.). Magazines on shelves are often overlapped, so the plugs must be on the correct side of the cover so that they are visible. We were concentrating on the plugs together at 2.00 a.m. when I said to myself, 'What's going to sell this magazine? What's going to make people buy this feckin' magazine?'

I was there with the graphic designer, who was a family man it must be said and was only putting in the hours, so he is absolved from any responsibility for my brainwave. I came up with a big headline on the front cover saying 'Sex at Sea'.

The reader would open the contents page and see 'Sex at Sea' listed at page 72, which was on the very last page of classifieds. In the smallest typeface possible, I think seven point was the smallest we could manage on our little IBM, we put on the bottom of the page, 'Sex at Sea. Ha ha, fooled you! If you are currently reading this we are quite a respectable family magazine, this is all we have about sex but please buy the magazine anyhow…'

Unprofessional? Totally. But the magazine sold out at the newsstand.

That issue also got some international notoriety thanks to my reciprocal subscriptions to all the English and American magazines (which was another good deal because I was getting hundreds of dollars worth of international periodicals for the cost of postage on a few copies of *Afloat*).

I subsequently met the publisher of one of the American magazines and he told me that they nearly died of laughter in the publishing house. 'Gee Enda, we saw your magazine this month. We wanted to call you up and say that we really like your article on 'Sex at Sea'. Wow, it floored us!'

In publishing, particularly in American publishing where they have very high circulation, there's a huge system of checks and balances. There's the editor, the sub-editor, maybe the lawyers after that, and so on, everything is double or treble checked. I was doing it on my own, without any checks or balances, at 2.00 a.m. when I was totally knackered – and it was a frequent occurrence. I would get it all done, go to bed for two days and forget all about it until the printer would deliver it four or five days later to remind me of my handiwork, whereupon it had to be distributed around the country.

With the 'Sex at Sea' issue I had proof that the old adage of 'sex sells' works – even in the Irish boating industry. So I repeated the exercise once again, this time for the 1982 Boat Show.

I had a female graphic artist designing covers, and it was done at the last minute, but I described what I wanted. 'Boobs and propeller. I want a mermaid with big boobs dangling over a three-blade propeller of a ship.'

So the designer followed my instructions, but unfortunately it didn't turn out exactly the way I had planned. Now had she done it beautifully and artistically it might have been nice, but instead it was done with a certain vulgarity, and it was an absolute disaster. And the first time I saw it was when it came from the printers.

Although I didn't suffer any repercussions from it, which still amazes me considering it was – of all things – the boat show edition, the embarrassment was enough. This time there was no humorous call from the US, though I dreaded to think what they must have thought of me.

Never again, I decided. It was a classic example of what not to do.

I did, however, encounter difficulty over a quite innocent sexual reference in the magazine at a later date.

Every £60–70 mattered to the *Afloat* accounts, and for two years that was how much I was owed by a client in Cork. I knew he had the money, but he refused to pay me.

I'd sent reminders and I'd made phone calls, all to no avail (the economy was so bad sometimes I'd only get paid if I called to people's homes). As it turned out, I had other reasons to be in Cork so I decided to drop by my creditor's house. Without a single word from him I was taken into his private study, where he got his chequebook out. Then he muttered under his breath, 'You fucking Dublin atheist, writing about pregnant nuns.'

What? Pregnant nuns?

It took a few moments but then it clicked with me.

I had written an article in the magazine about the Fastnet race, which is based around the Fastnet Rock off the south coast of Ireland. My writing style tends to be blunt and descriptive, and I noted that this rock stuck out. Now if you walked down the street and saw a nun who was pregnant, you'd remember it. So in my straightforward prose I described the Fastnet Rock as being 'like a pregnant nun, it stood out a mile away'.

It was purely descriptive terminology, there was no religious connotations or sexual subtext of any kind intended. But the power of the written word can be amazing, and this time it came back to haunt me in a business context.

Of course with my last 'Sex at Sea' issue of *Afloat*, he probably thought me to be some low peddler of sleaze. He had certainly built up a massive resentment of me at any rate.

In another instance, also centred in County Cork strangely enough, I ran afoul of the late Mary Doyle, the lovely wife of Denis Doyle who was a doyen of Cork and owned half a boat yard. Mary was a socialite, with a posh Cork accent and full membership of the Royal Cork Yacht Club to boot. She and her husband had been cruising off the coast of Spain when they met ex-King Constantine of Greece and Queen Sophia of Spain. Apparently, Queen Sophia then invited the two Corkonians on board the Spanish royal yacht.

Bringing them into their private quarters, Queen Sophia apologised for the mess whereupon Mary Doyle put her hand on her hostess and uttered the immortal words,

'Don't worry about that, we're well used to that in Cork.'

Thinking it an innocent little story I wrote it up and put it into a funny piece for *Afloat*. Boy, was I wrong. The next thing I knew I had Mary Doyle to deal with.

'It's all very well Enda O'Coineen but that's our personal lives,' she said in her polished yet unmistakable Cork accent. ' You don't go writing about our personal lives. Do you hear that? I'll have you barred from the Royal Cork Yacht Club, and what's more, I'll have no association with you ever again in the future.'

Now while the loss of Mary Doyle's association was a bitter blow in itself, the loss of a full page of advertising from Denis Doyle's Crosshaven boatyard every month was worse. Denis Doyle was a wonderful man, but Mary was implacable.

My blackballing in Cork soon began to border on the ridiculous. Denis had a big yacht and a crew of about fifteen people, all of whom I knew. Even so, I couldn't be seen talking to them when Mary Doyle was around in case they'd be castigated for talking to gurriers (I still identify with gurriers) from Dublin who would write about 'one's personal life'.

It took me a year and a half to make it up to her. I arranged to do an interview with her to profile the wife of a great sailor and she agreed to it on the condition that she could edit it and have full control over what went into the article.

In the interview, Mary told some fabulous stories of her husband Dennis, and one in particular hinged on the troubles in Northern Ireland. It was the tradition that the Royal Ocean Racing Club would enter every alternate year in the Fastnet Race to Ireland. But because of IRA violence, they refused to go to Cork one year, so being the sporting man that he was Denis Doyle suggested a race down to Spain instead. The motion was carried and, to cut a long story short, Mary Doyle and her British friends had only left the Royal Bayona Yacht Club in Spain by half an hour when it was subsequently blown to bits by Basque separatists.

Although the irony made it a great story, Mary refused to let us publish it. Of the three-page interview that we wrote she vetoed two-thirds of it, leaving us with a single page article, complete with a picture of her in her armchair in Douglas, the fashionable part of Cork where they lived. But at least it made the peace and ushered in a more normalised relationship.

By 1983, I was sufficiently well established to consider developing new products. I had the cash flow and credibility to expand, so I began to look around for a new sector where I could publish.

Security, sadly, was a big issue. Using the same formula as for *Afloat*, we sold advertising and used the credit to publish *Security World*, another trade magazine for the security industry. The primary market were about 200 or so firms who supplied alarm systems and products, such as automatic gates, electronic monitoring, video surveillance, personnel, and so forth.

I picked up all these companies from the *Golden Pages* and built up a database of potential customers. I then persuaded enough of them to buy advertising, used an overdraft to pay for printing and distributed the magazine free.

There was a lower print run on this publication because there were only about 2,000 clients who really mattered to the security industry. They tended to be large companies, most obviously banks, who required complete security systems for their premises. The first edition of *Security World* was more like a directory than a magazine because in it I listed the name of every security company in Ireland.

But I hated the topic, anything to do with security gives me the creeps. I hate locking things. I don't like locking doors at all and I don't like having anyone in my office that I can't trust. As it is, I generally don't lock things and people give out to me for it. I'm not a distrustful person and I tend not to take a negative opinion of others.

Therefore *Security World* was something fairly horrible to me because I found the subject matter completely repugnant. Every interview I did was a descent into the mind of criminals because the security operators were trying to combat the criminal element. In addition to this, there were a number of people in the industry who themselves had served time in prison. When I did the directory with the line of photographs, I could not stop thinking about police mugshots.

Having said that, I didn't regret starting the publication. There was market for it, it was satisfying a legitimate need, and security was unfortunately a necessary function, regardless of my own personal attitudes to it. Firms involved with the security industry, like any other businesses, needed to know what was happening in the sector. They needed information on the latest product developments, what companies were hiring what agencies, who was being promoted and who to contact.

I learned two fundamental lessons from *Security World*.

One was the importance of image. Given the murky backgrounds of one or two of the people in the industry at the time, there was an attempt to establish a level of respectability.

Security World offered them that respectability. The companies might take six pages of advertising in my magazine, including a profile of their firm and a picture of them in their shop surrounded by all of their wonderful products.

Now that firm might only have ten customers, but those customers were worth £100,000 each and one of them might have been Allied Irish Banks. So if you're the security manager in AIB, or any other bank for that matter, and you see this fine profile of Joe Bloggs and his 24/7 alarm systems in *Security World*, then you're going to be more inclined to purchase from that supplier.

Joe Bloggs looks professional. The very fact that Joe Bloggs was prepared to put his money into a decent advertising spread shows that he is professional, because Joe Bloggs is taking care of his image to the customers.

I was giving them respectability, and I was helping to confer legitimacy on what was a nascent industry at the time. Despite the fact that I loathed everything about security, my publication was helping the industry to mature in its own way. Those security firms would have to compete with each other and sell themselves through the merits of their services, which in turn would be displayed in the news and advertisements in *Security World*. Clients in need of security firms were able to better discern the professional operations because they had more information about the sector. It was certainly a lot better than going by the *Golden Pages*.

The second thing I learned from *Security World* was the importance of picking ventures on the basis of their returns rather than my personal attraction to them.

Unlike yachting, which was more of a leisure pursuit, the security sector was a real industry. The result was that *Security World* gave four times the return for half the effort and was overall a much greater success financially than Afloat.

Of course, because of my background I knew that the boating sector was the natural entry point for me, but it didn't mean I had to be tied to it for the rest of my entrepreneurial life, although I continued to open new ventures related to the marine market.

I liked travelling so I opened a travel agency called Anchor Travel in 1985, thinking that I would be able to get cheaper rates out of it. It was a good idea but needed a huge volume because you made small commissions of around nine per cent, and very often for a business account you had to split that commission in half. But it was a specialist marine industry agency, dealing in cruise liner holidays and that sort of thing. I never really made much or lost much in that business, though I did make a small bit of money selling it two years later.

To compliment the travel agency, I then started a marine insurance company. Irish boat owners had traditionally bought their insurance from UK companies but, after a very bad storm in 1985, they had a lot of trouble renewing their policies. Since the storm had only been a circumstance of freak weather, I thought that it might be a good time to enter the insurance market. I set up Aquabroker in 1986 with two insurance specialists – David Baines from Galway and Bill Cullen from Clare. That firm is still going and it has between forty per cent and fifty per cent of the Irish marine market.

Six years after returning to Ireland with nothing in my pockets, I had started three successful ventures – *Afloat* and *Security World* magazines and Anchor Travel (my interest in Aquabroker was non-executive).

In addition to that, I was printing specialist, one-off publications, such as an annual for the Irish Lifeboats and brochures for marine traders. I found a very economical way to do these brochures. Printing set-up costs were very high, but when companies wanted brochures printed I'd say to them, 'Look, I'll make you a four-page brochure, and I'll give you four pages in the magazine as well.'

They'd always agree to this, so I would print their brochure as part of the magazine. Then when I printed the magazine I'd run off my normal circulation figures, and then print an extra few hundred copies that I would then take their brochure from. This made sense because running off a few extra editions of the magazine was cheaper than the set up costs for a brand new print run.

But overall it was very, very tough. The marine industry in Ireland was about the same size as the marine industry in Manchester or Liverpool, and the money simply wasn't there.

As if my plate wasn't full enough at this time, I also started a project to put an Irish entry into a prestigious round-the-world race. Within a few years the project had taken over most of my life, and would lead me on to a completely new and different path.

But of all the deals that I struck during my time with *Afloat*, the best one happened by accident. I was always looking to add value to my various enterprises where I could, and as my businesses developed, I used more office space in the Dún Laoghaire premises on Marine Road, which I then sublet in turn. By 1987, I negotiated a deal to buy the entire building for £150,000 with a hundred per cent finance. I didn't even have the deposit, but I got a mortgage for £120,000 and a loan from a finance company (at much higher interest rates, over and above twelve per cent) covered the rest. But I had enough cash flow from the rental income to just cover the repayments.

I signed the contract but between one thing and another I didn't get around to fully closing it.

Then Conal Forbes came to me with the intention of renting some office space in the building. I was talking with him on the street in Dún Laoghaire when his brother, Cyril, the property investor, happened to be going past.

The property market was quite depressed then, but it was turning. I knew Cyril was an astute speculator, so I told him that I was buying the building and gave him the rental incomes on the spot.

Cyril did his sums quickly. 'I'll pay you £170,000,' he said.

'Here's the contract, step into my shoes,' I replied, which he did and paid me the difference of £20,000. It was the easiest money I have ever made.

That money was a hell of a lot to me at the time, and by far the largest sum I'd ever had in my hand at the one go. Up until that point, I had been living on margins and overdrafts. But it was the cash flow that allowed me to do it, so essentially I had created capital from nothing other than added value.

I reinvested the money in another premises on Haig Terrace, also in Dún Laoghaire, which I painted up and leased.

Then in 1988 an offer came up to buy *Afloat* magazine, my main flagship and baby. I thought it would break my heart. I had to wrestle with the idea of selling because it was my whole life. I'd eaten, slept, drunk it, and made it from nothing when I was on the dole.

Not only that, it had given me a lot of scope in contacts and networking. It gave me a platform and credibility in the marine industry and beyond, which was very important, and it could act as a catalyst to get other things going. But even though I was aware that I was about to lose these things I knew I had to move on. Some people do something and then they hang on and hang on. For me it was like going back to school and apologising.

You do something, you give it its time, and then you move on. Generally when you start your own business there is a beginning, a middle and hopefully a long and successful time before you retire. But to be an entrepreneur, you must be able to let go. It's not quick in and out. You give your life to building your venture, you get it up and running, you add value and then you take yourself out of the equation. If you have created a solid company, it will run along fine without you. Your value as the entrepreneur is the imagination, the catalyst and the creative art.

When you've set up your business others will run it for you.

Most jobs tend to be routine – not all by any stretch of the imagination, but most. You do a few weeks or months of training and then you are all set to repeat the processes of sales, administration, production or whatever. If the training and conditions for staff are adequate, the company should not encounter problems in that area. Even a lot of management comes down to routine. Regarding strategic direction, you, as the entrepreneur, will always be on hand to decide where the company is going, where the best chance for profit lies and what must be done to take you there.

However, if you don't let go then you will be welded to your enterprise for the rest of your life. This is fine if you are happy with the security, though bear in mind that the challenge will often disappear from it. If you are after serious wealth accumulation you have only two options:

- be involved in a sector where there is a chance of exponential growth; or
- replicate your entrepreneurial art to start and accumulate new ventures.

For me, there was limited opportunity with either of these options in the marine market, there was neither a growth potential nor the opportunity to keep replicating, plus I had become heavily involved in the Sail Ireland project. So I sold out and let go in 1988. For all the businesses, I received a few hundred thousand. It was a huge psychological break for me but once I got used to it I've never regretted it.

I didn't need security. In fact I've tended to dispense with it whenever I can.

In the final assessment, *Afloat* and everything that came after gave me a fundamental grounding in business. And the same fundamentals apply in any place and in any business, even if there's a different legal system, a different language, a different people, a different geographical location – and even if you have no money.

The bottom line is this: if there's a market, there's a way. If you are determined enough and you have a good product that you believe in, you can get in.

Don't let anyone tell you any different.

That said my next project – a round-the-world project – was to test my determination to even greater limits.

Chapter seven

Sailing around the World

In 1985 my businesses were doing okay and I was looking for a new adventure – and this time I wanted to combine seamanship and entrepreneurship together.

Merging my sport, my early love and passion with the practicalities of paying for it all – sponsorship, fund-raising and organisation – was to be the greatest challenge I'd faced. And the most rewarding. Ironically, it was also the least expected in my position. With my accumulating business interests, and my responsibilities as a husband and father, the natural thing to do would have been to consolidate my ventures and sort out our future income. But no. I was looking for neither money nor security. Somehow or other I had to assuage a desire burning inside me to find and get to grips with some new challenge; to take on some new impossibility. My love for sailing meant that I could never remain far from the sea or boats, but I was fed up with racing in non-Irish boats.

At that time, reports were coming in of the progress of the 1985–86 Whitbread race. Gradually I became obsessed with the idea that Ireland ought to be involved.

Of course it sounds grandiose, wanting to have your country involved in a prestigious race simply because you believe it can be done. But to understand why I wanted this to happen it's necessary to understand the way Ireland was then.

In the 1980s, Ireland was a grim place. Unemployment was almost twenty per cent, the national debt was soaring, political instability was rife, Northern Ireland was going its lunatic way and, in our time-honoured fashion, the smart people were bailing off the island in their droves to Sydney, New York, London and any other place that would give them a job and hope. Perhaps it was the harshness of the time, but I felt that the Irish had a certain mean-mindedness to them, a 'can't do' attitude if you will. We were thinking, acting and feeling like second-class citizens.

I believed that if we could build an eighty-foot yacht, paid for by sponsorship, and race it around the world in the Whitbread race, we could get the entire country behind it, lift moral and use it as a major promotional tool.

It was while this idea was jumping around in my mind – and seemed quite likely to remain there, because I didn't mention it to anyone else for fear of seeming crazy – that a chance presented itself for me to become involved with one of the Whitbread competitors as a journalist.

In June 1986, I joined the crew of the *Phillips Innovator* to help generate publicity for the round Ireland section of the race. The *Phillips Innovator* was skippered by Dirk Nauta, an easy-going but well-organised Dutchman who had been winning the Whitbread handicap division, and who eventually finished second over all. While happy to help with publicity for that leg, my secret motivation for becoming involved was of course to find out more about the Dutch Whitbread experience. At the end of this successful trip, my mind was made up – Ireland *would* participate in the next race.

Although the next round-the-world challenge was scheduled for 1989, I knew that four years was in fact little enough time to get a boat and a crew to the starting line. Now was the time to start the planning.

'You must be crazy. Where are you going to get that sort of money?' a friend asked one evening over a pint.

He had a point. While the money was available, it was not necessarily available to me. Quickly I realised that, not being a heavyweight in the business world, I would not be taken seriously. It was vital that I begin to build credibility for myself and the feasibility of the project. I put together a carefully prepared, colour prospectus that mentioned several notable Irish sailors who had made names for themselves in sailing circles worldwide, such as Joe English, Killian Bushe and Harry Cudmore.

Cudmore was a very colourful character. I sailed with him in the early 1970s and afterwards ended up in a party at the Royal Yacht Squadron in Cowes, the centre of the English yachting establishment. He smuggled all of his crew over the back garden walls and then produced a bunch of ties from his pocket to make us respectable. This was back before Northern Ireland got really heavy and a time when a load of strange Irish lads could still hop a wall and get into a place where British royalty was hanging out.

I'll never forget the time he opened the London Boat Show in 1988. Although he had a penchant for speaking with an upper class British accent, he did on this occasion lapse into his native Cork twang.

Cudmore had a good sense of humour, but for him to be successful he had to play up to the British. That was his way, and he got to the very top of British establishment yachting. He talked and sounded like one of them (most of the time) but he was really Irish through and through.

Although I had an impressive presentation, selling just the concept of Irish participation in the Whitbread was going to be very hard work. I put together a list of prominent people who had the influence and finances to support the idea and I began to contact them one by one.

Most of them liked the project, but still said 'No' when it came to actual assistance. It was demoralising, frustrating and painful but, like every salesman the world over, I did not give up. I believed that if I knocked on enough doors, eventually, somebody, somewhere would buy into the idea based on the promotional benefits being offered to them. It was just a numbers game.

One of the first rejecters was Tony O'Reilly. After I had written to O'Reilly several times without reply I eventually had to 'doorstep' him. Doorstepping is a journalistic term where you just show up at a spot where your chosen individual is and spring a question on them.

If you're an intrepid reporter who doesn't mind making enemies, it's not a bad tactic. If, on the other hand, you are trying to sell something to somebody then you should use this approach with subtlety and care.

My opportunity came when the Irish Management Institute was presenting Tony with an award. I made contact and spent half an hour with O'Reilly, outlining the ocean-racing background, my credentials and the project. Tony was polite, but felt that it wasn't for his organisation.

Shortly after this I approached Charlie Haughey, the then opposition leader. Haughey, like any politician looking to be elected, was sympathetic, although given the country's debt problems I doubted that he would promise funds. Nor did he, and he made it clear the state of the country's finances would not allow him to offer any public money if he was elected.

'If you think it's a good idea and would put that in writing, it would help us to sell the project to business people,' I said, and he kindly obliged.

Then I heard of another round-the-world challenge coming from Ron Holland, a yacht designer of Kiwi origin who was now living and working in Ireland. As it turned out, Holland had been working with the Fine Gael politician Hugh Coveney on the idea but both of them had given up. Like myself they had approached a number of prominent people with no luck.

On hearing of this new challenge, I decided that I had better compare notes with them. I met Hugh in Dáil Éireann and he gave me his file of rejections, wished me luck and agreed to put his name to the list of people supporting the project. He'd effectively given up on it. It wasn't much help, but it saved time and put me in contact with Ron.

With Holland in tow, I took over from where they left off.

Holland's name was good when it came to selling sponsorship. He gave credibility to the scheme, was known worldwide and had a vast range of experience to draw on. But we were still without any serious offers of funding and the rejections continued.

A phrase in the refusal note from one influential chief executive of a public company summed up the attitude of many: 'In view of the possible downside effect in image terms...'

In other words, however exciting the project may have been in marketing terms, it could be dangerous to be seen to be spending money on yacht-racing while unemployment problems in Ireland were so bad.

I was of the completely opposite opinion. I felt that projects like this would promote Ireland's name around the world and by the same token foster self-confidence at home. A 'can do' environment is the one that produces entrepreneurs, and entrepreneurs are the people who ultimately provide employment by creating new enterprise.

But, as I've said before, if you keep going and don't give up, things will turn around for you. Eventually Ron and myself had a breakthrough, in the form of Howard Kilroy.

Kilroy was the powerhouse executive behind the massive expansion and global success of the Jefferson Smurfit Corporation. With an interest in sailing and maritime affairs and no pretensions to any great knowledge of the technicalities of racing development, he was the ideal businessman to involve in our world challenge. He was also a member of Dún Laoghaire's Royal St George Yacht Club and when family and business time permitted, he enjoyed club sailing in a very low-key style.

I attended a few functions that Kilroy was appearing at, not to doorstep him, but to learn more about him. As it turned out he was such a busy man that it took three months before I could see him.

The day we met he was receptive to the proposition. In a note to me, dated 24 November 1986, he wrote, 'Your project for 'Round-the-World' sponsorship is fascinating. I will lobby it internally here for the next while and see what interest I can generate.'

However, full involvement seemed to be inappropriate to him, since Smurfit was not essentially a corporation that depended so much on public image-building as on product, price and service in their packaging and other business interests.

In addition to that, Michael Smurfit's big passions were horses and golf – perhaps symbolic of an island country which had withdrawn from the sea. But rather than throwing me out of the door altogether Kilroy gave his name in support of the challenge, and this started a ripple effect amongst other candidates.

Though the man had personally impressed me, I had never realised the depth of quiet respect Kilroy had in the business world. Whenever anybody saw the name Howard Kilroy, they gave their support immediately and by March 1987 I found myself with an impressive list of people from the business, sailing and academic worlds. It was time to give the group a name and I decided on 'The Ireland Sailing Trust'.

It was progress but there was still no real money on the table and the Whitbread was now only three years away.

After some discussion amongst the trustees we fixed upon a target of £100,000 as seed capital, and there were three good reasons for doing this. It would either: get us well on the way to buying a second-hand yacht; be enough to kick start a major fundraiser; or, best of all, show some potential sponsor corporation that we meant business and that there was low risk in putting their name on the side of an Irish boat. To attract the seed capital, we decided to go for ten people, each willing to put up £10,000 a shot. I was working on this objective when, one Saturday night on coming home from the pub with the Sunday Independent, I came across an interesting article on a Mr Dermot Desmond.

Now at the time neither I, nor most other people in Ireland, had ever heard of Desmond, but according to the Sindo he was blazing a trail with his stockbroking firm, National City Brokers.

Desmond seemed like an impressive entrepreneur. He'd been involved with the Investment Bank of Ireland, a few marketing enterprises and a stint in Afghanistan with the World Bank.

He then ended up back in Ireland looking for something new when he saw the opportunity to open a money-broking firm and make a profit from currency exchanges. In the early 1980s, telephone lines were virtually impossible to get in Dublin, but Dermot managed to land an office with fifty of them in Mount Street and soon after that he was into the big time. With ruthless efficiency, he made presentations to three top money-broking firms in London in order to get a partner and raise capital. One backed him, and he poached the best staff from the other two. NCB was born.

Unknown to us at the time, nautical themes had been running through Dermot's recent business career. Having renovated his offices one of the decorators, a retired lighthouse keeper, presented him with a ship in a bottle with NCB written on the side. Then after five years of successful trading, Dermot's staff presented him with another ship, a silver one this time, again emblazoned with the letters NCB. I contacted Desmond not long after with a view to presenting drawings of a maxi yacht with the NCB logo on the side.

My initial approach to Dermot Desmond, as it had been with other candidates before him, was by letter. As a subtle opening to the sales process I requested an appointment to discuss a proposition. Because I didn't want Desmond to prejudge the Sail Ireland idea, my letter was deliberately scanty on details, but intriguing enough to merit his interest.

I then followed it up with a phone call with a view to arranging a face-to-face meeting.

I was put on to Dermot without delay. 'Enda O'Coineen here . Did you get my note? Can I see you some time on Friday? I hope to have the yacht designer Ron Holland with me.'

'Sure, how about four o'clock?' Dermot replied, not knowing what the meeting would be about.

Immediately I picked up the telephone again and called Swift Couriers. Ten minutes later, they picked up my colour prospectus on the proposed challenge, a book and video about the Whitbread race and a freshly typed letter confirming the appointment, and delivered them straight to NCB. Apparently Dermot put it in his case and took it home.

Having learned from previous experience that it's hard for an Irishman to be taken seriously in Ireland, I saw Ron Holland as the key man to take to the Desmond presentation. To make Ron's visit to Dublin worthwhile, other appointments with potential £10,000 shareholders were set up. By this time, Ron had also made an appointment with Garret FitzGerald, so the next obvious choice was the Marine minister.

By this time, Ron was getting a little fed up with me. However, I persuaded him to take the plane trip from Cork for the meeting and I organised the tickets. Two days later, I picked him up at the airport.

So as not to ruin our image, I ditched my banger and borrowed my sister's car instead. We had a quick cup of coffee in Kitty O'Shea's and walked into Dermot's office at 4.00 p.m. on a Friday in May 1987.

Through the glass partition, we saw rows of computer terminals with sharp young dealers hammering away at them in rolled-up shirtsleeves. You could almost smell the money.

Sitting at Dermot's elbow was Kevin Barry, an economic analyst who had been headhunted by Dermot from the Central Bank. Formalities completed, we went straight into our presentation.

Ten minutes later, Dermot cut through our long-practised recitation with a blunt question. 'What will it take to build this boat?'

I looked at Ron. Ron looked at me. Precise costs, of course, depended on decisions we were not yet in a position to take, although I had round figures gleaned from my travels as a journalist and sailor. Meanwhile Desmond was thumbing through our list of people.

'Wally... I like him...' he muttered to himself. 'Hmm... Kilroy, I like him.'

Talking as if a difference of £400,000 was a minor detail, I heard Ron pronounce the bottom line. 'Between £1.2 and £1.6 million, depending on circumstances.'

'Right,' said Desmond without hesitation, 'I'll put up £1.4 million to build this boat.'

Just like that.

After all the effort, after all the presentations and disappointments, the Sail Ireland project had become a reality. The moral of the story – never give up.

Of course, Desmond didn't just open his chequebook there and then, there were some criteria he wanted observed. Even so, NCB's two conditions were straightforward enough.

The first was total confidentiality until they announced their decision, the second the presentation, within just two weeks, of a full written plan of campaign, including the structure of a businesslike organisation that would run the project.

With that, the meeting ended. We departed the NCB office with perfect decorum only thirty minutes after we had walked in.

We could not believe it.

'Unreal! Holy shit!' was Ron's first comment.

Barely able to conceal our excitement, but bound to secrecy, we raced away to our next potential sponsorship. We went through the motions of our next two presentations but after our NCB coup, it was a very lacklustre experience. Both FitzGerald and Daly were encouraging, but were not in a position to help very much. We now had to prepare and present a plan to NCB in fourteen days and I found myself in a dilemma. Several more people were needed to prepare the more detailed financial and organisational plan that NCB wanted, but I could not ask for their help because of the 'gag order' that Desmond had imposed on us. Allowing that situation to arise was a personal mistake because it crippled our ability to produce a document of the necessary quality – a real Catch-22 situation.

We worked hard on the plan but, predictably, it did not impress Dermot and Kevin at the meeting. The two NCB executives had also come up with a few conclusions of their own. 'You've come up with idea, you've helped raise the money, you've put the whole thing together, you've brought the people together, but you're not the person to run this project,' said Desmond to me. He then added, 'I'll fund it as long as you get Kilroy to head up the organising committee.'

The statement came as a bitter shock. After all the effort, all of the work that I had put in when others had given up halfway through, the project – my project – was being taken off me and I was being asked to get out of the way. I felt like I was being told to fuck off.

Later, I discovered what happened. After our first meeting with NCB, Desmond had sent out a researcher to gather information on the yachting scene and myself. One individual in particular had set out to assassinate my character and had met up with Desmond's researcher to cut the back off me, ensuring that I would not be the person given control of the project.

However, much as I didn't like it, there were harsh truths to be observed. What I couldn't see then, but came to understand later, was that I had reached the limit of what I could offer to Sail Ireland. The same was also true of Ron Holland and his office. The project now needed a seasoned executive, a person who could act as organiser, administrator and marketer. Quite simply I was the block between the money and the project.

I learned then never to underestimate the speed and ability with which financiers can get to the core of a project when they need to, and to tackle the necessary decision-making. It shouldn't have surprised me. After all it was their business – and their money.

Some people call it ruthless, and it is ruthless, but really it's only logical. What's in the best interests of the enterprise? You hire and fire as you require.

I won't deny that I was very close to an outburst when I was on the receiving end of it. I had two choices, go on the offensive and damage the project, and myself, or sit back and take the long-term view. I chose the latter. After all, I had started the project because I felt that it was something that would be good for the country, and although my pride was dented, the project was secure.

It was not long before I realised that it was a blessing in disguise to be freed from the prime responsibility. Although I had been ousted as the leading figure, with such an impressive group of people now committed to the project, it was a privilege just to be able to work with them.

While we recognised at once that NCB's condition regarding Kilroy was a stroke of genius, it left us with a big headache – how to persuade the head of a billion-pound Irish multinational corporation to take on full and active involvement in a relatively minor enterprise, when he had already specifically limited his commitment to the use of his name and perhaps a £10,000 shareholding?

I quickly set about bringing together the more prominent individuals who had loaned their name to Sail Ireland. My calculation was that if Kilroy saw the support and, more importantly, the money on the table, he could be persuaded.

The day after my shock meeting with Desmond, Howard Kilroy and the other Sail Ireland trustees met in Howth Yacht Club. I had arranged it so that Kilroy could attend the meeting, and could hopefully be convinced by the other trustees to take on the mantle.

We had permission from NCB to make a full disclosure to the members at this meeting. Naturally they were a bit nonplussed. One of our supporters, while wishing the project well, made his apologies and left. He was an executive with one of NCB's main competitors.

'Where is NCB coming from with this sponsorship? Is there room for anyone else, or should we all go home?' someone asked, probably voicing the doubts of most of our hard-won supporters.

'Who is this guy Desmond anyway?'

'Does he have the money?'

We answered as best we could. Then Holland dropped the bombshell. Looking at Kilroy he said, 'Dermot Desmond says you are the man to head up the committee,' adding that his involvement was in fact a condition of our getting the £1.4 million.

Kilroy raised his eyebrows. The other members present, thank Christ, unanimously agreed that Howard was the right choice, and began to build up pressure on him to accept at once. Some discussion followed, and Kilroy finally gave his answer. 'OK, I might give it a whirl...' there was a careful pause '... but let's crunch the numbers first.'

Ron and I allowed ourselves to breathe again. The corner had been turned and Sail Ireland was rolling. But now there was a lot to organise and little enough time to do it in.

Chapter eight

Sea Change

Sail Ireland was now two years from the Whitbread starting line and, as months slipped past, Ron Holland and I were constantly pressing for action. While appreciating that the organisational base had to be consolidated and the finances properly directed, we, of all the people involved, knew that sooner or later – and the sooner the better – we would have to get down to the nitty-gritty of the project and build a base of ground-level expertise.

Somehow we needed to plug in to ocean racing at world level to gain an insight into the contemporary thought processes, the technical development and the key people. The maxi World Championships were taking place in Sardinia and, with everyone who mattered in international sailing centred there, it was clearly the place to be. 'But you can't blow money on junkets to Sardinia', was the natural response of the accountants. In the end we succeeded in convincing them that all the money and organisation would count for nothing unless we could come to grips with the competition and make contacts with the right people. Finally Dermot Desmond, Howard Kilroy, Killian Bushe, Ron Holland and myself purloined the Smurfit jet and zipped off to the Mediterranean.

A sharp and fit Californian in his sixties, Jim Kilroy was chairman of Kilroy Industries, and was supposedly worth about seven hundred million by that stage (he was no relation to Howard). It wasn't his money we were after though, it was the experience and wisdom he had accumulated in building and racing several maxis.

How did you guys get in here?' Jim Kilroy asked us on our first meeting at Puerto Cervo.

'From Dublin on the G3.'

Jim nodded. The Gulf Stream Model 3 executive jet – a G3 to the wealthy – was an almost mandatory status symbol in Jim Kilroy's world.

'You realise its going to cost you two million bucks to build this yacht?' he asked, making it amply clear from his tone that he had no intention of contributing any of his own money to Sail Ireland. Desmond explained that he had put the money up, and that what we wanted from Jim was his ideas, interest and perhaps his maxi for training.

Within a day Howard and Dermot, having established our credentials for us, disappeared on the G3, leaving Ron, Killian and myself to hobnob with the maxi crews, watch the yachts in action and take a lot of photographs.

When I was ready to leave I had to get a ticket home on an ordinary commercial jet at short notice, and it ended up costing me a bomb. So much for executive jets, I would have been better off purchasing a return flight in the beginning!

The priority for us now was to find a technical manager who might roll over into the position of skipper or co-skipper. Harry Cudmore was convinced – and he ought to know – that there was no one in Ireland of the calibre required. Among several runners mooted, the choice boiled down to Bobby Campbell – recommended by Jim Kilroy ('He'll have to be on your payroll.') and Terry Gould.

Although Campbell's credentials were impressive, he was distant at our first meeting and said little. A Bostonian in his early thirties, he was very technically oriented, but projected all the personality of a brick. From our first meeting, there was little doubt in my mind that while his technical input could be invaluable he would not be the right choice for skipper.

By contrast Terry Gould was a much warmer personality. He had started sailing at the age of eight and since then had chalked up an impressive track record in ocean racing. In the end Campbell got the consultant's job and eventually became skipper, principally on the strength of his connection to Jim Kilroy, and Terry later joined us as one of the yacht-building team and then one of the crew.

Back at home, the technical aspects of the project were gaining momentum faster than the administration and marketing. Ironically for Ron Holland and me, after our months of sweeping people in to give our project credibility, the problem now was that there were so many involved that decision-making became more difficult.

What the project desperately needed was a co-ordinating chief executive, a role that I had been filling in a caretaker capacity. On secondment from Smurfit, Frank Gaughan, took over the job and was installed in an office provided by Bord Iascaigh Mhara (The Sea Fisheries Board) with secretarial support. Thanks to the support of Howard Kilroy and fellow executive John Bourke, I was made Gaughan's assistant.

For several years, Frank had been running Irish Paper Sacks for the Jefferson Smurfit organisation when suddenly he found himself transferred to Smurfit Management Consultants. He had gone on from an engineering qualification to study for a master's degree in business administration in the USA, so he certainly had the right sort of training and management experience. It was his job to see that Sail Ireland was run on professional, businesslike lines, and to assess and use the expertise available from professionals like Bobby Campbell. Still, even to be able to make such an assessment, Frank had a lot of learning to do, and not much time to do it in.

The organisation was structured in three committees, marketing, technical and finance, which were made up mainly of the original Sail Ireland Trust members. They each reported to a board of directors, chaired by Howard Kilroy, which rubber-stamped their decisions.

Feargal Quinn headed the marketing committee. With his extraordinary flair for public relations, Feargal had jumped in with both feet and characteristic enthusiasm. I was soon commuting to his office at 8.00 am for healthy fruit-driven power breakfasts and one of the first things the committee did was to agree on my provisional Sail Ireland name.

Robert Dix led finance while John Bourke took over the technical committee. Both men were accountants, and also consummate professionals.

By the time all of this organisational framework was in place and approved by NCB, we were into the winter of 1987. At last funds were released and things began to move on all fronts. Though the project had not been made public, there had been leaks in the press and the time was ripe to present the project to Ireland and the world with all the style it deserved. Charlie Haughey and Harry Cudmore launched it at a public reception.

Finding the correct premises to build the yacht in was our first problem. Symptomatic of our recession, there was a glut of industrial property on the market at the time, but it proved more difficult than we expected to find the right place. Finally, having looked over several unsuitable premises, we were offered rent-free the temporarily empty part of a Ballyfermot factory owned by Consolidated Plastics, a company part-owned by the Jefferson Smurfit Group.

Curing plastic resins demands an environment of high temperature and low humidity, as free as possible of dust. It meant building a factory within a factory – a hundred foot-long tent of bubble wrap plastic, with up thirty people working in and around it.

Boat-building is a cottage industry and is notorious for backhanders. We had to hire in some boat-builders from England and, during the interviews, I learned another little lesson in management.

One of the English candidates sat in front of us, and with his broad accent he cut to the chase with a sweep of his hand. 'Look, 'ire me matey, gimme the job. No fuckin' back 'anders, right? What I take, it'll all go back into the kitty.'

Jesus, that's just great I thought. We'll hire this guy, he's straight up with us, tells the truth all the time and he doesn't pull fast ones.

Then John Bourke pulled me aside. 'Look it Enda, when the guy comes out and says that, he's not straight. He's thinking about backhanders all the time, so now he has to prove that he isn't. The fact that he says he's not going to do it is a dead giveaway.'

It was the issue of honesty and trust again. Our English boat builder had been trying to impose his integrity on us, and while I was naive to it at the time, it didn't fool Bourke for a second.

Trust is earned, not demanded. Be wary of anybody who protests too much.

Being able to read people is another of the hallmarks of being an entrepreneur. No person is an island, and to make a success of a venture you are inevitably relying on many individuals, both above and below you. That's why you must choose with care, and you must be able to differentiate. Mistakes still happen, but you learn from that and keep going.

Of course there are still wankers who get to the top. Just make sure you know which ones they are!

The story of the Irish team's challenge in the Whitbread is better told in the 1990 commemorative book *Sail Ireland*, however suffice to say that in the end, while superbly organised, we did not win – or come close to winning. Ron Holland had gone for a conservative design and other contestants had simply walked away from us with their more outgoing ketches.

I'm not blaming it on Holland. It was a group decision to go with his design and therefore we shared equal responsibility. Though I felt a little more responsible for a couple of reasons. The Sail Ireland project was superbly run, it was administered by top-quality people and it was an example of brilliant organisation. No problems there.

Where it went wrong was the Irish psychology of the period. For whatever the reasons, the Irish felt like losers. The executives in Sail Ireland didn't think like that, but they were aware that the country did. How could we in Ireland build a boat that was going to win?

A lot to do with winning is psychological. It's in your attitude. I know about it in sport because I compete at a high level in sailing. It counts even in small things. A partner and myself played a game of championship tennis in Prague recently. The guys who came out against us had matching shirts and matching shorts, and immediately they had the psychological advantage. And they won. And got as far as the final.

Knowing how insecure the Irish felt about themselves, the Sail Ireland marketing committee came out with a winner's attitude. It was a powerful message and it invigorated the whole project and powered it forward. We can win. We've got the best designer, the best organisation, the best sailors, and we're going to win this race.

Then a huge paradigm shift happened with the design of the boat. Ron Holland put forward a conservative model, which you tend to do for round-the-world attempts, but it left-footed us. When you commit yourself to winning, you don't go along with a cautious design. That's like going into the casino, hyping yourself up to win big, and then laying tiny bets for the rest of the night. You'd be far better off putting it all on red.

When you think big, you don't mess around.

The design was wrong, and no matter what we did or how we psyched ourselves up, the design was always going to be wrong.

That's where I should have put my foot down. I saw that the project was failing to have a meeting of minds between concept and design. There was only two ways it should have gone. If we sold it as a winner, then we had to design as a winner and we should have got Holland to give us something speedier and less sturdy. If we were going to go with a cautious model, we should have promoted it as a great adventure and a great achievement.

But we did a 50–50 split and set ourselves up for a fall. Because of our yacht's poor performance in the race the likes of *Phoenix* magazine got going on us. After all the effort and success it was perceived as a failure because we didn't win.

This was something else I learned. No matter how many great experts you have around you, if you fundamentally feel that something is wrong, you must say so. Granted, how you say these things is sometimes an art in itself, but say it you must.

You can always deliver a difference of opinion in a non-combative and non-embarrassing way. In fact it's your duty to do so for the sake of the organisation. On a personal level, I regarded the entire Sail Ireland project as a success and an extraordinary experience. I managed to pull together a bunch of Ireland's finest business people and in doing so learned a huge amount. Seeing top-class professionals in action always makes a person aware of their own limitations, but knowing your limitations is one of the keys to success. For myself I had gained a new level of entrepreneurship, and I learned that there are many different ways in which people can contribute.

A few of them stand out in front. Des Bourke-Kennedy for instance was the king of positive thinking. The man never said a negative word. When Dermot Desmond delivered the verdict that I was not to run the project, it was Bourke-Kennedy who called around to my house and explained just how much I had achieved.

When you are intense about something, you go hard one way and go hard the other way. Passion is a very powerful thing and we need it in our lives if we are to succeed. In the early days of entrepreneurship, there has to be a feeling, a filling of a need, something so strong that it will continue down the line and invigorate all those connected to it.

The downside can happen if the entrepreneur believes that he or she is being removed from the object of their passion. I was passionate about the project and I was really down in the dumps having been removed as the lead guy. But Des really turned it around for me by explaining what had already been accomplished.

Another figure who stood out was John Bourke. I learned that he was the type of person that I didn't want to be.

Now that sounds unflattering, but it isn't. I don't want to be like John Bourke because I know just how good he is at what he does, and I know that I could never match his style because I just don't have the reservoir of quite patience that he has. He would think nothing of enduring a situation that I would find interminably tedious. As a professional banker, John was very much a committee and consensus man. Once he told me that he wanted one of his top managers to do something, but didn't want to give him a direct order. Instead he wanted the manager to see it for himself and have ownership of the concept.

John waited a full year for it to happen, but once his manager came up with the idea the guy was immediately full of pride. It was his idea, his thought and his imagination. He would implement this concept with more enthusiasm and success than if John had given it to him in the form of an instruction.

He had therefore the perfect gift for running bureaucratic structures, something that most entrepreneurs would never have because they are just too impatient and fast moving. But even Bourke knew the significance of gut feelings.

'The Duke of Wellington never lost a war,' John once said to me, 'If he woke in the morning and things did not feel right, he might retreat and delay battle. The grass might be wet, he might be uncertain about the terrain, or he might just not feel right about it. The enemy would laugh, call him a coward, and insult his manhood or whatever. He didn't care because if he didn't like the conditions, or wasn't sure of victory, he didn't commence.'

Another exceptional individual on the team was Feargal Quinn. In addition to his natural enthusiasm and flair, what surprised and impressed me far more was his genuine modesty. Although he was head of the marketing committee, he put himself completely in the background during the launch of the project. Most others would have been out glory hunting, but not Feargal.

Years later when I was setting up a company in eastern Europe I came across a very bright girl who was selling souvenirs in a market. I noticed that she had an amazing talent for languages and that she was picking up English almost as soon as it was being spoken to her.

I hired her as an assistant in our office and then called up Ann O'Broin, Feargal's personal secretary, and arranged for the girl to go and work in his office. It was a two-way deal, Feargal got a very bright and enthusiastic employee for a while, and I got my new assistant trained in a superb public relations environment. After she was finished in Dublin, the girl came back and taught everything she had learned to my staff.

But if I had to pick the biggest all-rounder in terms of colour and 'cop-on', it would have to be Harry Cudmore from Cork.

Harry gave me a number of tips regarding Sail Ireland. 'Enda,' he said, 'get the big players in, wheel them out front and have them put in some money. If you do, it can't fail because their name is associated with it.'

And he was right. Once we had showcased our corporate sponsors, we were still £1 million short, but we knew that we couldn't go wrong by that stage. Once people have committed a certain amount to a venture they are not inclined to see their investment go under for the sake of a little more cash. Ultimately the entire project cost £4 million, which was spent over two years on logistics, sales, consultants and employees.

While Harry was a great guy to know, he also was aware of the need to apply more Machiavellian strategies in order to get a decent grip on something. He advised me once that if you are running a team of, say, fifteen or twenty people and you need to assert your authority without question, pick somebody and fire them. It sends the required message instantly.

And who do you pick? Generally the person that nobody else likes because that person is usually unpopular for reasons of incompetence or laziness. If two objectives happily coincide, you've trimmed the fat and put the rest of the team in line. If you are going to run a team you must be prepared to lay down the law and command respect, should it come to that. Sometimes, of course, you might be sacrificing a good worker, and while it's harsh it can be necessary. Everything has to come back to the same basic principle – what is in the best interests of the project?

Overall, Sail Ireland was never just about doing battle with the elements; it was a major battle of economics, logistics and sheer willpower. Sailing was the easy part. I cut my teeth at the higher level of business without really being at the higher level, and I would soon have to use everything that I had learned.

Chapter nine

Executive...

By 1990, with the Sail Ireland project wound up and no businesses requiring my full-time attention, I was free to pursue some sailing of my own. The Whitbread must have had a real effect on me because I entered the BOC single-handed round-the-world race. This was an enormous challenge and, in retrospect, did not have a lot of logic to it.

I wanted a very fast yacht and I set my sights on a sixty-footer, which in reality was too large for me to be able to handle on my own. To get it I had to enter a lease purchase agreement, buying the boat over time for $180,000. I used most of my own remaining money, pretty much everything I had, and sought sponsorship from many sources before eventually winning support from Smirnoff.

I started with the distributors of Smirnoff in Ireland, but their executives just couldn't see any value in it for them. Undaunted, I stepped on a plane and went to Connecticut in New York and met with the group's global marketing director. Paul Murphy, a good friend and supporter from the National Yacht Club, to whom I'm still very appreciative, flew over with me to assist in the negotiations.

The GMD heard me out and I finally secured a sponsorship for $100,000. Just like that. You should have seen the faces on the Irish guys when I told them. They just couldn't believe it.

In fairness to them, though, the advertising budget for the Irish market was pretty small. A hundred grand to the global director was probably a fifteen-second television commercial somewhere. To the Paddies it probably represented their marketing budget for the year, or longer.

Between that cheque and some other things I raised most of the money. But I still had another problem. A key condition of the race was that I get insurance cover. Not surprisingly, this is not a thing you drop into your local broker and arrange. So eventually, after intense shopping around, I was offered cover for about $60,000 – thirty-three per cent of the value of the boat. In simple terms, the insurance company was taking a three-to-one bet that I would come to grief.

This is probably a good time to talk about risk management. When you trace the history of risk, in fact, you trace the history of civilisation itself as we have come to know it. The story of risk is well told in Peter Bernstein's excellent book *Against the Gods – the Remarkable Story of Risk*, and the management and understanding of risk is a necessary understanding to have if you intend to develop your own enterprise.

Let me explain.

It's 3,000 years ago, a bad storm leads to the destruction of a merchant, his ship, or even an entire coastal village. It's a total loss.

There is nothing in the kitty, and insurance is a term that the merchant has never heard of. It may take a century for the town or the merchant's family to recover from the loss. If ever.

So unless he had something squirreled away, he's done for. There's no such thing as an insurance policy that provides funds to recover the losses for the village, ship or individual so that trading can recommence.

It is only in the last 300 years that society started to study, analyse and manage risk in a systematic fashion – and began learning how to calculate the actual probability that a person or venture might encounter a terminal disaster. Modern insurance as we know it started at Lloyds, the famous London coffee house where merchants met and discussed the likelihood of dangers befalling their ships. Many individuals might opt-in to share the risk of a particular voyage so the loss, or the profits, was spread.

So what does all that have to do with my BOC challenge yacht?

Despite being the founder and shareholder in an insurance brokerage business, it took a personal experience for me to really get an understanding of how the risk market works.

The $60,000 I needed represented a fortune at the time and just was not possible for the budget within which I was operating. So to solve the problem, I came up with a neat little escapade that insured my boat and provided a little amusement for the underwriters on the floor of The Lloyds of London Insurance Market.

Located in a futuristic building in the heart of London, this market is something of a risk casino, staffed by armies of pinstripe buccaneers. My introduction to the market came when I personally took my risk onto the floor.

I got an underwriter to take five per cent of the risk, and then I went around to all the other boxes – almost forty in all – selling between one and five per cent of the remaining risk. The underwriters were essentially sponsoring me but instead of giving cash they were taking a little bit of my risk upon themselves.

In return, all I gave them was a little publicity and a few minutes diversion from the humdrum of the market. It was something for the 'city types' to chatter about over their beer after work. I think I got a good deal...

A person's decision to take the entrepreneurial route is strongly influenced by risk and is based upon the same risk/ reward trade-off.

If you leave your job and spend all of your resources on a new enterprise and it fails, you risk losing everything and becoming destitute. The more you have progressed through life – and the more assets, responsibilities and creature comforts you have accumulated – the bigger your risk. Likewise, the later in life you expose yourself to risk, the harder it will be for you to recover when things go wrong. So if you are a few years from the expensive watch and golden handshake, perhaps it's the wrong time for you to think about starting something new.

Success can strongly depend on your management of risk. I have almost always had 'what if' scenarios mapped out. Being better able to understand the risks related to my venture gave me stronger personal security, reduced tension and gave comfort to those around me.

'Don't do the crime if you haven't the time.' This is the catch phrase of crooks everywhere. A friend of mine heard it from a petty criminal he met in London. A thief by profession, he had a young wife and family to support. For this reason, although tempted, he kept away from bigger crimes. His logic was that bigger crimes were too risky when measured up against the longer jail sentences he faced if caught.

So it's quite clear that risk management is a fundamental of business. How can it not be when it's universally understood by everyone from the lowest criminal element to the highest financial institution?

After my own risk management, I finally got into my beautiful sixty-footer and sailed across the Atlantic to qualify for the BOC race in September 1990.

Just as I was getting into the US on the qualifying leg, I got caught in the tail end of a hurricane and suffered damage to the rig of the boat. This delayed me in getting to the start in Newport Rhode Island, and I started the race a day or two behind the rest of the competitors.

It was about 2 a.m. in October and I was down in the bilge trying to fix a problem with my self-steering system when a deep-sea trawler struck me. By rights it shouldn't have happened because I had a radar system that was supposed to go off when other ships came too close, but for whatever reason, I never heard the alarm.

When the trawler struck the boat my hundred-foot mast got pulled down and the boat was holed, putting an end to my BOC round-the-world attempt. As the trawler took me back to the US with my punctured yacht in tow I began to evaluate where I was going in life. 'What the hell am I doing... What the hell am I doing?' I remember saying to myself as we chugged away somewhere between Bermuda and Norfolk, Virginia.

As it was, my Lloyds insurance police did not cover the loss of the mast and hull damage. The policy I had only covered me if the boat was entirely destroyed, leaving me to seriously consider scuttling the entire vessel.

Since I had been operating the boat single-handedly when I was struck by the fishing boat, I did not think I would be successful in seeking compensation. Then by chance, in a bar on the mainland, a local man suggested to me that I should claim off the fisheries co-operative that owned the trawler. At sea, power gives way to sail and therefore it was the trawler's obligation to keep out of my way.

Armed with this knowledge, I promptly got the local *Yellow Pages* out and kept ringing until I found a lawyer who would take my case on a success only basis. Most didn't want to know and I finally settled with one lawyer who agreed to take the case for forty per cent of the settlement.

Within a week the lawyer settled for about $50,000, leaving me with $30,000 – allowing me to walk away, debt free.

After that I thought I might do a single-handed record from New York to San Francisco around Cape Horn, and between that and a few other ideas I made another attempt to raise money. But this time it just wasn't happening. The ideas were there but I didn't have the resources, and truth be known my heart was not really into it as much.

I had become a little tired of living in a false world of raising money for one-off record attempts and competitions. This period of my life was a turning point and a time for a reality check. A very patient and understanding Suzanna and three wonderful daughters were waiting for me back in Dún Laoghaire, and I had very little money.

Although I did continue to sail, I decided then that I really had to get back into the real world and straighten out my priorities. My more adventurous days were now behind me.

I returned to Dublin and found myself unemployed again. I did a weekly sailing column for *The Irish Times* that paid between £80–100 a week, and I did a little freelance journalism work. It kept us going, but it wasn't exactly a life of disposable income.

I was at home one evening in spring 1991 when the telephone rang. 'Could I speak to Mr Enda O'Coineen,' a slightly accented voice said.

'Enda here.'

'Good evening Mr O'Coineen, my name is Susi Huber and I work with IMPAC. We are taking part in the Miami-Montego Bay Race and we want to know if you would like to participate.'

Now a couple of things had conspired to bring this about.

Ted Turner's son, Ted Junior, had just bought an eighty-foot maxi that had been in the Whitbread Race. Then somebody saw a copy of my book, *Sail Ireland*, which was an account I had written of the Irish experience from start to finish.

Now in Ireland if you write a book the response is typically, 'That wally, what would he know?' But globally if you write a book you are suddenly an expert. Susi had seen my book on the Irish Whitbread Challenge and decided that I was in the latter category.

Now along with the Fastnet Race, Bermuda Race and Sydney-Hobart Race, the Miami-Montego Bay Race is regarded as one of the ocean classics, so there was no way I was going to turn it down. And besides, my yachting column for The Irish Times was going to suddenly get a lot more interesting.

I hooked up with Ted and his crew in Florida and raced down to Jamaica, learning a lot about the crew and the people who had invited me.

Turner Junior was twenty-six and half of his crew were made up of other twenty-something rich kids. I can't really say much for them except that they were quite spoilt, although Ted himself was a decent guy. He was capable of leadership, but he could never be a great entrepreneur like his father. He was simply was not made that way.

The other half of the crew was more intriguing. They consisted of IMPAC executives and their invitees, myself included. IMPAC is the acronym for Improved Management Productivity and Control, and they liked to call themselves 'management engineers'. They despised the term consultants, although most people would put them in that bracket. Knowing something about the varying quality of consultants, I actually prefer the term management engineers, because IMPAC really were that good.

The CEO and founder of IMPAC was Jim Irwin, a big Irish-American businessman with little sailing experience, though he owned a motor yacht. Irwin had gone along with the group and had taken his wife Linda and four executives from the company, including Susi Huber. He wanted to learn more about ocean sailing and get an understanding of it – in particular the management dynamics so they could examine the relationship in running a large yacht and running a business.

No doubt they also wanted to get close to Ted Turner, which would be a normal corporate strategy in the circumstances.

IMPAC had a free hand to invite me along with some other crew but, although I was one of their choices, I was more into the sailing side of things. The other IMPAC people were business types, for example Susi turned out to be a German industrial psychologist.

There was also Susi's fiancé, Tom Doyle, together with senior IMPAC executive Colm Hendrick with his wife, Eileen. Linda Irwin joined us too. A very accomplished lady in her own right she was intelligent, beautiful and very politically correct. She later got it into her head that I was a little in the male chauvinist category and I really did not have a proper regard for the female sex. At that time as a man with a wife, three daughters, five sisters and one mother, I had not lacked female criticism or respect at any stage of my life. But a woman can be different to a man. This is not supposed to be a sexist comment, I think the difference is a reflection of life, art and beauty itself. But I must confess to being bewildered by a lot of the PC stuff that I hear these days.

I actually think that Linda's interpretation of my jokes, perceived attitudes, comments or whatever was just a classic misunderstanding of English. 'We are divided by a common language', as George Bernard Shaw put it.

It's all in how you say it. America is a more direct society with less subtlety in language and what you say is often taken literally. It is hard to explain to Americans, however, a European-style humour may often say something in a conversation while meaning the exact opposite.

It's called irony guys. Look it up.

However, despite my levity, it's true that the wrong comment can cost European companies a lot of money. So much so that now there are several examples of executives (very cultured, sophisticated, educated people with normal relationships) having to do intense courses on political correctness regarding what they can and cannot say.

By the time the voyage was finished, psychologist Susi had me so analysed that I did not know what to make of her. Amongst other things, she decided I was vain. So be it.

There were twenty-two of us on Turner's yacht. We raced this ocean-going machine off the coast of Florida, upwind out around the Bahamas, down towards Cuba where we 'hung a right' for a spinnaker run down to Jamaica in some of the most beautiful sailing waters of the world. Six hundred wonderful miles in total.

I had a ball, though I'm not sure about everybody else.

We were running down the Windward Passage between Jamaica and Cuba when a tropical squall hit us. We had a full spinnaker up, roaring along at fifteen knots – very fast for a sailboat – and it was a dark night. As each wave crashed, the yacht was getting more and more out of control. Then a big mother of a wave came and shook the yacht a bit. Turner and his crew panicked.

Up to that point, I was happily mucking in as part of the team. But since it was turning into a crisis situation, I got hold of the wheel without bothering to ask permission and took command of the yacht. I had been through tropical fronts like this before and it was no big deal. It's pretty standard stuff for most experienced ocean sailors.

Asserting my leadership came naturally and did not cause me a second thought. On that eighty-footer there just wasn't anybody else capable of it at the time, Turner and his buddies really didn't have the experience, and the IMPAC people knew very little about sailing. So that left me.

Without wasting time I got the big spinnaker down, kept the yacht going and generally got things under control again. I wasn't even scared. Don't worry, there have been a load of times when I was but this was small potatoes by comparison. Though it must be said that there's nothing like a bit of turmoil to sort the wheat from the chaff. In times of peace and stability, we tend to be content with a fairly mediocre standard of leadership and management. By that I mean you get bland leaders, middle-ranking people, who just conform and drift through society.

Dig through history to times of uncertainty, when gaps need to be filled and when societies have problems – it is generally then that strong leaders emerge.

Unfortunately, strong doesn't have to mean good. Think Hitler or Milosevic. The rest of the race went fine and we had no more incidents. Jamaica was fantastic place to arrive at and we did a great performance in the race. We were closing land at Montego and I began to consider my next move. I had thought no further than finishing the race, writing up my column and moving on.

'What are you doing when we get to Jamaica?' It was Jim Irwin speaking. He was exhausted from the trip just like the rest of the non-sailors. Sleeping accommodation in tubular berths in the open plan vessel was primitive and the seas had been big.

'Em... nothing really. I've just my newspaper column to finish.'

'Come and join me on my boat. She's here in Montego.'

'Sure, fine.'

At that stage all I knew of Jim was that he was just another friendly American. I am always curious to see other craft as well, so I happily went down to the bay with him.

Moments later, this enormous yacht came in. His boat turned out to be an American-style motor yacht called *Tai-pan*.

It seemed like a mega-vessel to me, even though it was only sixty-feet and not in the big leagues. With her captain and professional crew who maintained her in immaculate condition, she had been shadowing our racing yacht all the way from Florida. Jim has upgraded many times since, but even back then *Tai-Pan* came complete with satellite phone, jacuzzi and exercise bicycle. Wow.

I had not realised that Jim was a multimillionaire type with almost more money than he knew what to do with. I put the emphasis on 'almost'.

The various costs of my communications back to *The Irish Times* via the yacht's satellite phone probably cost more than what I was ultimately paid for the article, but Jim insisted I use the facilities and the comfort was just grand.

Jim said he had been impressed with my taking charge of the yacht during the squall and he wanted to know more about me. We got along well and the more we talked the more fascinated I became by his thinking, perspective on life and his team on the yacht. In addition to his core management engineering business, he had interests in hotels, property, travel and even a yacht brokerage.

I discovered that Jim Bill Irwin, or JBI as he was known, was an extraordinary character. Growing up as a poor Irish-American family in New York City, he was fuelled with ambition and a desire to get on with it. He was a tough guy and quite a contrarian, who I took to immediately. His corporate culture was as tough as he was and with him you were only as good as your last month. Very often IMPAC would get into a company and reduce the headcount by forty per cent and do the dirty work that top management were unwilling or unable for.

'I would like you to come work for us,' Jim said over dinner as the evening sun radiated majestically over Montego Bay.

The offer was totally out of the blue. 'I'm an entrepreneur, I've always run my own business. I'm not really a good employee,' I said. Despite the fact that I had shag-all lined up for me in Dublin and I was in dire need of cash.

I suppose Jim liked the honesty and directness. 'Enda we need people like you in our organisation.' He explained that companies like his wanted lots of different types to input different things. His constant challenge was to create and maintain an entrepreneurial culture in what was a large organisation (I'll talk about this in more detail later).

For a time I hesitated, not actually sure if the guy was for real. Eventually, with an attractive base salary of $30,000 a year, freedom to continue my newspaper writing, some perks and a $100,000 sponsorship for the Irish Ocean Youth Club, of which I was a director, I flew home a happy man. Needless to say, my wife, Suzanna, was over the top with the prospect of steady income as I worked as a management engineer.

Suzanna also came to like many of the IMPAC people as well as Jim Irwin's extended 'family'. I thought I might last six months in the job, maximum a year, but to my genuine amazement I was still there two and a half years later.

That's a long time to survive with this demanding man and company. But it was a wonderful learning experience. Jim Irwin was good to me, I developed a high respect for him and his methods and I hope I gave back something in return. Working for IMPAC was fascinating. I learned a great deal about the theoretical aspects of management and it complimented what I learned with the Sail Ireland team. Not only that, but it was my first experience with an organisation as progressive and as radical as IMPAC.

According to the marketing literature IMPAC had a thousand consultants worldwide. When you joined the company you got a portable computer, which was way ahead of its time in the early 1990s, and the company had its own intranet that you could plug into no matter where you were in the world as long as you had a telephone line. So I was using an Internet of sorts in 1992, at least five years before it was accepted practice within other companies.

Irwin's philosophy also dispensed with offices. As a 'consultant' with IMPAC you were one of three things: working with clients; at home with your family; or on the bench awaiting a call. The only staff in offices were administration or accounts people.

Jim was a futuristic person who was running a virtual company. And he was doing things years before the larger corporate world had even considered the possibility. It was a business concept that could only have been developed by a person who was ahead of his time.

But IMPAC's approach was as clinical and as remorseless as the circuitry it was operating on. The company had little time for smooth MBAs and McKinsey-type 'touchy-feely' consultants who go in and charge big fees for fat reports which often accumulate dust on administrators' desks. Rather Irwin looked for practical, streetwise people who earned their 'studs' as implementers.

We generally only went into companies that had more than 1,500 employees, and when we did we were usually the axe men. When a company needs radical restructuring, very often it's too late by the time management get around to doing it. The people in charge of the firm know the executives personally, they are emotionally attached and they shirk from sacking anyone.

Sometimes if you want the best for the company you must have a clinical and ruthless attitude. Your primary consideration is the balance sheet and the profit and loss margins. It sounds cruel, it sounds inhumane, but it's better to sack half of your staff and preserve the organisation than mess around indefinitely and see the entire workforce ultimately laid off at a later date.

And very often that's exactly what your choices are.

We went in at the shop floor level and began to investigate the entire firm upwards. Our approach was also unique. We didn't go in and get paid for a sheaf of paper, we went in and guaranteed that if you didn't make savings as a result of our work, you got your money back.

You see Irwin, like other great businessmen, thought at the strategic and long-term level, which is unusual. He knew that the added value was not achieved in writing the report, it was achieved through its implementation.

Not only that, he also allowed for a large capital investment on the part of IMPAC before the client was even committed to employing us. We offered, at no cost to the potential client, a complete analysis of the business from its management structures all the way down to the number of nuts and bolts they held in stock. Doing that for a company of 1,500 employees might mean an expenditure of $50,000–100,000 on the part of IMPAC.

Not surprisingly the middle and upper management of the client companies despised us. We reported only to the chairman of the board or the CEO of the firm, and anybody below them was considered expendable. If the client wasn't prepared to give us that type of freedom, we didn't entertain them. It was a pretty brutal business, and we were akin to a Spanish Inquisition of the corporate world. We went in, found out what we needed to know, stripped the poor-quality executives and idle from the workforce, and then nursed the corporation back to fiscal health.

It was do or die. And we did.

I was fortunate insofar as I was sent in at the top end of the business. I was taken in primarily because of my adventurous side, but my skills in communication, marketing and business development all fitted well. I ended up reporting to JBI on the corporate board. Jim's first assignment for me was developing some new products that mixed outdoor, adventure and physical activity with psychological training techniques. The goal was a combined product that would create long-term behavioural change in organisations. He also wanted to build training products and services in team building and leadership training.

Whether Susi Huber was given to me to work with, or whether I was given to her to work with, I was never sure. It didn't matter, we had a ball regardless. Our research took me to the Center for Creative Leadership in San Diego, Sportsmind in Washington and Outdoor Pursuits in Colorado. It was a fascinating experience to visit these places and look at their activities. I arrived at the Centre for Creative Leadership just at the time that the book *Breaking the Glass Ceiling* by Ann M. Morrison was published. It identified how women executives could only get promoted so far in organisations before being halted by an invisible barrier, an effective 'glass ceiling' that nobody could see, but was there nevertheless.

I also learned then the enormous difference between the training and development necessary for a leader and what was required for team building. The leader had to be a team player in some respects, but was not a team member. Leaders tended to be strong individuals and, although they often understood the dynamic of personal relationships and the value of cooperation, they were best suited to giving orders rather than receiving them.

That on it's own doesn't make a leader, but it's one characteristic. In fact I think that it's impossible to define what kind of person a leader should be and what makes them. Some leaders are cast into the role by accident, many learn and refine their style of leadership over the length of their career, and a few are just naturally good at it.

Leadership of course is critical for entrepreneurship. However not all leaders are entrepreneurs and not all entrepreneurs are leaders. So if you are an entrepreneur and not a leader, to succeed it will be crucial to 1) know that you are not a leader and 2) correct this by attracting key personnel who are good leaders. The most important thing I have learned is that few, if any, leaders are the same and that personal styles are unique. However, the list below, drawn from studies and personal experience, gives the traits that I associate with good leadership:

- Have clearly defined goals. Know to where you want to lead.
- The chosen goals should be simultaneously beneficial to the group and individual members of the group so that internal conflict is avoided.

- Have the ability to communicate these goals effectively.
- See your leadership as an obligation rather than rank and privilege.
- Accept responsibility when things go wrong and do not blame others.
- Harness the energy of strong associates and subordinates. They should be encouraged and given credit for their contributions rather than viewed with suspicion.
- More than anything you must earn trust. You can't lead if you have no followers.

Unfortunately there are some who lack the confidence, competence or people skills to be a leader yet want to have the position because they are attracted to either the status or the financial rewards. Often what they lack in ability, they compensate for with a mixture of cunning and aggressiveness. They are simultaneously bullies, sycophants and freeloaders, and are detrimental in every way to the functioning of an organisation because they act as a bulwark between management and workers, leaders and followers.

If an organisation has an individual like this in a leadership role, everything below this mediocre person will be negatively affected. Good workers will be viewed as a threat and cronies will be promoted. Anybody who doesn't fit the culture will depart, the rest will conform and stagnation will occur.

Good leaders, ones with the right people skills, will avoid this happening no matter how large the organisation is. However, when things are going well people motivation in the organisation is often academic. Motivating people during setbacks is the real challenge.

Fads come and go, but as I've regularly said and will always maintain, the fundamentals do not change. In what *Business Week* magazine termed 'Sanitised Lunacy', the fad of the 1990s was to take teams of executives on mountain survival courses and put them through the worst physical hardships conceivable. The objective was to get them out of the work environment to play, have fun and develop a team mentality. The best example of this that I came across was an adventure school in Scotland. They would take a group of executives, say from a London bank, and leave them on their own in the hills with survival rations and a couple of blankets. And while they could charge city rates, their operation costs were incredibly low since they had no accommodation, catering or service costs of any consequence.

Invariably these outdoor trips created behavioural change on the ground, but it only lasted for a brief period back in the organisation – eventually people went back to their own ways.

Let me give you an example from a famous Harvard study.

A management team goes into a factory. They raise the lighting, adjust the furniture and in a short time the workers respond positively to the new environment and the productivity level increases. Some time later, after productivity has dropped to the previous levels, the management team go back in, lower the level of the lighting and put the furniture back where it was before.

Behold! Productivity goes up again.

Of course, after a period of time it reverts – making your Feng Shui routine as useful as a time out in the Highlands.

At IMPAC our brief was to properly diagnose the change necessary to make organisations work better, facilitate that and – most importantly – quantify and sustain the long-term benefits. Fads were no use.

We had to isolate the factors that would lead to improved teamwork and productivity, and then deliver them in a package that a corporation could employ to keep up the higher standards.

Jim specifically was interesting in correlating my adventure, ocean and team-building experience with that of the experience of running a large company. He was also interested in training methodologies that would quantify what was needed in advance for a management team to achieve something concrete, such as merging two cultures in a company or creating and managing change. This involved assessing what the company needed, be it a merger, change of working habits or whatever and then implementing those changes, evaluating the experience and then conducting a follow-up.

IMPAC would do an analysis of the client and then speak to the CEO or the chairman of the board. They might have merged with another company, or made a recent acquisition, and found that their new staff were unresponsive or hostile to their working culture. So what do you do when you've got people who are set in their ways and you want them to change? Based on what the company wanted to achieve, we did individual analysis with each of the target employees and created profiles. Then we put them through a suitable programme designed to achieve what the company needed.

Drawing on my experiences at sea, I developed a product called *Teamship*, which used the maritime setting as a catalyst for changing habits and thought processes. In fact, a boat is the perfect place to effect behavioural change because it's such a captive environment. For that reason we ran *Teamship* on an 80-foot maxi that operated from the coast of Florida.

To begin with, it makes you tough because you learn to go without certain comforts. You are living for days on very little food, you are not getting much sleep and you are totally at the mercy of the elements. There's not much that's rougher than being with ten people at 4 a.m. when your energy is totally spent and you're cold, wet, hungry and miserable, and you still have a very long distance to go before it's over. And that's only the physical challenge. There are also the human relations to grapple with.

Compatibility is a very strong part of sailing. For instance if you're on a crew in an ocean race, you have to share beds. That is a somewhat repellent thought when you are used to fresh sheets, or at least your own sheets, every night in your own home. On a boat it's different. You finish your shift whenever and find a spare bunk. It has a sleeping bag still warm from the last occupant. You get into it and go asleep. You don't pussyfoot around thinking about the body fats and odours of the last person who slept there because you are just too tired and it doesn't matter anyway.

That environment builds tolerance because it eliminates pettiness and superficial dislikes. Everyone has a common goal, a common desire, and that's to get back to port as soon as possible. It renders everything down to the essentials. Can I rely on you? Can you rely on me?

People who don't have the right social skills don't survive in that environment. But in general sailing, and this is one of things that I love most about the sport, tends to draw those social skills out of a person. You really learn how to relate to somebody else when his or her needs and desires are identical to your own – and when you relate on that level, you begin to trust. Once you have achieved trust there are no more problems.

In the same way *Teamship* was designed to remove all the negative attitudes from executives and give them better teamwork skills and habits. The experience worked a lot better than sending people off to a weekend of courses in a hotel or dumping them in some desolate wilderness. For starters, there's a strict hierarchy on a boat, and within that hierarchy there is a basic minimum expected from you. So unlike survival courses where a lot of bickering occurs and time is wasted while potential leaders are sifted out, on the yacht you already had your brief. This was pretty much the same as in an organisation and therefore the environments closely matched in that respect.

The demands of operating a sailing ship were also a lot more effective than spouting a load of waffle at staff in some anonymous hotel lounge.

The crucial difference was that, on a boat, the perceived risk is much greater than the actual risk. You're moving around on a very unstable platform and for someone who's not used to that it feels very insecure. For a load of hotshot executives on a ship for their first time, it was like their lives were in constant danger. Which is just how we wanted them to feel. It made them practical and more dependent on each other. That in turn fostered the key value of trust, and developed the group into a team.

It was for these reasons that IMPAC really did earn the title management engineers, and it placed them above and beyond the standard consultants. And the proof of Irwin's flair for business was apparent when he rolled out his concepts in other countries such as France, Spain and Germany. He'd go to France and they'd say, 'Oh no, we're different', and he'd go to Germany and they'd say, 'Oh, no we're different', and so on. And while the nuances of local culture meant that Jim had to implement some things differently, he understood that the fundamentals of human relationships, management and business did not change, and that's why he succeeded.

You think locally, but you act globally.

Chapter ten

Entrepreneurship in Organisations

Although it may be a contradiction in terms, the most successful large companies are actually a composite of a lot of smaller ones put together. Because of this, all organisations need to have entrepreneurs inside them. Successful companies always recognise this. When I was offered a job by Jim Irwin one of his first comments was, 'If my organisation was full of people like you, we'd have big problems. But at the same time we need people like you to create change, to make things happen, to come up with new ideas and new concepts.'

Jim was right. While you certainly need an organisation to conduct business, an entrepreneur should not cloak himself or herself with just the organisation. A really good entrepreneur will surround himself with a select group of other entrepreneurs to keep that vital idea generation going at all times.

Naturally, it's a careful balance. We are all familiar with these two oft-repeated phrases, usually said by someone trying to get something done: 'There's too many chiefs and not enough Indians' and 'Too many cooks spoil the broth'.

If you have a team of nothing but entrepreneurs, it will be an absolute disaster. Everyone has their own ideas, the group is not working toward anything central and it falls apart. But if you cull the entrepreneurship out of the organisation, it can also lead to disaster.

America might be thought of as massively entrepreneurial, and their society is definitely more respectful of the entrepreneur, but ironically it is American companies that are killing the organisational entrepreneur or 'intrepreneur'. Particularly in large organisations, which rob the employee of individuality through slavishly enforced, soul-destroying corporate cultures.

The end result is that the organisation ends up with a lot of very unhappy people who stay working simply for the pay. The organisation has lost contact with its entrepreneurial roots, the get-up-and-go attitude that made it successful in the first place, and the company begins to atrophy.

Put simply, if the organisation cannot keep some level of entrepreneurial culture within its walls, then it will always have difficulty effecting positive change. The company will become change resistant, and this is death for a business because you always have to be able to respond to the market.

So who are the entrepreneurs?

The entrepreneurs are simply the employees or managers who can see a way to do something new or better within their organisations. They may have small ideas, or they may have big ideas, but they will have ideas that can save or generate money. But why should organisations need these entrepreneurs if they have good management I hear you ask? Isn't it the job of management to have and implement new ideas? Isn't that why they are so highly paid? The fact of the matter is that many managers are never as well placed to understand the processes of their own organisation as the employees who actually carry out the tasks. Managers are also as prone as anybody else to overlook the obvious and be stumped for new ideas, regardless of how much experience they have under their belt. For that reason, it is imperative for a company to make use of their human resources. Why have ten brains devoted to solving a problem or seeking efficiency when you can have five hundred? The organisation is simply stacking the deck in its own favour by incorporating the abilities of its latent entrepreneurs.

Unfortunately, instead of listening to their own staff, most companies will hire expensive consultants to come in and interview the staff, learn about the processes, take suggestions, and then write a fat report to be delivered back to management in return for a hefty fee.

They would rather do all of this than simply give their own employees the opportunity to speak and be valued.

I believe that the creation and maintenance of an entrepreneurial culture inside an organisation is one of the greatest challenges a company can ever face. However, I also believe that it can be achieved successfully by adopting a number of simple principles.

But before I discuss how this can be done, let's examine the workings of a company that has no entrepreneurial culture.

Take a look at the diagram below.

Organisation A. The Rigidly Bureaucratic Company

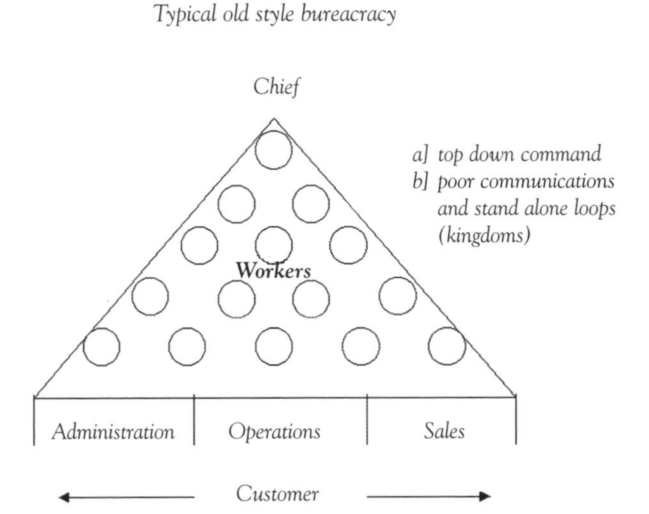

There's a big chief presiding over layers of middle management leading separate teams. Each team has a specific role in the company that lies within a certain division, and at the very bottom is the customer, who receives the company's service or end product.

The actual physical hierarchy of this company is not an issue, all organisations have to have a single leader. No problems there. The problem lies in the bureaucratic culture that has formed within the hierarchy.

Because we are conditioned from birth to accept authority, status becomes a hugely important thing to us. Inside an organisation, this sense of status is reinforced, and quite often as a means of dominating and controlling the workforce. We learn to fear those of a higher status and to do as we are told. The relationship is simple and uncomplicated. Management speaks, workers obey. Exactly like the military.

At first glance, this might seem to be an efficient system which delivers perfect control. With closer inspection however, we quickly discover the inherent weaknesses.

To begin with, communication is terrible. Because of the status driven culture, information will be distributed in the organisation in *direc-*

tives that travel from *top* to *bottom*. Information coming from the top of the pyramid will always be deemed to be more important than information coming from the base of the pyramid. This is tremendously detrimental to the company because the customer usually makes most of their contact with the base of the pyramid, leaving management critically removed from the most important sources of information.

Within the separate teams this culture is replicated. Kingdoms are formed, separate territories within the company that have isolated interests. Lateral communication becomes irrelevant as these kingdoms seek to preserve their existence, and status, within the pyramid.

If you work at the base of the pyramid you are of lesser value than somebody closer to the top. Naturally, an individual trapped in that position believes that they owe the company little or nothing. Only the guarantee of a regular pay cheque motivates them to work, and to work without much enthusiasm.

And finally, last *and* least in the pyramid is the customer who is on the receiving end of the goods and services offered by the organisation. If the organisation has disinterested staff and low morale, the customer will know it by the quality of service they receive.

So how does the entrepreneur fit inside this culture?

The short answer is, they don't.

Remember, entrepreneurs make *ideas* into *reality*. To make an idea into reality inside an organisation, the entrepreneur first has to share it with the management who can make the necessary resources available to implement the idea. However, the culture of the typical old style organisation will usually discourage the employees from sharing ideas in the first place.

The status mentality-driven mentality means that the person who has the idea may be afraid of having 'ideas above their station'. New ideas can bring resentment. Suggestions for improvement are often perceived as criticisms of existing processes and therefore, more sinisterly for the employee, criticisms of existing management.

Secondly, because communication channels are poor, the entrepreneur will be discouraged from sharing the idea because he or she believes that it will have little chance of reaching management. Another fear is that their idea will reach management, but will be credited to another person.

Thirdly, the new idea may be viewed as threatening by others within the organisation because it may mean that their working environment, or their kingdom, may have to be changed.

And finally, there is often little or no tangible incentive for the entrepreneur to actually share ideas, other than perhaps a momentary cash reward, a perfunctory congratulation and a gold star on their employment record – if they're lucky. The recognition of the employee's contribution is short-lived and so is their role as an entrepreneur.

In the rigidly bureaucratic organisation, changes are dictated from the top by senior management, or from the outside by consultancy firms. Employees have little to contribute to the organisation beyond narrowly defined labour, and because of this they will begin to see their needs as increasingly divergent from the needs of the company. The 'us and them' mentality increases, and nobody really benefits.

In summary, the characteristics of the old style organisational culture are:

- Status driven;
- One way communication;
- Kingdoms;
- Lack of individual recognition or incentive for the entrepreneur;
- Money the only incentive to work;
- Change is driven only from the top or from the outside.

One very frustrating experience I had with bureaucratic mediocrity was my involvement with the *Coiste an Asgard* national sail training scheme where I serve as a director on a voluntary basis. *Coiste an Asgard* is the committee tasked with running *Asgard 2*, a purpose-built sail-training brigantine owned by the Department of Defence.

Unfortunately, while the *Asgard* is a fantastic program, a lot of this type of maritime training is still locked into a style that is centuries old. You take the kids out, shake them around, they have a great experience and they talk about it for the rest of their lives. Full stop.

That's all good stuff but it has the potential to be so much more. We can keep the informality, keep the adventure, keep the fun while at the same time reinforcing the themes of cooperation, tolerance and mutual trust. If we can teach kids those concepts and how to live by them for the rest of their lives then we have managed something amazing, particularly in the reform and assistance of troubled or problematic teenagers and juvenile offenders.

I've worked with these kids and I'm convinced that if you stuck them on a boat and sail them off to the Caribbean for a year they would come back totally different people. A project like that could look after fifteen or twenty kids for maybe half a million euro all-inclusive. It would be cheaper than incarceration (average cost in Ireland is around, €100,000 per child) and far more humane.

In the early 1990s I started and ran a youth sail-training project of this type for three years. We did up an old, ninety-foot sailing boat and called her the *Pride of Galway*. The highlight of the project was a voyage up the Guadalquivir river to retrace the route of Christopher Columbus and visit the great World Expo in Seville.

During the run of that project we successfully took a few hundred young people out to sea, including juvenile offenders from Trinity House detention centre, while promoting Ireland and Galway at the same time. What was incredible about the young offenders was their high levels of intelligence and energy. They were hyperactive and neither their families nor the police could handle them. They certainly weren't bad kids but they were up to devilment – just like I was when I was their age. The experience proved to me beyond all doubt how there are better ways to handle juvenile offenders and since then I have been lobbying to introduce something similar into Irish sail-training. This type of project needs long-term monitoring and professional management but it's been used in America and Scandinavia with better results that simply banging the kids away.

My concern with the *Asgard* program was, while it was a very successful program, we were only scratching the surface in terms of what it might be able to deliver. Unfortunately I could not even get members of an Coiste to listen to the idea, because they got it into their heads that I was trying to put delinquents and juveniles on our lovely brigantine.

That was never the point and it would be unfair to mix young offenders with other kids in a haphazard way.

My actual point was that the Asgard program was subsidising kids from mid-to-upper income families when there was a desperate need for resources for other pressing juvenile projects. Those projects are being choked by a civil service mentality and political leadership that only pays lip service.

The reasons for this come down to the fact that the leader of the department – and this holds true for any civil service branch in any similar political system – is an elected politician who usually has no experience with the sector he or she is responsible for.

Below the minister are varying grades of status conscious civil servants who, without any incentive schemes to reward creativity, will never connect to a guiding mission or shared goals.

The result is an organisation that has no inspired leadership and an apathetic workforce. I want to be clear that I am not attacking civil servants on a personal level, but I do believe that the organisation of the civil service fails to bring out anything beyond mediocrity. It's the rigid bureaucratic system which is at fault – not the people.

Regarding the *Asgard* programme, as far as I could see the department was simply mumbling along with only sporadic strategic direction. If it attempted to survive in market conditions it would be bankrupted.

One of the biggest problems with *Coiste an Asgard* is that it's filled with geriatrics. Some of the very people responsible for youth sailing are over seventy years old! Nice people, don't get me wrong, but they've been running the program the same way for twenty-five years and I think the chances of them coming up with something new are probably slim.

When making a pitch of any kind to an organisation, you must find a champion, someone who can connect to what you are trying to sell. With the civil service it was almost impossible to find a champion because of the kingdom mentality. Why would anybody champion a new idea when they feel they have nothing to gain from it? Reform is urgently needed to develop a youth training program but while I've been lobbying for change I found myself constantly under suspicion. There's no dynamic in the department and the civil servants I encountered were quite territorial.
While bureaucratic structure and hierarchy is unavoidable in organisation, it has to be tempered with proper communication, engagement and respect between those in the organisation or else it will produce nothing but conformity and pettiness.

People don't want to feel like irrelevant, disposable components, they want to feel valued as individuals. Proper managers will recognise this and will make special efforts to reward followers and reconnect them to the overall goal of the organisation. By doing this, they will bring out the natural intrepreneurs who will be able to contribute to the company's objectives.

Organisation B. Dynamic Organisation

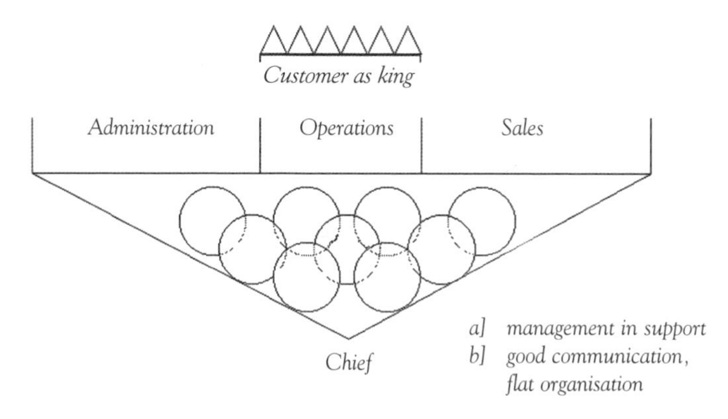

At the top, instead of the big chief, you find the customer. That's because this organisation recognises that the customers needs are paramount, and that the organisation must be flexible and respondent to those needs. Employee efforts are overlapping, forming a network of shared responsibility, not isolated kingdoms. Finally, senior management operate in support of staff, assisting staff to do their tasks better and more efficiently.

This inversion is possible because the culture of this company is meritocratic, not status driven. Authority is traded for responsibility, and change is constant and a positive force in the organisation, not an enemy at the gates.

The following are my four guiding principles to fostering entrepreneurship in organisations:

1. Pave the way by committing to intrepreneurs.

First of all, introduce the concept of entrepreneur to the organisation. Explain to your employees what an entrepreneur is and how entrepreneurship benefits both the organisation and the entrepreneur.

Don't just give lip service to the idea either, back it up with a clear and defined plan as to how you intend to manage, reward and resource your entrepreneurs. There's no point, particularly in large organisations, in being subtle or coy or just creating channels for the 'right' people. If the 'right people' can not get on as well as the next person, then they aren't the 'right people'.

The goal is to make entrepreneurship a constant theme in the culture of the organisation. Do this and you'll be creating internal buy-in for all employees and banishing destructive 'them and us' attitudes. Each person in the organisation will see more clearly how their goals and the goals of the organisation are inter-twined. Unfortunately, most attempts to foster entrepreneurship are usually 'flash-in-the-pan' stuff that doesn't really encourage a cultural change. The most well-known and conventional format for encouraging entrepreneurs is a straightforward staff suggestion scheme. Employees are asked to submit their ideas and will get prizes of some description if those suggestions are implemented.

On the positive side the prizes can be generous, the scheme is well intentioned and generally good at finding small efficiencies. On the negative side it is short-term, small scale, and has no lasting impact on the culture of the organisation. It's better than nothing, but the format is passive and is similar to conducting a survey. It hasn't really done anything to create long-term change in attitudes or get employees to consider themselves in any more ambitious light than their job description.

2. Management in the organisation must keep a permanent, direct channel of communication open to all staff.
Part of the entrepreneurial program must involve genuine, two-way communication. While the general running of the organisation will still be achieved through directives, you should establish a hot-line for entrepreneurs so that they can put their ideas across to the right people.

When an entrepreneur has a good business idea but no money, they need a financier. When the intrepreneur has a good idea but no authority or resources, they need a champion in senior management.

In both scenarios, the entrepreneur/intrepreneur needs access to the people that can give serious consideration and resources to their proposal. Without this line of communication inside an organisation, entrepreneurs will be forced to send their ideas up through the many layers of middle management where, sadly, it only takes one person's prejudice to stop a good idea dead in its tracks. To prevent this from happening, entrepreneurs must be able to submit their ideas directly to senior management, or at the very least, a dedicated admin team that is only once removed from management.

The dividend of this approach is that you can develop a constant stream of information from the base of the organisation while at the same time breaking down destructive status barriers. You also increase morale in the organisation because you are telling staff that they are worth listening to.

3. When employees do share ideas the organisation must congratulate them.
Often it's not possible or worthwhile to put ideas into action, or to give awards for every idea submitted. But sincere words of praise, on the other hand, cost a company nothing yet can have surprising results. Many individuals are simply seeking the recognition that they have something more to offer than their nine-to-five job allows. If the organisation offers this praise, they are giving confidence to the entrepreneur and grooming them for future success.

When it comes to rewards, something I have learned is that giving money to a person is not always the best recognition. Money goes into a bank account and changes the digits there for a few weeks, and then it's gone. There is little emotive impact on the person receiving it, other than the quick buzz of debt alleviation!

But if you reward somebody with an all expenses paid holiday, they'll remember the fun of the holiday and the reason they received it. That's a powerful emotional charge, and one that the entrepreneur will feel hugely positive about.

4. Give ownership of the idea to the entrepreneur, including financial control if possible.

Having an idea taken from you, as I discovered during the Sail Ireland project, can be hugely demoralising. When a person has an idea or goal they should also be allowed to develop it, because that idea is born out of their entrepreneurial art and is a sacred part of them.

Allowing somebody to retain ownership or even input into the development of their idea is also a superb way to boost confidence and commitment. It was for this reason that John Bourke waited a year for one of his managers to see an opportunity for improvement within their organisation. When the manager did see the opportunity, he became excited, enthusiastic and committed to making it work.

But notional ownership will not be enough to sustain the entrepreneur if other resources are lacking. What happens very often in management is that a person thinks that they are being allowed to realise an opportunity, but then discovers that they are so restricted in what they can and cannot do, that it ends up not being worth the effort. If you seriously want to nurture the entrepreneur, make sure that you give them real support and real resources. Otherwise, you are only wasting your time and theirs.

The ultimate goal of developing an entrepreneurial culture is to reconnect the organisation to its entrepreneurial roots, and to be able to introduce and handle change to your advantage. When nurturing the entrepreneur in your organisation, bear these maxims in mind.

Change is an ongoing process, not an occasional event, and it can be used to your advantage. The catalysts for change can come from any direction – internally or externally, top-down or bottom-up. The only question is whether your organisation can respond properly.

The benefits of developing organisational entrepreneurship cannot be underestimated. You have a fitter, leaner, more agile and more enthusiastic workforce, genuinely committed to making a success of your company while advancing themselves at the same time.

Even in my own ventures I have found that people whom I hired for positions in one company turned out to be absolutely great in new and more challenging positions in other companies, including start-up enterprises.

Success breeds success. With a mixture of the right people and the right plans, properly resourced, there's no reason why a company or organisation cannot expand. Based on this idea I have developed the concept of the Entrepreneurial Loop.

Think of the Entrepreneurial Loop as a wheel, perhaps like the flywheel of an engine. To begin with, it may be tough to get your project or business up and running. But once you build up speed there is a momentum that you can tap into to start new enterprises and projects.

The hardest thing of all is to get your wheel moving. My first Entrepreneurial Loop was *Afloat* magazine. It took tremendous effort to get the business turning, but eventually I succeeded and spun more enterprises out from it.

Let's take a typical project or enterprise. The loop has four quadrants which are:

Plan – what is the goal, the objective of your enterprise?
Resource – how do you fund it and where will the revenues come from?
Execute – work, work, work and don't give up!
Evaluate – is there another opportunity you can exploit?

Plan 1

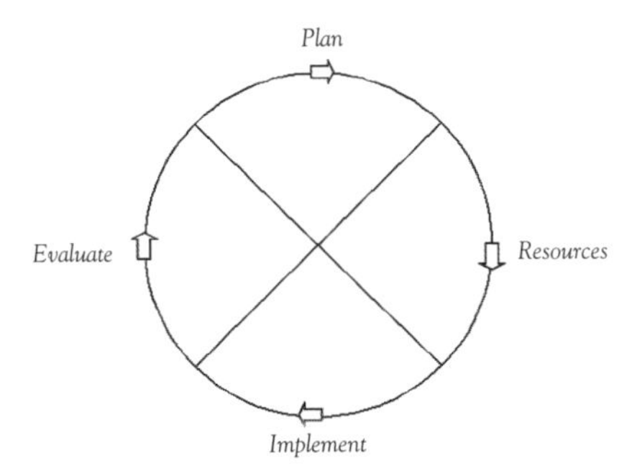

Once you've achieved cash flow and got your business on some kind of level footing, it's time to think about expansion. The more enterprises you can build, the more secure they will be. Remember, a very successful company is in essence a lot of very small enterprises rolled together, many of which were originally leveraged from the success of their predecessors.

Most importantly in this loop relationship is the entrepreneur or intrepreneur in charge of developing the new enterprise. A classic example of this is the Czech Credit Bureau, a financial services company that I set up in the Czech Republic and will describe in more detail later. The managing director of the company started as a part-time analyst when he was a student, and worked his way from there to becoming a co-ordinator, a project director and then a manager. He now runs a strong enterprise which has spun out yet another similar enterprise in Slovakia.

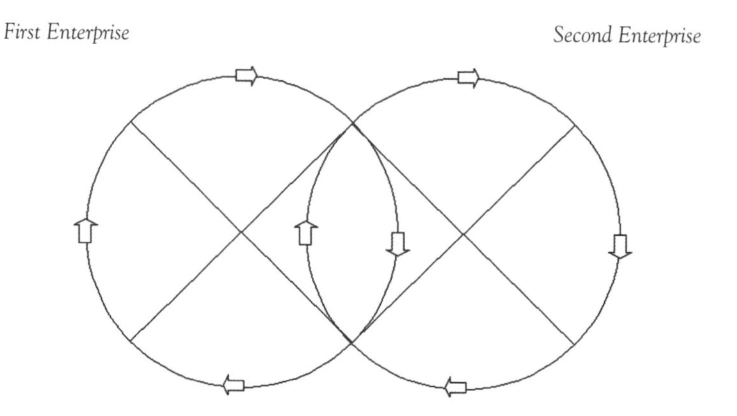

In the overlapping areas between the numerous enterprises – which can be in totally different sectors – are the shared finances, marketing abilities and strategic understanding. Essentially, the entrepreneurial art in action. You can then interconnect organisations sharing common resources, while still supporting and generating new enterprises from the synergy.

While these are my guiding concepts for the utilisation of entrepreneurship in organisations, I still have to make it clear that entrepreneurship is not something that you can simply cook up according to set rules. The most you can do, both inside and outside of the organisation, is to take away the worst barriers and work on creating an entrepreneurial culture and environment. However, it takes entrepreneurs to be able to create that culture to begin with. You can't give what you don't possess.

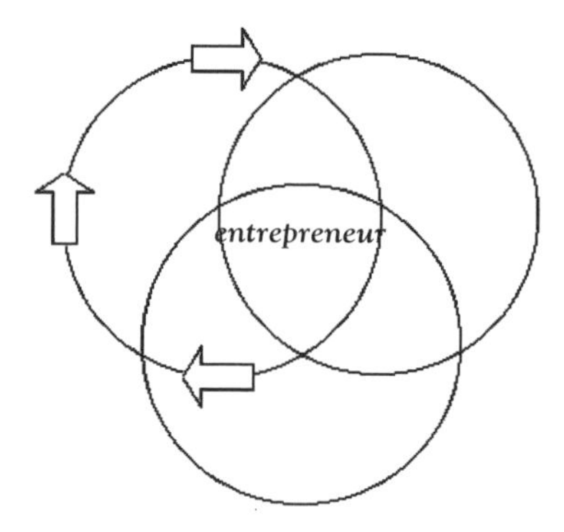

Some people inside organisations aren't entrepreneurs, and they don't want to be entrepreneurs. It's a very uncertain life because you're pushing out the boundaries and constantly moving beyond your natural comfort zone. There's both risk and reward with that, and it's definitely not for everybody.

However, if the entrepreneurship has gone from inside acompany, then the company has essentially become brain dead. It will still persist as a bureaucracy for a time, but only until a fitter and more agile enterprise, driven by persistent and committed entrepreneurs, takes its place.

Chapter eleven

The Corporate Life

I developed a tremendous respect for Jim Irwin, his company and his philosophy. His approach was nothing short of a revelation. The fact that a large and successful company could harness misfits like myself and put them to good use was something I had never anticipated.

Frankly, when Jim gave me a job, I would have been very reluctant to hire myself. What I mean is that there is little room for somebody like me in an organisation that is built on a rigid structure where individuals are focused on specific tasks all day. Naturally, that type of constancy is a key ingredient for success in any business or project but, if I were running the show, I would not hire myself into that situation. My attributes are best applied elsewhere in the process.

Because I aware of this characteristic in myself, it really impressed me when I was offered an executive position with such a well-respected American firm as IMPAC. It impressed me even more when I realised that the person who hired me also recognised that I was not the steady-going worker type. It was not the fact that I got a job when I needed it, but the idea that there is a future for different types of entrepreneurs within organisations. The knowledge and skill base was there. All it needed was the right idea, the catalyst, and the creative art of entrepreneurship. With that spark you could leverage all of your financial and human resources into new directions.

IMPAC was an organisation that offered the scope to develop new ideas and launch them without fighting bureaucracy or negativity. Of course when it was explained to me that Irwin needed people who could break moulds and stir things up, it began to make sense. You don't hire somebody humdrum for that type of thing, and while there are many criticisms that could be levelled at me, being humdrum is not one of them.

A cartoon of myself on the ocean having been successful on the second attempt at the Atlantic.

Kilcullen 3 – A twenty-one foot boat which I sailed 10,000 miles and completed the Mini-Transat Singlehanded Trans-Atlantic race to the Caribbean where I met Suzanna. After the dinghy, the new Kilcullen seemed a large yacht to me. It wasn't, as the photo shows...

Our Czech publications. A simple business model moved from one market and sector to another, but leading to much more opportunities.

The launch of our Polish business in Warsaw - complete with golden Kilcullen warrior!

Understanding that had made Jim Irwin a very wealthy man, and it restored my faith in large organisations – the most successful of which of course are often a collection of small organisations.

Although IMPAC's headquarters were in Florida, its European centre was based in Dublin, allowing me to be based at home, yet work for the global organisation. Like many second-generation Irish-Americans, Jim was not well known in narrower Irish circles, although he identified strongly with the Irish. He didn't need to be better known, but I knew it would mean something to him to be given further recognition in the Irish community. To improve his profile, I talked with Niall O'Dowd of *Irish Voice*, the New York newspaper of the Irish expatriate and Irish-American community. He had never heard of Jim Irwin, but he reviewed his background and Irwin was included him in the paper's list of the Top 100 Irish-American businesspeople. It meant a lot to Jim because, despite his strong Irish identity, he had lost contact with his community to an extent. All I had to do was nominate him and his credentials stood out on their own.

Of course even more important than Irish-America was Ireland itself. Though Irwin never mentioned it I knew that he would regard recognition here as a major honour. I thought I had just the opening when I was assisting with our corporate review meeting, which was rotated from places as diverse as Bermuda and Hawaii to dear old Dublin. I tried the Irish Management Institute, wondering if they could offer Irwin something in the way of an honorary title.

'And *who* is this man?' came the reply. It was clear that they would not be extending any honours to Irwin. A poor grandson of Ireland who created a $100 million company? Obviously the IMI had bigger fish to fry.

Whatever the reasons, it was probably a loss on their part. Jim was the sort of guy who might tell you to sod off if you solicited a donation from him. On the other hand, if he were exposed to the situation where money was needed but he was not specifically asked for it, he might surprise everybody with his initiative and generosity.

At the time of the Irish Management Institute's rebuff, Irwin had been particularly generous to Ireland's Olympic bid campaign, which was the result of a meeting with, initially, Gay Mitchell. In 1992 Gay Mitchell was the lord mayor of Dublin. With advice from IMPAC's sales director, Peter McGibney, who had contact with Mitchell, we asked the mayor to host a lunch for the IMPAC board. We had intended doing this with the IMI but that idea was dropped.

Gay said, 'Sure', but his hospitality budget was spent so I organised some outside caterers.

The board meeting broke at midday and Jim and I walked to the Mansion House to meet up with the mayor. Irwin knew nothing about the mayor but Mitchell had been in the newspapers for suggesting that Ireland should put in a tender to host the Olympics. Many had laughed him out of it for having such a ridiculous notion. I thought the criticism was both shortsighted and narrow-minded. When you really analyse the concept, it is not nearly as absurd as it might seem. I discussed all this with Jim.

We had some soft drinks and started lunch. Mitchell started talking about the Olympic idea, thinking perhaps a small donation might be possible.

Ten minutes later Irwin stands up. 'I think gentlemen we should donate £50,000 to Mayor Mitchell's Olympic plan.'

'Hear, hear,' was the partially nervous response from the crowd. Our PR man went bright red. Some of the IMPAC people were scared that the money would be slashed from their own budgets.

'As a matter of fact gentlemen, I have decided to donate £50,000 from my own money to match it.'

There was more applause. Gay Mitchell had a grin from ear to ear. For the following twenty-four hours we had massive media coverage, including television interviews, talking about the donation and the Olympic project.

A few days later, I was organising the money transfers and was amazed to discover that there was not even a bank account set up for the Olympic project.

While the Olympic campaign eventually fizzled out, Irwin's donation provided seed money to DISC, the Dublin International Sports Committee, which helps attract major sports events to the city. I asked Irwin later how he felt about his money going to a non-starter. 'I really don't care if the Olympic project never happens,' he said, 'the important thing is to try.'

It was a response worthy of the founder of the modern Olympics himself. As Pierre de Coubertain said in 1894, 'The most important thing in the Olympic games is not winning but taking part. The essential thing in life is not conquering but fighting well.' However, there was some dividend in the Olympic venture for IMPAC. Dr Tony O'Reilly had listed his name in support and it facilitated a contact between himself and Irwin. The plan originally was for Irwin to visit O'Reilly in the Bahamas on *Tai-pan*. Fortunately I researched the harbour at Lyfort Quay where O'Reilly lived and discovered that the harbour was too shallow for Irwin's motor yacht. I don't like to think of the embarrassment that would have been caused to all concerned if he had run aground on his grand arrival. (This was something that happened to a boat I was on during an official visit to New York and I can still hear the laughter ringing in my ears.)

Instead, a private plane was chartered (Jim could have bought his own but he just wasn't bothered) and he flew into the Bahamas to meet with Dr O'Reilly there. I'm not sure if IMPAC ever conducted any subsequent work in any of O'Reilly's companies, although it would have been quite usual for that to happen after such a meeting – that being the purpose of such networking.

O'Reilly later invited Irwin into the Ireland Fund network at a Washington dinner. Through the Ireland Fund, O'Reilly has made many great contributions – and he also built up an amazing network. However, when Jim saw Tony up on stage being applauded for contributions of other people's money, he decided that he wanted to do his own thing.

When Gay Mitchell came up with another idea, the Dublin Literary Award, Jim Irwin sponsored that with a prize fund of a €100,000 (originally punts now euro) annually, making the IMPAC Award a prestigious international event. Looking back, I am proud to have played a role in all of this, and to help open people's minds to the fact that it is totally achievable for Ireland to host the Olympics – if we put our mind to it.

Of course, networking events can sometimes go awry, and the one that stands out clearest in my mind as going the most awry involves our very own Charlie Haughey. Jim Irwin had been an early financial backer of Bill Clinton, thanks to Al Gore being a friend of the late Joe Ruggario, a senior man in the IMPAC organisation and a personal friend of Jim Irwin. One of the payoffs of his donation was IMPAC receiving two tables at President Clinton's inauguration in 1992. Irwin gave instructions to his worldwide staff to get fourteen prominent businessmen and politicians lined up as guests and have them flown in to Washington.

My colleagues produced Brian Burke, the former Prime Minister of Australia, and also some top Finnish businessmen, and then I got a call to organise two Irish people. *Business and Finance* had been out the previous week with a picture of Stephen O'Connor on the cover. The Waterford Foods CEO had just been awarded the title of Irish businessman of the year, so I called him up.

Who could possibly resist a trip to the White House? One down and one to go. Because I had the previous connection with Haughey, he was the natural second choice. He had retired shortly before, so I decided that his schedule might allow for it. Would he go? Haughey agreed. I arranged to meet him at the airport that Saturday and, although he was officially just an ordinary citizen by this time, I managed to swing one of the two VIP lounges at Dublin airport for him. Haughey's name still held clout – this was before the scandals that were later attached to him. I knew very little of Haughey's other dealings and, even if I had been aware, I certainly wouldn't have delved into them.

Now the same day Mary Robinson, only recently inaugurated as the Irish President, was also about to board the government jet to visit Scotland.

So it happened that our ex-Taoiseach was in one VIP suite and our new president was in the other, a complete coincidence. That necessitated some to-ing and fro-ing between both suites as the other underlings and myself tried to work out the protocol for this type of thing. Who was going to say hello to whom?

Charlie was the ex-Taoiseach, but Mary was our serving head of state and therefore it was decided that he would go into her lounge to make the greeting.

I walked in with Haughey.

He took Mary's hand. 'How are ya, Mary,' he said in that distinctive voice. Still holding her hand he looked at the government jet parked outside. Robinson had no other choice but to follow his look.

'Look what we left ya,' said Haughey with a grin.

And that was that. The ad hoc protocol had been honoured and nothing further was exchanged. It was something of a relief because their mutual dislike for each other was palpable.

So with that out of the way, Haughey flew into Washington DC for Clinton's inauguration dinner the following Tuesday.

Now amongst the notables at Irwin's table that evening were Lord Anthony Churchill (it was good for Jim as an Irish-American to have a British Lord in his pocket, especially when dealing with other British executives, even if Churchill did fall asleep during meetings), and Michael Stacpoole, a friend of Churchill's and the IMPAC public relations executive. On Stacpoole's CV there was the more dubious position of being photographed whilst handing over an envelope of cash to prostitute Monica Coghlan, a bribe to keep her quiet about her tryst with Lord Jeffrey Archer.

Also in attendance was a very attractive woman in her late forties and a complete trophy hunter into the bargain who probably had a notch for every famous guy she took down.

So the inauguration went ahead, the meal started and the serious hobnobbing began. Then Haughey came into his own, and with that magic aura of his began to pull all the right people to Irwin's table. Senator Ted Kennedy, T.P. O'Neill and pretty much everyone else who mattered.

Jim couldn't believe it. This was brilliant. Haughey's inclusion was an instant payoff for IMPAC. The man, even in his retirement, had a fascination and fatal attraction for fellow politicians and other movers and shakers. All they had to do now was get Haughey out and about on the three-day corporate social programme they had lined up.

Then this attractive older lady decided that she wanted to get know Haughey some more. A lot more. Kind of 'know him in the biblical sense' more, and the end result was that the two disappeared almost totally for three days – surfacing occasionally for air.

Haughey's social circuit was thrown in the bin, and IMPAC dusted their hands with resignation. So much for showing the old guy off around town.

Now I don't know for sure, but if you ask my opinion I'd say that Haughey was probably shagging this lady day and night for the whole seventy two hours.

Or maybe the two just had a culturally interesting time around Washington's many fine galleries and institutions. I couldn't say for sure. What do you think?

At the time I was amazingly naive and innocent, so much so that I might even have subscribed to that latter version if I had been pressed on the issue. I was even afraid to talk about it for five years afterwards, but now that Charlie has passed away I don't think anybody really cares anymore. More power to him anyway, as he was almost seventy years old at the time...

After a successful US outing and becoming one more trophy for our PR ladyfriend, Haughey then returned to Ireland.

And then I began to get these calls from Charlie, and they were somewhat roundabout.

'Hello Enda, how are you?'

'I'm fine, and yourself?

'Fine, Fine... Tell me, the IMPAC executives, when will they be in Ireland again?

'I'm not sure, I'll have to check the diary. Why do you want to know?'

'Oh, I'd just like to invite them to my house, you know...'

And the telephone conversations would go on like that, with Charlie beating around the bush and not really getting to the point.

Then I got another telephone call. This time from Haughey's ladyfriend.

'Enda. Under no circumstances are you to give him my phone number. Do you understand?'

Yes ma'am.

Haughey must have been sniffing around her, but it was obviously a once-off deal for her.

Subsequently I learned that Stacpoole was fired from his job at IMPAC. It appeared that this same lady was shagging three or four others in the company around the same time. The net result was a big scene and all the IMPAC wives clubbing together to get both of them chucked out.

That wasn't the end of the matter though, because I rather cheekily took Haughey up on his invitation. The following year Jim was in Ireland to go to the Irish Derby, and it was the perfect opportunity for Haughey to make good on his offer. Which he did, although he was very cold about it. Even so the cocktail reception in his home at Kinsealy delighted the Americans.

Working for IMPAC got me out and about in quite a few countries, including those of central and eastern Europe where it was dealing with some very large companies in Poland, Slovenia and Czechoslovakia. One client that really made an impression on me was a shoe manufacturer called Zvit that was based in Zlin in southern Czechoslovakia (it's now in the Czech Republic). Zlin was a one-company town, literally, thanks to the very famous Czech industrialist Thomas Bata (pronounced 'Batcha').

Zlin as an urban centre didn't exist until the 1930s when Bata put his massive shoe factory there and then proceeded to build his town around it. His administration building alone had 2,000 people working inside.

Now Bata was something of an eccentric, but there was a method in his madness. Instead of taking the usual top floor offices, Bata placed himself in the corner of the building. To be precise, in an elevator. Every morning he would step into his office, sit down at his desk and press the 'up' button. Now every one of the twenty floors of that building was divided into a different department, so when old Mr Bata drew level with a floor, his managers had to report into him immediately.

First floor. Sales. How much did I make today?

Second floor. Design. Where's my new loafer?

Third floor. Accounts. Add this to the tax breaks list.

Fourth floor. Production. Work harder.

Fifth floor. Purchasing. Who's robbing me?

And so on from floor to floor. And not only was this Czech guy keeping tabs on each separate team within the company, he could also watch the complex from the windows of his office. If somebody had spilled glue, he was going to know about it. If rubbish wasn't cleared away, he was going to know about it. If someone was leaving work early, he was going to know about it.

Bata's factory was an extraordinary vision and he ran it with an iron fist. But he wasn't a heartless man and he didn't neglect the human side of his enterprise. He built houses and schools, even churches for the employees. He reasoned that when you look after your employees, it flows the whole way through. If they are happy, they work better and are friendlier to the customers. Production and sales go up.

Then after the Second World War, the communists took it over.

Ironically Zlin was a perfect example of what the communists wanted in a centrally planned economy. One town will make shoes, one town will make excavators, one town will print books, etc. And by virtue of his unique business concept, Bata's factory went on producing shoes for forty years.

IMPAC were invited into Zvit in the early 1990s to help modernise it and get it up to scratch for a market economy. By now, it was typical example of a communist enterprise. The factory was rundown, the process was wasteful and inefficient and the end product was poor quality. Shoes were coming out the other end, but it was just raw production.

It was another huge irony. The raw materials that went into the shoes were all worth something, such as the leather, the oil, the glues and rubbers. But the shoe itself was worth very little, at least in the western market. It was simply not made to a standard that would survive.

Working with all these ex-communists and nouveau capitalists could also be a fairly standard experience insofar as we would often be meeting the same types of problems again and again. As usual IMPAC did its preliminary report and knew the client's business inside out, so we had a host of improvements to implement for a disbelieving management.

We would say, 'We will save you $500,000 a year on energy alone.'

Management would say, 'How can you do this? We are good management. We are not so wasteful as that!'

But of course they were. Electricity was supplied free under the socialist system and therefore the factory administrators were in the habit of using it with complete abandon.

So IMPAC designated someone to go around at 6.00 p.m. each evening to switch off all the lights and machines. Ditto with the heating. The office staff in the administration building had been opening windows to let the heat out instead of turning down the radiators.

We had to educate our clients in even the most basic aspects of running a business. Issues like quality and utilisation of labour had to be addressed. The factory had people on the payroll that never actually turned up for work. Efficiency was ratcheted up just by implementing sophisticated time and motion studies on working methods, workers and equipment.

But there was one aspect of the business in the post-Soviet states that tripped us up. As I've mentioned before, IMPAC didn't deal with the tail of the dog. We had to take our orders directly from the head honcho in order to receive maximum freedom. And we did this in eastern Europe as well. We only dealt with the CEO or the chairman of the board.

But it was a period of rapid transition between two completely different political and social systems, and that left us with a headache. Who the hell were the shareholders? Almost every company was being privatised. And it was a very, very complex task to actually pinpoint either the owner of the company or the person who made the key decisions. It was straightforward in a western capitalist model. You just went to the top of the company hierarchy, or maybe a bit above it, and that was that.

Not so with the old comrades. You would do your business with the managing director, thinking he was the person in the driving seat, only to discover that there was some senior communist party official behind him who was pulling all the strings. Or else there would be a committee decision-making matrix of some description that was completely impenetrable. Very often decisions were not made in the way you would think that they were made. Of course, it was all insane. Perhaps it made sense in the closed socialist society, but in a free market world, it was terrible. But we were dealing with countries going through tough changes, and you can't make the old way of doing things disappear overnight.

We persevered and soon we became adept at tracking down the right people. It was one of our major challenges, to discover who and where the key personnel were, especially given our style of service. Unless we had total permission directly from the boss, we couldn't do our jobs correctly.

Doing this type of work taught me a lot about how eastern and central Europe operated. Quite often one of our team was assigned to some remote town, such as Zlin, and would be stuck there, working on one project until it was completed, however I was quite privileged to be involved in a range of projects across a number of different countries.

And at the same time I was developing attitudes to specific countries. Prior to that time, they were just names on a map to me, if even that. If the country was behind the iron curtain you just didn't think about it anymore, they were just part of one big, mysterious, red blotch. In particular I came to like Czechoslovakia, its capital Prague was dynamic, progressive and buzzing, and I enjoyed it best of all.

But more than anything I wanted to get back into business for myself.

Chapter twelve

Torn Curtain

If there are too many people like me in a company there will be trouble because you have too much idea generation. Sooner or later there comes a time when you just have to focus and get down to the nuts and bolts of things. Jim Irwin always knew that, and just kept enough of us so that he could feed off the idea generation and the leadership skills.

For the same reasons, Jim also understood that you could not tie down entrepreneurs indefinitely. Ultimately, they have to work for themselves – it's what they are cut out for.

That's the challenge that I always loved. It was the only thing that would satisfy the contrarian in me.

The other thing that I needed to think about was that I was not making real money. I was making a salary, and an okay one, but a salary nevertheless. I was just getting by. Unashamedly I wanted to make real money and I knew that I would never do that as an employee. The economy was dead in Ireland. There seemed to be little opportunity for somebody with no capital and who was not prepared to, or in a position to, 'work' the system. It was time to go out on my own again and make a fresh start.

I wanted to live – and to live I needed freedom. Money is meaningless in itself, it won't make you happy, but it does give you freedom. Freedom to pursue your goals, develop your ideas and basically do whatever you damn well want, as long as you don't inconvenience other people in the process. Sailing had been my adventure and challenge for a lot of my life, but the challenge of paying for it all had made it difficult to pursue.

I'd had a taste for freedom in my life and I was never going to give it up. It was what I really wanted and it was the largest motivating factor for me as an entrepreneur. To have the freedom to be in control of my own life. That, and the adventure and challenge of making it big.

Whatever 'big' is. I never really gave it much thought.

Life is short and precious. You have to live it in the way you want and need to, because you'll be a long time dead. Of course, there are responsibilities that you have to recognise along the way, but a lot of those are the ones you choose to have.

Now being an entrepreneur is definitely not for everyone. In fact, I think most people would be afraid of following their dreams because their fear of being insecure is greater than anything else in their lives.

You wake up everyday, your radio goes on, you have your breakfast, you go to work, you meet people, you live in various patterns. Your life is generally mapped out. There's a time where everybody you meet breaks for lunch, you go away for weekends, you get together at Christmas. It's the normal life; those are the things you do. And there can be tremendous pleasure in that. Many people have stable employment so that they can pursue their passions in other activities, and that's where they develop their entrepreneurial spirit.

Your job also helps to define you in other positive ways. It gives you a sense of purpose and a sense of belonging.

When I was alone in a sixteen-foot dinghy for a few months of my life with only the Atlantic Ocean as far as the eye could see, I was away from all normal controls. It sent me stir-crazy in the latter stages. Working as an entrepreneur can be a similar experience. What is your work? How do you define it? How productive are you? Could you be doing more? What contribution are you making? What yardsticks can you apply to your life when you are the one who's totally in control of it?

So there has to be a passion, an all-consuming desire that will always drive you onwards through the doubts and uncertainties. One of the things that spurred me on to set up *Afloat* was my dread of remaining on the dole. I didn't know how I could exist on it any longer when life was just a long procession of nothingness. But that's exactly the type of prospect that you can be faced with if you go out on your own. Greater than my fear of ending up on the dole at some stage in my future – however unlikely that may be nowadays – is seeing my life dripping away into mundane routines that have been dictated to me by others.

Just to do a job nine-to-five is impossible for me. But taking the entrepreneurial route is highly insecure and highly unstable. You'll never know what's around the corner. There's no predictability and that makes it difficult for the people around you, especially your family. It's a difficult trade-off. But it was the route I had to take – and take it I did.

Eastern and central Europe was hot for entrepreneurs in the early 1990s. As the Soviet Union became history and communism died out across Europe, the iron curtain was drawn back to let in all who were willing to enter. What would take the place of the inefficient socialist governments and their centrally planned economies seemed to be anybody's guess, although we in IMPAC were attempting to give them something sustainable as fast as possible.

On a personal level, the region spelled risk and opportunity, virgin markets with all the allure that America had perhaps held for my great-grandfather Cormac O'Coineen over a century before. From working in the ex-communist bloc, I knew there were two ways things could go for those who tried their luck – you either went home broke or became very successful over time through hard work and sheer doggedness.

There was a buzz in the air that said 'Go east young man', and I willingly followed this invisible pied piper, ready to make my fortune or go bankrupt trying.

By this stage in my life, I had made a clear decision to identify myself as both a European and global citizen, and I use the term 'global' as distinct from 'international'. To my mind people and companies in the international category tend to view the world from their home base, and they perceive anything outside of their own locality as being foreign.

If you are global, you have the capacity to view the world through the perspective of whichever culture you are in. So if in Spain, you must think and act as the Spanish do, otherwise you run the risk of making cultural mistakes that can prove costly.

For me, this sense of being global coincided with the arrival of the Internet in the 1990s. Previously we were defined by connections with our family, village, town, region and country. Now technology had opened up a planet-wide network and exposed us to things far removed from our immediate geography. Whether we realised it or not, the Internet liberated us from our primary affiliations and made us all truly global citizens.

As a global person, I passionately wanted to be successful. Behind me were my sailing exploits, a stint as a journalist, a publishing enterprise of limited opportunity and three and a half years as an executive with IMPAC. Now I wanted something new, the stimulation and fear of voyaging into the unknown once again. Central and eastern Europe offered that unknown, and enormous opportunities besides. But before I left IMPAC in 1993, I decided to seek some guidance from Paul Murphy. He's a great big man with great business experience and at important points in my life

I've gone to him for advice. Generally Paul will listen to me and, whatever big idea I had in mind, he would advise me not to do it. That was pretty much the spiel he gave me about leaving IMPAC. 'Enda you'd be crazy to leave IMPAC. It's a good company, a good job, it has great prospects, and you just want to ditch it and go out totally on your own?'

It's a real irony that I keep going to Paul because I never actually follow any of his advice. But it's not a reflection on Paul, more a display of the contrarian nature of an entrepreneur.

I left IMPAC on good terms and remained a part of the team on a consultancy basis for certain projects that I was involved with. In fact this was something of a success in itself as Jim Irwin drove IMPAC in such a hard-nosed way that it was more usual for people to be fired than leave of their own free will.

However, before I could disappear eastwards, I had to raise some cash.

'You want to borrow money to what?' my local bank manger exclaimed. I had just broached the idea of starting a business in Czechoslovakia, a place that many were confusing with the more sinister state of Yugoslavia. My bank manager later admitted that he didn't know the difference and had been forced to consult his atlas. I didn't expect the bank to fund the business completely, but I did need support for working capital and to plug holes. But there was to be absolutely no assistance from him. It seemed that, while the banks could understand the needs of multinational and international companies entering the post-socialist states, to get their heads around a smaller entrepreneur operating in eastern Europe appeared to be the banking equivalent of moon-walking.

I had about £15,000 of my own money and a few credit cards that stretched working capital to £25,000. That type of money wouldn't cover much else beyond travelling over and back from Ireland to eastern Europe, but it was a start.

With the transition from communism to capitalism in eastern Europe came exciting business stories of fast development, change, opportunities – and enormous profits. It was all a powerful stimulant, later to be dented by the horror stories that filtered through. It was an ugly capitalism, thrust upon the people there without any of the checks and balances that evolved in established democracies. Although the socialist countries of central Europe may have been more advanced than the Russians prior to the Second World War, their annexation into the Soviet empire ensured that they ultimately shared the same fate because they came to be as backward as Russia itself. I looked as far east as Moscow, and then at the countries of Slovenia, Poland and in particular Czechoslovakia.

Of these locations, the Russian capital appeared to be the obvious target. The Russian economic system went more or less from agricultural serfdom in the late-nineteenth century, to communism, brutal industrialisation and centrally planned economics through most of the twentieth century, before being hurled into raw capitalism in the 1990s.

In economic terms, people tended to lump both Russia and Moscow together, but this was a mistake. There is Russia and then there is Moscow, and I quickly learned that the two should not be confused. A city of eight million people (fourteen million including the suburbs), Moscow has an economy and politics all of its own. By contrast, the country of Russia is a sprawling mass. With 147 million people it has little more than twelve per cent of the population of China, yet almost twice the territory. You can fly seven hours directly east of Moscow, go through as many time zones, and still remain in Russian territory. It is a country of vast resources, but also of vast problems.

I had a friend who flew to Moscow on a commercial trip in the early 1990s. He was a marketing director with his company during that period, and was a gregarious and outgoing salesman responsible for business development. Clever and nobody's fool by any stretch of the imagination, he is the essence of a sharp and professional businessman. But despite all of these qualities in his favour, he fell foul of Russian criminals and to this day remains acutely embarrassed over what was, in more ways than one, 'revealed' on that trip.

It all started as soon as he touched down at Moscow airport. 'It seemed smart for me to share a taxi to the city centre for $25,' he told me, describing the offer which greeted him on exiting the arrivals hall at the terminal. 'I was not keen to pay the minimum $100 extortion rate and a deal is a deal.' Although he could have claimed the $100 as expenses, he believed that it was his duty at all times to save money for his employers. 'So I got in with three other well-dressed men and the driver. Not a lot was said when I exchanged greetings, other than a grunt. I assumed it to be just cultural reserve and language differences until,' he explained, 'we seemed to be driving away from the city centre.'

This brought some anxiety at first, but he shrugged it off, thinking he was over-reacting. Then as the car accelerated he became concerned, and then downright terrified as the vehicle raced through anonymous Moscow streets. Deathly silence reigned inside the speeding car until it took a sharp turn on to a side road, slowed and he was jumped.

The next thing he knew the car had stopped in a field. Other than a few grunts, little was said as an army of hands started to strip him of all his clothes and possessions. 'I remember thinking that this must be the end. It's true, my whole life flashed past. My wife, family, holiday plans... I should have called my mother... until suddenly I was alone.'

Meanwhile the surly men were divesting him of almost everything on his person, including patent leather shoes, $1,000 suit, watch, wallet, credit cards, passport and luggage. 'They even took my wedding band and that was it!' he recalled. Eventually the car and the men disappeared with all that he had been carrying and wearing with one merciful exception – his underpants.

Stunned, he wandered aimlessly for a while. Fortunately, the weather was warm and eventually he got help, despite being avoided by the locals who were naturally suspicious of a mostly naked man speaking in a foreign language. He got back to the airport and, after more adventures and embarrassment, got the next plane out of there. And that was it. My friend left Moscow and, to my knowledge, has not been back since.

Of course, there were many more stories like this from Russia and their former satellites. In addition to the type of ruse that happened to my friend there were more subtle ploys, such as agreeing the detail of a contract in English and having it translated to the local language with a totally different meaning. Of course, legally, it is the local language that counted, leaving the expatriate high and dry. In Russia a degree of brutality was even expected from the investor. At some meetings you would lack credibility unless you arrived with mean-looking minders who had firearms concealed in their bulging pockets. In short, Russia was not a civilised place to do business.

However it remains an enormous market and I believe that someday, sometime, it will sort itself out. Of the 147 million people there, the top ten per cent of the population hold fifty per cent of the state's wealth, money that could be further distributed amongst those who are enterprising and brave enough to engage with Russia's opportunities. Despite the country's chequered history, there are an enormous number of decent people who mean well, wonderful human beings and some very clever people who have been messed up by dint of history, greed, bad leadership and, for want of a better word, 'quickmoneyitis'.

From an entrepreneur's point of view, Russia made me both laugh and cry. It brought to mind Oscar Wilde's great wisdom, which we often follow in the quest for success, 'I can resist everything but temptation.'

I admit it was difficult to resist the temptation of the fortunes to be made there, but also I realised that Russia was simply too ambitious for me. If you are going to enter Russia, you must enter it in a big way. And unless you are prepared to be as mean, tough and ruthless as the rest of them, stay out.

Next in line were Czechoslovakia and Poland, the former subsequently splitting into the Czech Republic and Slovakia the year I arrived. In contrast to Russia and Poland, the Czech Republic was much closer to western Europe in culture and style. Set on the Vltava, its capital Prague is one of the most beautiful cities in the world, radiating a mystique all of its own. And throughout most of the 1990s it was very cheap. Students could go there for the summer, get merry on about five beers for the equivalent of a pound, and get absolutely blasted for two!

Most importantly though, compared to Russia, it felt very safe and friendly – despite the fact that the people were under the Russian yoke for over forty years. Soon after I arrived the country split, with the new Czech Republic becoming a separate state of ten million people, with just over one million inhabiting Prague. Despite the favourable comparisons to Russia, the Czech Republic also posed its own unique problems.

I initially found it a very complicated place, complete with the third most difficult language in Europe and a totally different legal system to the one I was used to. In the US, UK and Ireland, we have a common law system based on precedent, case law and, excepting the UK, a constitution. In the Czech Republic, the law is based on the Napoleonic Roman code, a system I wasn't familiar with.

For example, we once carefully drafted a shareholders agreement with a US company in the Czech Republic for a business partnership. While it was fine by US and Irish law, it was meaningless in the Czech Republic because it was not written in accordance with the Czech commercial code. Therefore the whole process had to be started again from scratch.

David Beattie, a friend and senior partner at O'Donnell Sweeney (whom I consider to be one of the best law firms in Europe) described the difference to me in this way: 'In Ireland we can agree what we like, so long as the law doesn't forbid it. There it's the reverse. We can only agree to do something if the law approves it'.

I had a particular interest in the Czech Republic's financial institutions, and promptly discovered that its banking procedures, as was the case in all of the transition countries, were messy to say the least. Bank

Bohemia, now gloriously bankrupt along with several other Czech institutions, is a fine example of what happened to a reputable bank after deregulation and exposure to the free market.

Unlike some of the other examples I described previously, this wasn't a crude Mafia style grab, but a disaster that sprang from the naivety of people who equated capitalism with doing what you wanted. In banking, this translated into the local lending manager taking a percentage of your loaned money as his 'commission', a norm that encouraged corruption and destroyed what could have been otherwise viable business ventures.

A Czech lawyer told me about four acquaintances of his who got together and started a hotel development. They all came from engineering backgrounds but had no real experience of running a commercial business. With the fall of communism and the influx of tourism they decided, logically enough in many regards, that building hotels was the sure way to make money. The whole thing was a no-brainer, or so they believed.

The cost of the entire project was put at about forty million Czech crowns (about €1.5 million) so they went to their bank manager for fifty million. He arranged the loan at a high interest rate to be repaid over a three-year period, in itself an absurdity in property finance which generally requires repayment periods of at least ten years. He also slipped in a request for five per cent of the money to be paid back to him, his 'commission' on the loan.

However, all of this was fine with the four partners, who took the money and some more for good measure. Capitalism must have felt truly marvellous. They would build the hotel and make lots of money in the process. With so many tourists flocking to Prague, they could pay the entire sum back in double quick time and line their pockets on the way. The whole thing was foolproof.

Unfortunately, unlike more genuine capitalists, they had no detailed cash flow projections that balanced revenues with income, or any of the other normal business plan calculations regarding market, advertising and management. And the bank official, far from pointing out these deficiencies, was simply waiting on his kickback.

As the money flowed and construction started, so too did the 'fact-finding' business trips abroad, the new executive cars, the hospitality bills and, of course, the extensions to the family homes. For the budding entrepreneurs, it was perfectly fine to cheat on their own company since it happened under communism all the time. It did not register with them that they were the sole shareholders of the company and were therefore responsible for full repayment of the loan. Likewise, the bank official carried on as if he were lending from a state-owned bank with unlimited funds. The whole venture had become a merry-go-round for the aspiring hotel developers and their bank manager, and many more were now climbing on. It was at that stage that our mutual lawyer friend wisely advised one of the partners to invest his cash 'dividends' and spread the risk. 'Perhaps US mutual funds or some German banks', he suggested.

'No, no, I prefer to stick to a Czech share, like Komercni Banka,' the partner said. As the largest bank in the country he had full confidence in it. At that time the shares were worth 2,800 crowns (about €107).

One year later, the hotel was finished. Of the fifty million crowns that had been given, only about thirty million crowns had gone into the building. The engineers had cut corners and 'tunnelled' out the rest of the money. The hotel was badly built, there was little proper marketing, and few customers. With all of the original loan squandered, the resulting cash flow from the hotel itself was unable to support the loan to the bank.

So what did the bank do? In a stroke of genius it loaned the company more money in a process known as 'rolling over'.

Extraordinarily this time the bank gave sixty million crowns (about €2 million), twenty per cent more than the original loan for a project that was finished. With the sixty million crowns the four entrepreneurs paid off the fifty million owed on the first loan, gave some more to the bank manager and continued on with their lavish lifestyle. In a complete absence of marketing sense, they naively believed that because the hotel was so new business would improve of its own accord.

Everybody was a winner. The partners had a business that was just waiting to make money, the manager had his second commission, and the bank could now profit off a new loan, secured with a fine hotel valued at sixty million crowns plus on paper. Except that bank's first loan had been paid off by the bank itself.

This rollover by the bank made its balance sheet look good for investors and regulators. For a western financial institute asset-backed finance based on real estate is low risk and therefore, for outsiders looking in, everything was kosher. Of course the reality was that Bank Bohemia had given out sixty million crowns for a shoddy and unprofitable hotel that had been put up at cost of only thirty million.

Ultimately of course, it all caught up with the budding entrepreneurs. The hotel did not make the required money and the bank repossessed the property, the cars and all the other trappings of fake success. The only things left were the KB shares (now down in value by eighty per cent) and the partners' home extensions, which we hope were better built than the hotel.

Surprise surprise, Bank Bohemia was later declared bankrupt.

Another fine example of post-Soviet Czech entrepreneurship is the flamboyant Vladimir Zelezny.

Zelezny was the prime mover in establishing TV Nova, the first privately held television station in the Czech Republic and apparently an outstanding success story.

Unfortunately, the profits were partially blown in other central and eastern European countries by New York backers Central European Media Enterprises, or CME.

CME had worked on the assumption that because the business model had been successful in the Czech Republic it should then roll out easily in the rest of the region. This might have been the case if cultural differences had been taken into account, but there was a lack of understanding which led to a big blowout in Poland and the project went off the rails. They had thought global, but not local.

Zelezny was guest speaker at one of the US Chamber of Commerce monthly lunches when the guests included the US ambassador, many heavy-hitters of the Prague business world and myself.

Zelezny spoke of the marvellous success story of TV Nova, stating that it had about 700 employees, sales of $145 million, profits of about $40 million and that it had captured seventy per cent of the market share in three years.

It was an impressive achievement partially accomplished by good business. The former state television company still had 12,000 employees and was being totally thrashed by this upstart. Taking on monopolies and big establishment players was something close to my own heart and I was enthralled by the TV Nova story.

Of course one of the other major reasons behind Nova's quick success was Zelezny's wall-to-wall broadcasting of pornography, something that the communists had prohibited. If you switched on your television set after a certain time of the day during the early transition period, you were guaranteed to find the screen filled with people jumping up and down and bonking non-stop. From the strictly controlled and boring communist media, which had constantly reported (falsely) increases in agricultural production and the like, this was a total change. And naturally a controversial one.

After his speech, the president of the Chamber of Commerce called for questions. There was a pregnant pause. Everybody had one question in their mind, but nobody was prepared to ask it.

Nobody but me anyway.

I rose to the floor and asked Zelezny two questions in my best North Atlantic American accent. The first being about his vision for the future of television in the Internet and e-commerce age and then a second question which went something like this: 'You know, Mr Zelezny, here the standards of public decency and morality are higher than in other countries. Yet I am sure that because of the strict controls on national TV and public broadcasting that what is shown on TV Nova might not be accepted in countries like the United States. What is your view on this?'

Quietly around the room I could see the heads nodding quietly in approval, including the US ambassador. Zelezny got up and said he would respond to the second question first. 'Firstly I would like to apologise for the poor quality of our erotica models. We plan to improve it! Secondly, I would like to ask, which does more damage to society? People on television making love or violent movies showing murder, rape, shootings and violence?'

Zelezny then added that they would rather not show violent Hollywood movies, but that sometimes they had little choice. The answer probably wasn't that surprising coming from Zelezny since the man used to front his own TV show entitled *Call the Director* to trot out his own political lines.

Subsequently the station's ownership became the subject of a very difficult battle between Zelezny and Ronald Lauder, the scion of Estée Lauder and chairman of CME, with Zelezny using his *Call the Director* show to heap scorn on the Americans. Nothing much good came out of it for either party and Zelezny ended up attempting to run a very shaky independent channel of the same name for a while.

Since then he has had some interesting experiences, including spending a night in jail on fraud charges, becoming a senator and having his political immunity stripped to allow an investigation into his affairs. Zelezny eventually won back his television station only to be booted out by his new investors.

Ultimately the Czech government ended up carrying the can when an arbitration court ruled that they should have protected Lauder's investment and were ordered to pay CME $350 million in damages.

Despite all these shenanigans, it must be said that the Czech people are a good bunch and very practical. They like to drink beer with the highest *per capita* consumption in the world, tell jokes and live with a sort of black humour. The split with Slovakia, for example, was very matter of fact and passive.

Before the split, Czechoslovakia had been a federal state in which the Czechs and Slovaks had attempted to run their own affairs yet remain a unified state. However, the Czechs favoured faster reform than the Slovaks did, so the Slovaks declared a separate state in July 1992. For the next six months, the Slovaks, led by Vladímir Meciar, and the Czechs, led by Václav Klaus, negotiated the disbandment of the federation.

It was not unlike a civilised divorce, with the national treasures being divided and two countries being created. The logic of the separation from the Czech point of view appeared to be that if the Slovaks wanted to split, fine. Why force people together when they do not want it? This was a very sharp contrast to the aggression of the former Yugoslavia, inhabited by a totally different kind of people, even if they all stemmed from the same Slav tree.

While one might interpret the Czech approach as being 'unmanly', I personally take the view that the Czechs are practical and non-violent. However, they also embody a German-style discipline in keeping to the rules which I must admit is not in my character. I dislike a preponderance of rules and bureaucracy, and I am a natural-born rebel. That doesn't mean that I'll openly oppose or be combative, but I'll usually just do my own thing. Entrepreneurs have to have their creative freedom and they burn with the desire to make their mark on the world.

I liked the Czech Republic, and I was determined to make my money there – and that was exactly what I did.

I found the whole thing an extraordinary adventure. Starting up in Prague was not unlike the adventure of leaving from Boston to Europe in my little dinghy. I was going into the vast unknown. I knew nobody, had few contacts and I didn't even have a place to stay...

Chapter thirteen

Prague, Year Zero

It was now January 1993 and I was fresh in Prague.

Had I arrived one month earlier, I would have been in Czechoslovakia. Now the country was called the Czech Republic, with the new neighbour of the Slovak Republic. Everything was new, but at the same time old. Such were the contradictions of a region in massive socio-economic flux.

Each step you take through Prague is a step through time. In Old Town Square stands a statue of Jan Hus who, in 1415, was burned at the stake on the orders of the church hierarchy in Rome. He was a true heretic in the eyes of the Church and a true hero in the eyes of the Czechs – and in my eyes too – for he dared to translate the bible from Latin into Czech. He wanted to bring religion closer to the people and give the bible to them in a language they understood.

A true visionary, a true entrepreneur and look what he got.

With no delusions of grandeur or religion to preach, I considered myself somewhat safer. I was simply an Irish capitalist prophet looking for adventure and the chance to make an honest crown. By the million.

Back on the streets of Prague, as chairman, CEO and first employee of a new Czech company in formation, I started to develop a strategy.

Very often people end up in business because they know somebody and that person gives them a break, and it had been no different for me back in Ireland getting my start in journalism. *Afloat* came swiftly after and was a labour of love. It was successful because I was passionate about my sport and my subject. But it was a tidal market, operating in a remote island in western Europe in a very specialist area.

This time I intended to be more analytical and get into a business which I believed had upside and the potential to be huge. I took my time and looked around for just the right model and market. I knew that I could set up a successful business, but I wanted it to be one that could make big money. So I needed something that wasn't capital intensive – because I didn't have a lot of money to invest – and that I could get stuck into immediately.

The areas that were of interest to me included software development, communications, technology retailing and financial services. Seeing the growing popularity of PC sales in the west, I considered starting up a computer retailing business, but I decided that the market wasn't right for it yet. The ordinary Czechs couldn't afford computers, whilst the larger firms would be serviced by the multinationals, leaving me with just a narrow – albeit growing – affluent middle-class market.

Retail printing was another idea that was in my mind. I had marvelled at the success of a neighbour of mine who opened a ProntoPrint franchise business in Dublin. After three years, and with just three other staff in the business – he was both manufacturer and direct retailer – he was making a turnover of £300,000 a year, thirty per cent of which was profit.

I had slaved at publication and consultancy work which involved much greater brainpower, much greater skills, a huge diversity of disciplines and I hadn't generated near as much profit or returns.

Financial services was the most attractive sector by far. A lot of people I knew had made money in that area, including Dermot Desmond, and I was keen to emulate their successes.

Why?

Well if you are selling jumbo jets, and one jumbo jet is $1 billion, all you need is 0.01 per cent of that deal and you have a nice little commission. When you are selling soccer boots, you might have to sell one million boots to make the same commission. I was deliberately looking at areas that were lucrative.

The bottom line is this – if you are close to the big deal, all you need is a very small part of it. Deals of that type are happening constantly in the financial sector.

That basic concept of scalable opportunity became the driving logic for my quest to get started in financial services. I didn't know much about the general area, my insurance experience was about the limit of it, but I had selected it as my starting point in this new city and I was determined to get on with it.

What I decided to do was treat it in the same way as any other sector and apply the business fundamentals that I already knew. I was simply going to take a formula that was applicable to other markets and then spend time listening to what the customers wanted before launching the first product of my new enterprise.

To listen is the essence of good marketing, good business development and downright good sense. The discipline of the listener is the greatest discipline there is and there is wisdom in the old proverb which says that, 'he who listens well, learns well.'

A very good example of this is the story of Denis O'Brien's KISS 98 FM radio station in Prague. O'Brien later became a major player on the telecommunications scene but, at this stage, was involved in less spectacular enterprises. Denis and his team, having determined to start a 'popular' radio station, went out and spent a lot of time listening to their potential audience.

Europe 2, run by a French company, was the leading private station, coming in soon after the fall of communism. There was a hunger for anything foreign, and young Czechs (the little contrarians, more power to them) immediately devoured one of the so-called 'evils' of the western world – pop music!

It started well for Europe 2, as they rolled out a diet of all the latest pop. Then all of a sudden Denis O'Brien grabbed a big chunk of listeners – in a market that had gone from state broadcasting to having nineteen private stations. Denis had done his research and it told him that Czech people in the eighteen to forty year old category, the prime consumer bracket, liked local news and the pop music of the 1970s. Although the Czechs would eventually graduate into racier things, in the early 1990s, they simply weren't ready for the modern stuff. KISS 98 FM gave them what they wanted and enjoyed the spoils, although it was a tough fight and the market eventually consolidated.

Getting going involved an awful lot of listening and meeting people to find out exactly what was needed from potential customers. As it happened, a man called Frank Haughton, a former money broker in Dublin with Dermot Desmond, had just started the first Irish pub in Prague. It attracted all of the expatriates and was full to the gills every night. Frank charged three times the going rate for his drinks and did so well that he paid for the entire venture six months after opening.

I went there frequently to meet with all the top foreign executives who had been posted to the Czech Republic, to make friends and acquaintances, network – and to listen.

I spent my time picking up knowledge, asking them what did they think of this, what did they think of that. I learned informally what I couldn't afford to find out professionally. For the price of a few beers, I could pick the brains of senior consultants from all of the then major firms, including PriceWaterhouseCoopers, Arthur Anderson and Deloitte and Touche.

One beer cost me maybe fifty cents (even at Frank's inflated prices) and it lasted about thirty minutes depending on the consultant. If I had gone in to talk to them in their offices it might have cost me $200 for one hour.

I also picked up a lot of hard luck stories. For example, there was one guy who went into business with a Czech and together they built up a very successful bar and nightclub. The westerner thought he had a 50–50 partnership agreement, but he had read the contract in English before it had been translated into Czech. Unfortunately, what the Czech version said was entirely different, but it was the Czech version that stood under the law – and it gave total ownership to the Czech 'partner'.

But I wasn't interested in anything of that level anyway, it was too public and too prone to exactly those types of cutthroat individuals. I wanted to get into a white collar, blue chip and top level enterprise.

I didn't have to wait very long to find my niche.

Prior to November 1992, the Prague Stock Exchange didn't exist, there had been one before but the communists had closed it. Within a relatively short period of time, it had more than 2,000 listed companies. It was way too much, especially when you consider that the London Stock Exchange is the oldest in the world and it had roughly the same number. That was for a country of almost sixty million and one that had been the centre of an empire not so long ago. By comparison, a country the size of Ireland had maybe ninety listed companies on its exchange, of which only forty or fifty were really serious.

The Czech Republic was much nearer the Irish end of the spectrum than the British so it was obvious to any outsider that most of those newly listed Czech companies were going to disappear rapidly. But which ones? How would it be possible to tell the difference between a reasonable investment and a dead horse?

Again it was the crux of risk management. To manage risk, you need information. Investors needed information on these companies before they could commit funds and become embroiled. To get the bigger strategic picture, they wanted not just information on the company they might invest in, but also that company's competitors, both existing and potential.

Eventually after all this listening, a plan for the new business started to take shape. I decided on the idea of setting up a financial information company based on the lines of a cash rich New York organisation called Valueline, and a similar operation called Hemmington Scott in London. There had also been a publication in Dublin called *Aspect*, in which an Irish Stock Market guide was published, which was another possible model.

The guide and directory reference publication I had decided on could be done with incomplete data, it would be made to look good and would be funded by advertising. The idea was to print the data on the 2,000 so-called stock exchange companies in limited form, state clearly it was only sixty per cent accurate and post it free to the companies in question. The companies whose data was wrong could send in corrected data if they wished.

The idea was not capital intensive and I knew that I could make it work. My first enterprises had been based on information, and I could roll out a similar service for a different sector by following the principles that I had learned in the past. I knew what the customers wanted and I knew that theirs was a market for the taking.

But first I had to raise some cash. I had completed some rough figures and I knew that my £15,000 savings, already being nibbled at by the cost of flights to and from Prague, was inadequate. Banks were not an option, so I was considering my other options (or lack thereof) when David Beattie, introduced me to a client of his called Jimmy McShane. I met with Jimmy and told him about my plans to start another business in eastern Europe. While Jimmy had no expertise in my proposed enterprise, he had a good head for business. We subsequently became friends, and he gave me terrific advice that I still hold to in business today: 'Make a turn, don't be greedy, and leave something for the other guy.'

At that moment, however, Jimmy was listening away and I was getting two impressions. First that he related to what I was trying to do, and second that he really had no idea what my venture would entail. We closed the deal in the car park of Jury's hotel in Ballsbridge as we sat in his car. He opened his cheque book and gave me £20,000 for twenty per cent of the business.

It was a big break. I had no shareholder's agreement or even a receipt to give him, but based on that meeting, McShane decided to trust me – and he did it without having anything on paper in return. Later, I am proud to say, he was rewarded handsomely for his investment.

Now for some that might look like an incredible gamble and, in some respects, it is. But in other ways it's not. As I mentioned before, one of the fundamentals of business is being able to read people. McShane could tell that I just wanted to set up a successful venture and that I had no intention of doing a runner with his money. Being semi-retired, I think he also enjoyed the involvement. These days my investments and partnership are significantly bigger, but the fundamentals of trust and confidence remain. I had earned Jimmy's confidence and he put his trust in me.

Sometime later, courtesy of David Beattie, he got a shareholder's agreement. With some money in the kitty, I could now move on to my next fundamental requirement. As before, I intended to build an enterprise of quality from the top downwards, and now I had to find just the right employees.

If you get the right people at the start of an enterprise, you will have formed a peer group that will operate a self-selection process. They will set the culture and the standard, only bringing in other people who are of equal or better standard to them.

Any successful venture that I have been involved with has had the right theme, the right culture and the right people from the very start. Any problematic enterprises I have encountered have been ones where that dynamic had gone wrong, or was never instigated properly.

When things get rough, the right people will form a solid core and stick together. The wrong people will cause embarrassment and hassle, and they will drag your enterprise down. Even firing them causes disruption.

Where did I find them? In the Irish pubs of course.

In Frank Haughton's Irish pub, I met Ian Smith, an expatriate Englishman who mentioned the name of a young Czech, Petr Kucera.

Petr was in his early twenties and worked with Resources, a foreign information firm. Petr was mentioned as having great attention to detail, being good, bright and smart. It took a lot to persuade him to join me because all I had to sell to Petr was a concept, a vision if you will. A vision of a successful start-up company where he would be the prime mover from the earliest stage. But the biggest thing that I sold him was trust. The trust that I was going to make a go of a serious enterprise and not allow it to fail.

There's no magic answer to what you have to do when you are selling a vision. You simply have to believe wholesale in that vision yourself. I knew that I was going to make it successful because I needed to be successful. Petr could see by my actions and demeanour that I was going to make the business work, and so he came to believe in the business too.

For Petr it was also a challenge. He was young and driven, willing to try something new, and perhaps he also didn't know any better. In the old socialist countries, it was difficult to find open-minded people for this sort of thing – anybody over the age of twenty-five would have been too busy saying that it wouldn't work.

That might sound like an extreme example of ageism, but the fact of the matter was that the people in their thirties had known the security of working under the Soviets. They were much less likely to take to a free-wheeling enterprise where you put your faith in your own abilities rather than some great, over- arching system that dictated everything to you from cradle to grave.

Of course, you don't have to have lived under a communist system to develop that type of 'can't do' attitude. We only shrugged it off recently in Ireland, and in general most people see the difficulties before the opportunities when a potential enterprise is put before them.

Lack of confidence in starting anything is a potent mixture for failure. All you have as an entrepreneur is belief, belief in your own ability to succeed. This must be transferred to the team you build – they must have belief in the product or service they offer. If not the customer will detect it very quickly and you're dead meat.

So that they could see who I was, my background and, above all, my commitment, I later flew Petr Kucera and a friend of his, Daniela Kafkova, to Ireland and arranged for them to participate in a sailing race to France on the boat of my friend, John Killeen. At the time, this was an extravagance for me, but I felt that it was important. We never got around to finishing the race, instead we cruised the south coast of Ireland. Petr got a small scar on his face, which is on him to this day, but he eventually decided to join me.

When Petr came on board, it was a breakthrough, because with him he brought Daniela and also Ian Smith. While I also had to sell the dream to them, it was much easier. Petr was the natural leader and when he came, the other two followed. We couldn't have achieved what we did without each other.

I had been thinking about a company title, and I liked the name Aspekt. The title of the Irish stock market magazine had grown on me and I discovered that the word (spelled with a k instead of a c) had the same meaning in Slavic languages. To this I added Kilcullen, after a grand aunt of mine and an old family surname. Kilcullen originates from Cuchulainn, the ancient warrior and adventurer from Celtic mythology, and it was a name I had always given my boats on various adventures. I like to think the Kilcullen part also puts a little personality into the business name. And so, Aspekt Kilcullen sro (which is the Czech equivalent of ltd or llc) came into being.

With my business concept defined and a team in place, it was time to get serious and establish ourselves as the main financial information provider for the Czech markets.

This is the stage that many new enterprises fail. They can have a great plan, great product, great team and everything else – but the spending gap between their kick-off to the point where their cash flow begins is what kills it. The reality is that everything takes much longer than expected and there are always problems. With my limited funds, I was acutely aware of this and I structured things accordingly.

With our office space, I did two things to maximise the image of the business and reduce overheads. As I would be meeting with senior managers and executives I knew that I had to communicate a positive and professional image. If I left them with a business card with an office address at a cheap address, they might judge the quality of the operation by the location. Naturally that would not at all reflect the real circumstances, but when they would only have one meeting with me and my card to go on it would be a plausible conclusion to draw.

Of course, if anybody asked, I would not have lied or misled, I would have told them there and then how we were structured. However, few, if any, did ask. When you present your business card to a person, it generally goes like this. You give them your card, they see your address. You look well, you talk well and – most important of all – you smile. You are acting and thinking professionally, they see that and they accept it. Professionals want to deal with professionals, and therefore much of what you do in start-ups is about confidence and conviction. If you are starting, everybody will wish you well and wish to support the new business – but not at their risk or their expense. It's a fact that most new businesses fail, and nobody wants to have one of their service providers drop off the radar screen at a critical moment. The natural inclination is for them to give you the line that means 'come back later after you a re established'. And you can't get established when your client base is waiting for you to become established.

It's a terrible paradox that you must avoid. You must go in strong, ignore the fact that you are new and just sell the benefits of service as you would for any other company. I wasn't willing to take the risk of having the company image damaged inadvertently, and so I did a deal with a serviced office business in an expensive and prestigious location in Prague for just a nameplate, registered address, postal drop and the use of a boardroom when needed.

The second thing I did was to arrange office space to work from. For an actual office, I briefly used an apartment, but then I decided to rent the entire floor of one building.

Overkill?

Not at all. I had seen that a lot of people were in Prague looking for one or two-room offices, so I decided to cater for them by taking more space than I needed. I had little difficulty finding tenants and I asked for cash up front. I sublet three-quarters of my space for a cost equal to what I had to pay my landlord for the entire floor, and effectively got my own office for nothing.

There were also other benefits to this. I refined the lessons I had learned from outsourcing and gave priority to those tenants that I had a professional relationship with. For example, I wanted a professional graphic design studio to produce our publication (again the emphasis was on quality), but we also needed to be close to the production process and to be in control of it – often a difficult thing to do when outsourcing.

We knew Vladimir, a very good designer, who worked from his apartment. Speaking with him one day I said, 'Take a space in my office and I'll give you guaranteed work. You can use it to service your own clients too.'

He did so and we enjoyed a mutually profitable relationship. He could operate from our premises, while I had a service with no management problems or diversion from my core activities.

Vladimir outgrew his one-room office at the same time as Aspekt, and we all moved together to bigger premises. I took my other tenants with me so as to continue the rental arrangement and I kept that cash-flow cycle going.

When I last spoke to him, Vladimir had a thriving business with over fifteen staff working for him. Because of bonds and working relationships formed with us, they understand their customers well and continue to do a lot of work for Aspekt.

However, it took some time and an awful lot of effort before we could even consider moving offices. I was putting in by far the most hours. My staff would leave in the evening and notice that I was staying on. Then they'd arrive back in the morning to find that I was already there.

They even began to suspect that I was actually living in the office. A ridiculous notion, but unfortunately one that was quite accurate. Although I had tried to hide the fact, it was becoming painfully apparent that I didn't have any other place to stay. The combination of impenetrable language and the amount of time I was devoting to putting the business together meant that I hadn't got around to organising my own accommodation. Instead I had brought a sleeping bag with me to the office so I could sleep on the floor each night.

While my own discomfort didn't bother me (I have endured a lot worse in my lifetime), it was still an embarrassing situation. On the one hand I was trying to build confidence and sell the idea of a market-leading company, on the other, my staff could see that their manager couldn't afford to live anywhere else. I have no doubt that they were wondering how in God's name would I pay their salaries at the end of the month.

However, there was an upside to the situation because it demonstrated the level of my commitment. It was putting the message across very clearly that the venture had to work and that, in turn, contributed to the working ethos and culture of the team. After a few weeks I was offered a bed in somebody's apartment, but by then I doubt if my staff cared one way or the other.

During that time, we concentrated on the actual venture. The vision of the business was to build a database of the financial markets and, out of that database, to build products. In that way the concept of the database was not unlike a forest with the data as the timber, the raw material so to speak.

Naturally I wanted to add value to this raw material, just as the entrepreneur should do to maximise returns. Although you can make money from pure extraction, it's usually far better to do this at the refining or manufacturing end of things.

Consider the timber metaphor again. You'll probably sell a finely crafted wooden chair for twenty times what you paid for the wood itself. By integrating high skills and creative art, both in your treatment of the raw material and your conceptualisation of the business, you have added considerable value.

And that's what I wanted to do with our data. I wanted to create a directory product, gather all the available information on the various companies, their vital statistics and contact details, and sell it back to them. It was a business model I had used before, but this time I aimed it at the financial sector.

To refine our product, we first had to be able to manipulate the data, and to do that we needed a software application. I couldn't afford to employ software developers from big companies, so I decided to get Czech students to do it for me. But how could I meet them and select the brightest? I had to make a contact in the field, so I made friends with the professor of computing science in the Czech Technical University. As it happened, the professor really wanted his daughter to learn English, so I arranged for her to go to Ireland with a friend to improve her language skills, and in return the professor gave me access to some of his top students.

Led by Petr, they got to work on the data-gathering software package immediately. The system they created would flow our data into a directory magazine, so that we could give it to banks, broking firms and leasing companies. There were maybe a hundred of these firms all gathering this data separately. But why should they expend all that effort and expense gathering it when really they could just get it all from us? We would also sell the database on disk, which would be an even superior product because then we could sell an update service to the database on a regular basis.

It's worth pointing out now that the confusion caused by the changing politico-economic system in the eastern European region, made even the most mundane information worth money. Deals were happening fast, hundreds of companies were being privatised and put on the stock exchange every few months, and shares being traded on the basis of who knew what. Nobody had any knowledge of these companies – not even the basic contact details. With the monopoly phone company introducing extra digits, the speed of privatisation, ownership changes and so forth, most printed directories were out of date almost as soon as they were distributed.

The monopoly phone company, though it was to their financial benefit, were not great at responding to directory enquiries either. Sometimes it could take twenty minutes to check one phone number – if you were lucky. It was a huge problem all round, more so for us because we were supposed to have that information en masse for clients. Accurate addresses, fax and telephone numbers were basic to our core database. We didn't have ten minutes to waste for the phone number of just one company, so how would we update our data on time?

Then I came up with a solution.

'Petr, keep calling until you get a friendly operator and invite him or her out for a beer.'

Petr did as I asked and, sure enough, he eventually made contact with an operator and invited her and several of her friends out for a drink. We showed them a good time, developed a relationship with them and asked them if they could do some work for us. For the girls it was new and interesting to meet our people, it was something different and gave them a chance to earn some extra income by checking all of our addresses and phone numbers.

Whether or not they did it during their time working for the phone company was their own business. In reality, I would be surprised if they did it at any other time, they were getting paid twice for doing the same work, albeit for a single customer. Why the hell should they answer calls for customers when they could update the database for us and get paid for it?

OK, there is a moral question here, perhaps some people would take the line that we 'bribed' the girls to 'steal' the information. But although the information was commercially valuable, it was also supposed to be in the public domain. The state phone company had rotten management and motivation systems in place, and their existing directory enquiry routine was pure and simple exploitation. We just needed to get this information efficiently, and had the monopoly provider been anyway decent, the situation simply wouldn't have arisen (or we could at least have approached them through regular channels). That wasn't the case, so we had to work around it.

It wasn't the last run in I was to have with Cesky Telecom, but I'll get to that...

We did, of course, require far more than just numbers and addresses for the database, and that meant face-to-face meetings with company leaders and executives. It was nightmare getting the information because that was how the communists had exerted control, by restricting the free flow of knowledge between ordinary citizens while at the same time gathering information on everybody and everything for their own use.

Although the Czech companies were now officially public, they remained paranoid about giving any material about themselves. Dealing with them and other post-socialist entities was an art in itself. One of my most memorable early 'first meetings' was with the president of the Russian Kazakhstan Bank. It was part of a decision to meet all the main players in town. I went in at the most senior level to build contacts, to listen and to learn.

It might seem strange that a person in my position – someone who most certainly wasn't a main player at that time – could be so cocky as to seek appointments with all these industry leaders, but it's simply a matter of perception. What difference did it make if I was a representing an established enterprise or not? I had a good product for a needful market and it was irrelevant whether my company was twenty years or twenty days old. I had to consider market research, distribution and client base, and that necessitated one-on-one meetings.

However, how I could actually be granted time with such high-level personnel without any firm credentials to back me up, is another question.

I didn't mislead or misrepresent myself. I didn't have to. That old line about 'familiarity breeding contempt' can also work in reverse. Most people I met had no idea of my business, who I was or what I wanted from them, but because I was a foreigner I was taken seriously. Eastern Europe was full of hotshot foreign investors and to the bewildered ex-soviets I was probably just another one of them. It was a sign of the times that any expatriate, regardless of status, could get access to the most senior level of business.

Any non-Czech contacting a company was put straight through to the person in question without much hassle ('A westerner? He must be important!') while the unfortunate native had to undergo a filtering process. It's a phenomenon I have witnessed in Ireland too and it's an indication of an immaturity in business thinking. It's the quality of the product, concept or person that's important, not their nationality.

Think global.

What attracted me to the Kazakhstan Bank was the chance of selling advertising space in our directory to them. The Pvní Investioní Bank (First Investment Bank) was offering a twenty-five per cent return on savings deposited with them – every month. Now in a normal economy it might be a good thing to be sceptical of returns like this, however, at that time some of the eastern European countries had a thousand per cent inflation per annum, and therefore returns like this were not necessarily absurd.

I decided to bring Anna, a Russian translator working with Aspekt, along with me. Anna was one of these brilliant Russian intellectuals and linguists and I later gave her a full-time job for a while. She had worked much of her life in the Academy of Sciences in Moscow, could rattle away fluently in eight or nine languages – but had zero business sense. Quite the reverse in fact. She could talk all day and all night on marvellous and intriguing topics but afterwards it dawned that you have achieved absolutely nothing.

Although that level of intelligence is wonderful in a social context, in business things must be target-oriented. You must be productive and achieve something with the time you have available for your various duties. It's another of the contrasts between the market forces of capitalism and the push economy of communism. If you are in the performance-related, market-led system and you don't do your work, it eventually comes home to bite you in the ass, and you get sacked or lose revenue. If you didn't pull your weight under the soviet system chances were that: a) one of your comrades did it for you; or b) your shoddy work went right down the line into a product that was forced onto the push economy market. There wasn't much of a comeback either way. (Until their entire system went belly up that is.)

Our meeting with the bank president was scheduled for twelve o'clock – or rather 'High Noon'. All of a sudden the new east took on an unnerving resemblance to the Old West. At the entrance of the Kazakhstan Bank, the security guard was polishing bullets, an activity which I hoped he was doing out of boredom. Several boxes of ammunition were piled up by his immaculate machine gun. The weapon shone and reflected the rays of the bright winter sun, the light of which cheerfully pierced the bullet and bomb-proof glass of the security guard's enclosure.

What a confident feeling the investor must have had, knowing that such weapons were keeping his money secure...

Of course, anyone with even an average knowledge of the industry would understand that cash banking of this nature had gone out with Butch Cassidy and the Sundance Kid. Whatever about other parts of the ex-communist bloc and Soviet Union, things had never got bad enough in the Czech Republic to merit such an aggressive façade.

Still, it concentrated the mind.

We made it past the security guard without being riddled with any shiny bullets and the bank staff showed Anna and myself into the boardroom.

Like the Steppes of Kazakhstan, it was vast and expansive, and we took a couple of seats at the massive mahogany table like a pair of isolated nomads. Ten minutes later, there was still no sign of the president, though we had been offered the customary cup of treacle coffee.

Then possibly the most exceptional looking woman I have ever seen in my entire life entered the room. Long legged and large busted, she sat down in front of me, crossed her legs, took out a new notebook, new sharpened pencil, and smiled at me. The huge crystal chandelier sparkled (either that or I was beginning to see stars) and that huge room suddenly felt a lot bigger.

Now by this stage in my life, I had long surrendered to conformity regarding conventional business dress and the wearing of suits, shirts, ties and not really a whole lot more. It's simply another part of a professional image. For this meeting, I was most certainly acting my role and my part as a conservative businessman. Correspondingly one expects the personal assistants of other business people to also look a particular way. The secretary of a banker generally does not look like a lady out to make a living from an investment in her personal assets. However, this lady was a billboard for sex from top to bottom.

Now bucking fashion trends is often seen as hip and courageous and being something of a maverick I do sympathise, but I wouldn't recommend it in commercial life for one simple reason – anything out of the ordinary is viewed with instant suspicion.

Business people want stability, not surprises.

For example one friend of mine, Ric Barroilket, a high level salesman, once told me how he had a colleague flown 4,000 miles at short notice to assist him in a pitch he was making in Spain. Although his colleague arrived just in time for the meeting, Ric refused to let him enter because he noticed something that he didn't like about his colleague's attire. Although he had most of the usual formal wear, he was without one thing – cuff-links.

Now cufflinks are not important in most countries but Ric, aware of Spanish dress code at that level of business, was not prepared to risk suffering even the slightest negative impression in his limited time. So much so that he ditched his partner and made the sale himself.

Similarly, I asked Anna not to bring our business papers to meetings again in a plastic shopping bag. It would be much more professional, I suggested, if she could use the briefcase I had bought for her.

As an entrepreneur, I have become quite particular about dress and in fact I've made a total reversal on my thinking from twenty years ago. Whereas I personally don't care about appearance in general (I regard it as a person's lifestyle choice to make for themselves), when it comes to the welfare of my enterprises, I believe that it's important to go that little bit extra. Psychologically, it has been proven that people like to do business with those of equal or higher status. Even if you don't have a lot of money, you can still look the part of a winner, and that will make people more inclined to deal with you.

After what seemed an eternal wait at that mahogany table – it had only been twenty minutes but I had been melting under the strain of the overpowering secretarial legs and the girl's constant chattering in Russian (the one-time official language of all the Soviet states) about things that almost certainly had no connection with banking or business – the head of the bank made his entrance.

As he waltzed in, my image of what a typical bank president should look like was shattered.

He wore a bright-coloured suit, the mandatory Rolex watch, charm bracelets and an open necked shirt revealing a hairy, sun-tanned chest that reminded me of a line from a song: 'That was my bother Sylvest (What's he got?), A row of forty medals on his chest (Big chest!)... '

To round everything off, his teeth were studded with enough gold and diamonds to make his mouth sparkle like a constellation – and like the stars they probably came out at night. He was in every way as gaudy and as over-the-top as the institution he was presiding over.

'I am pleased to meet you', he said in Russian, translated by Anna. He clapped his big arms around my shoulders in friendship and he boasted, 'Sources close to the president of Kazakhstan have a stake in my bank.'

Talk about the hard sell. He was telling me that the bank was watertight because Nazarbayev's cronies had invested in it. For the next four hours, there was a slow yet constant information exchange and relationship-building exercise. Precisely the way business had been conducted under the old communist system. First you got to really know a person, to find out where you stood with them and whether they thought like you – and if they were amenable to bribes. Then you probably bribed them in return for specific cuts of the project. While all of this was happening, the basic logic of the original project began to get warped and was turned into something devoid of logic and market needs. Money was creamed off and enormous inefficiencies crept into the system.

My Kazakh encounter was a complete contrast to my earlier meeting that day with the president of Citibank. There had been no machine guns, no opulent boardrooms, no pneumatic secretaries and no boasts about Bill Clinton's friends being shareholders. Instead the conversation went along the following lines:

'What can we do for you?'

'What can you do for us?'

End of meeting.

And it only took twenty minutes.

It was after 4.00 p.m. and a very liquid lunch that afternoon before I could extricate myself from the banker and his centrefold secretary. I left Anna as a decoy to keep them all chattering away whilst I tried to regain lost time on serious business.

Needless to say, I never did any business with that specific institution. It became the centre of a scandal before going out of business, whilst its larger-than-life president hit the papers amidst a storm of allegations. His wasn't the only bank to go bust in that period before the Czechs cleaned up the sector, although not before many investors were badly burned.

Chapter fourteen

Counter-revolutionary

The Kazakhstan Bank was one of many meetings clocked up on the meter as I beat the pavements of Prague's business district. Going in at the top level of these companies provided me with a valuable insight into the needs of the market and clients. At the same time, however, a weird formula evolved in my mind. It might sound crazy, but I began to believe that the bigger the CEO's desk and boardroom, the worse the company.

It was an absurd correlation, but it was only a little later that I recognised why it was actually a sound principle. Under the communists, you couldn't always give somebody more money, so instead you gave lots of rewards, one of which might be a bigger desk. Therefore, a successful bureaucrat (there was not much room for anything else under the system) was not measured by the size of his salary or profitability – he was measured by the size of his office.

I always remember one manager who headed the research department in a bank. He had an enormous desk, meeting room and over seventy people reporting to him, yet he could not authorise an expenditure of more than $100. By contrast, Petr Kucera who was running my company from a room shared with others and with fewer employees, was producing several times the amount and could make much larger expenditure decisions.

The companies that were still in the old mode of thinking were patently the ones that hadn't made the psychological jump to the dynamic of the free market. The four senior managers of my company operated out of the one room. We didn't give a hoot whether it had grandeur or not, we just needed a workspace to get our stuff done. More than a decade after transition, there's still a gap, and it doesn't just apply to post-soviets. You still have organisations where people are trapped by status. They are caught in their own position and perception, and end up in a narrow groove. To be in that state in business is death, there's always evolution and you must go with the flow. New ideas, new consumer tastes, new and better ways of doing things. Sure, some are fads, but others are genuine improvements and you must be savvy to them.

Within a few months the software that the students had developed was able to merge the multiplicity of information that we had collected into one single database. The combined data could then flow from that master database into a publication and it gave us the bones of a business directory.

We probably could have sold the directory on the strength of the data alone, but then we would have missed out on lucrative advertising revenue. We had by this stage gathered the names and contact details of 10,000 opinion leaders and decision-makers in the Czech Republic and we intended to post the publication directly to them. Postal rates, relative to advertising rates, were quite cheap at that time so it was a perfect method of distribution. It was practically the same formula for my past magazines. The important difference was that this directory was guaranteed to attract premium business-to-business advertising.

We started working on the quality and feel of the hard copy directory and thought up a scheme to attract more interest. The first publication would do a short profile of the 'Top 100 Managing Directors'. This would be a welcome departure from the old communist style directories, which were very impersonal and gave no interesting details. The information in the old directories was out of date anyway and nobody knew who the top 100 MDs were.

It was typical of a faceless, committee-run system, and communism was disappearing fast. In its place, free market capitalism was firmly rooting. One hallmark of the free market system is individuality. Stop and think about it and you'll realise just how much we link the efforts of groups, organisations and governments with one individual. It doesn't matter if successful diplomacy is due more to the efforts of countless diplomats and civil servants, it's the minister in charge who is congratulated. It's the same in business. A CEO will be rewarded when his company performs better, regardless of whether the improvements were brought about by lesser executives– or had anything to do with his efforts.

Of course, the reverse is also true. Figureheads will also suffer if circumstances beyond their control conspire to bring failure. In our society we simply want nice, bite-size personalities who we can identify, either to praise or blame, as the situation merits.

Industry leaders particularly like to know who they're dealing with and, even more so, want themselves to be known. We knew that if Czech business people saw their photos in our magazine, they would be inclined to buy advertising space. Not only would a positive reputation generate more business for them, it would massage their egos no end – a factor not to be underestimated in business. Since the mid-1990s, when we did this in the Czech market, it has, like all markets, moved on and massaging the CEO ego this way works less well today.

There are now alternative ways and more CEO egos to massage – thus the heart of the capitalist system!

By now, I had outsourced everything I possibly could, and I had an operation that ran off eight separate, and mostly remote, parts:

1. researchers gathering data;
2. an accountancy firm dealing with accounts and invoices;
3. a designer creating the publication;
4. a typesetting and layout company;
5. a film studio for colour separation;
6. a printer for plate-making and printing;
7. a postal company to print labels and post magazines; and
8. freelance journalists to write the articles.

The full-time staff of Aspekt (now at five) had to look after the toughest part – selling advertising in a publication that did not yet exist. Putting together a top-class presentation and high-quality colour brochure, my sales team dressed to the teeth and hit the ground running.

And ran into a brick wall – they didn't know how to sell.

For my Czech workforce, the process of sales was a real learning curve. They were all great individuals, but they still needed training in how to be good salespeople. It was also the first time that I had a sales team reporting to me. Prior to working in the Czech Republic, I had usually sold my own ventures or projects.

In reality, of course, the entrepreneur is competing and must sell to achieve everything that they need, including staff, financial resources, credit from suppliers, and so on. Only after they have successfully sold themselves time and time again can they get around to selling their own product.

Because the free market system involves intense competition, the sales process in the west has evolved into a sophisticated element. However, under communism the limitations of central planning and distribution eliminated much of the competition, and their knowledge of sales, therefore, was extremely crude.

In should have been no surprise to me to find that that local knowledge of sales and marketing was appalling. Vast fortunes were blown on advertising and exhibition space by Czech banks, who either thought they were dutifully copying capitalist tactics or on other occasions were just satisfying egos. Their naivety and huge advertising budgets represented yet another hole in their financial sieve.

Likewise, the first salespeople I hired in Prague were not salespeople at all. Like the old-style communists, they would go into a room and say 'Here's my price list here's my product, do you want to buy?' which was probably the biggest turn-off ever. Our natural conditioning is not to part with money, and when someone approaches you like that it's very easy to say no. Maybe it would have worked with commodities, but definitely not for the sophisticated financial services information we were offering. To rectify this I had to invest a lot of time and energy in training. There are hundreds of books to be read on what makes a good salesperson. If you are the budding entrepreneur, I suggest you go read them all. I have read lots and I have learned something new in every one. From all those books and from my practical experience I have learned one thing.

The fundamental of sales is this – people buy from other people. No computers, clinical analysis, sales pitch or motivator detracts from this fact. While price, benefits, convenience, reputation, service and so forth are important, the bottom line is people. Even on the Internet. When you purchase goods from an automated site such as Ryanair or Amazon there is still a human element. Although your transaction is completely electronic, the material on the website is written in a 'person-to-person' fashion in common, everyday language that you'd expect to hear from a normal individual. When you complete the transaction on your credit card, the screen even thanks you for your purchase.

Now, in reality, the jumble of circuitry that transacted the sale is unable to care one way or the other, but the perception is that the company has thanked you for your purchase, and that makes you feel good.

For the entrepreneur, direct one-to-one selling is the most important. For my team, I always placed specific emphasis on building personal relationships. Your skills in this area will determine whether you can sell your project to venture capitalists, bankers, potential employees and, ultimately, customers.

Selling is a process. In the same way that a car is manufactured and just doesn't materialise out of nowhere, a sale is also made in different components and stages. The following is a distillation of what I have learned about selling, and it's based on five elements each drawn from common sense. This process can take two minutes, two hours, two days, two months, two years or two decades. It depends on what you are selling.

Jim Irwin at IMPAC called it his AIDDA formula and he compared it to men and women meeting for the first time, starting from the chat-up line:

- *Attention*
- *Interest*
- *Desire*
- *Decision*
- *Action*

Attention

To get favourable attention (you don't want any other type) you must start with your research – for example, the local talent in a bar. Does this person catch my attention? Are they someone I can like and respect?

It could be a minute reading a company brochure in the lobby or a month researching every detail of the person and organisation you are approaching. Your effort in this respect should be relative to the importance and potential return of the person whose attention you are trying to attract. Do your research properly, and you might discover a unique angle or opportunity that will get you inside. If the person in question is the decision-maker for what you wish to achieve, do your very best to make the contact. Don't set your sights any lower – chances are someone else will present your request in an offhand manner and ruin it for you.

To make personal contact, you must first set an appointment. This request, either by letter, phone, fax or email must say as little as possible so that your business can't be prejudged, but be specific enough to be relevant to them and justify your claim on the person's time.

If your objective is to get a one-to-one meeting, avoid explaining it on the telephone or posting the material. People buy from people, so make sure you are there in person to sell it. Get the meeting first, and then refer to your supporting materials. Once you are given a tacit consent for a meeting, you should work around the subject's schedule.

I once met an arms dealer (I actually had no idea what his business was until he told me) who wanted to make contact with Russian General Alexander Lebed, a hero of the Chechen war and later a governor in eastern Russia. To get the general's attention the dealer sent him a fax inviting him to a Rolling Stones concert, which Lebed accepted.

For your meeting, dress accordingly – you will be judged by how you dress and present yourself. Unfortunately you rarely get a second chance to make a first good impression. You have too much at stake to appear in outlandish clothes, or anything else that the prospect may take a dislike to. It is best to be boring, steady and conservative. If you want to brighten your appearance, go in with a smile.

Your dress is almost like a uniform insofar as it suggests your role. If you want to do business and you go in dressed like a rock star you will not be taken seriously.

Likewise if you are dressed like a businessman and are performing as a rock star, you will not be taken seriously either.

When a target didn't have much time, I often suggested meeting for breakfast. This was a little unusual in eastern Europe and caught attention. Depending on the level of contact, I might even book a top-class hotel. If the meeting was for two, I would reserve space for three since it would guarantee more space and avoid us being crowded in with strangers.

I did the same when attracting employees. I had a very poor office but I would arrange to meet in the best hotels. There is no room rental cost, maybe a cup of coffee in the lobby, but it gives a good first impression. Eventually, you have to show your little office, but remember that on the first meeting you are selling a dream and ideas are greater than things.

Don't be afraid to be creative in setting a meeting. Once I had been trying to hook up with someone for a whole year, but he never had the time. Then, at Christmas, I sent him a very large desk clock and asked that he make a little time for me...

Interest

Now having attracted favourable attention (assuming you have not at this stage been ejected from your target's office), the next thing is to generate interest. You must say something that will generate interest in what you can do for them in their current situation. You may be funny, mysterious (to a degree), or have something in common with them like an acquaintance or hobby – anything at all that will generate interest.

As in all meetings, the warm-up is almost always critical. Avoid going straight into the subject of the meeting. If you start too soon it's very difficult to get back and build that personal contact because soon it's just business. You must get to know the person and they must get to know you. When you speak, it breaks down barriers and makes the person more receptive to your presence. If they are not receptive to you, they probably won't be receptive to anything you have to sell them. At the beginning of the meeting talk about anything except what you have really come to talk about. This may take thirty seconds or thirty minutes. I have gone into sales meetings and spent the first forty minutes, of a planned forty-five, talking about anything but the subject and still come away with an order in the final five minutes.

When you first meet a person, you must scan for clues as to what interests them. A tie, badge, photos, the newspaper on the table or whatever else might get the conversation going.

Jim Irwin gave me a classic example of this type of opening. He once went to make a sale in the office of a German executive. The executive was clearly the functional type and had nothing in his room other than the desk, chair, computer and writing materials.

Jim sensed that the German wanted to get straight into the subject at hand, which he knew would probably kill the sale. It looked as if he had little choice until he spotted one unusual picture on the wall that was all white with a small dot in the middle. Jim quickly asked what the picture was.

It transpired that the picture was an aerial photograph. The dot was the executive and a group of other men walking up the side of a mountain. For thirty minutes, the German enthusiastically described how he and his old school friends would meet in the mountains for a reunion every year. Jim's one question had opened up the prospect to him and, by the time it came to the sales presentation, they were both talking away like old friends. Needless to say, Jim got the order.

Only after you have broken the ice can you get into the service or product that you have to offer. Describe it in full and outline what it will do for them. You should know in advance from your research what your customer wants, and your description of the product must fit closely with expectations. Generate interest by describing something that you know your customer is already receptive to.

Then *shut up*.

And be quite

And listen, you must listen.

It's now time for your target to talk and you to absorb. You need to find out what their needs are. You can probe a little to extract the information, but remember that this is the time where your target should be talking the most. Listen to what the customer wants and when they are finished, offer them what they want if you can provide it. If you've done your job correctly, they should be interested in you and what you have to offer.

Desire

OK, so now they are interested. This is the time for you to generate real desire. Point out the benefits. Point out what they can get from the service or product in question. Remember that *benefits*, not features, create desire.

You may be selling a simple chair. It looks good, it has padding, it is built from quality materials, there are plenty available, and so forth. These are all features. Benefits are what the features will achieve. This chair will make the prospect more comfortable, it is something they can sit on, they will be less prone to repetitive strain injury because the chair is ergonomic. The chair is easy to maintain, it folds for easy storage and transport so will save them time if they move office.

Keep asking what can you do for them in their situation, and what they want from the product. At this stage, it's all about wants and needs.

Some products appear to be straightforward commodities. A bag of coal is a bag of coal. But if you are to be a good salesperson you must look at the features closer and understand how they create benefits. The coal is smokeless (no pollution), it lights quickly (timesaver), it does not burn too fast or at too high a temperature (economic and comfortable). Learn all of these benefits and then give the person what you think they want based on your research. After that, the decision is easy. You must also build on the emotional side. Tell the subject this is a really good investment for their organisation right now – and tell them why. The customer will begin to equate your product and service with security (or insecurity if they don't have it).

Keep probing and keep asking questions. Create desire by telling them what they want to hear. It is at this stage that you will be working hard to overcome objections. Below are some tips on handling objections.

Anticipate it. If you have been selling this product or service for some time, you will be aware of the objections and can work them into your pitch.

Isolate the objection. Find out if this is the target's principle objection of many others, or the only one. If they agree that everything else is fine – then you have them and you merely have to handle this one objection.

Ignore it. Sometimes this can work. Some people simply want to air their views and are content when they have done so and will not bring it up again.

Feed the objection back. Ask the prospect to elaborate more on the objection and in doing so they may answer it themselves, or present it in such a way that it is easier for you to spot a solution. If possible, try to get them to suggest the solution themselves, they can't argue with that.

Don't interrupt. Do not be impatient – hear them out, even if you think they are talking rubbish. Everybody has an opinion that must be listened to. If the target is not allowed to get their point across, they will become frustrated with you. If that happens, it's goodbye sale.

Don't argue. Remember, the customer is always right – even when they are wrong!

You can disagree in different ways. It is important to keep in mind that you are not there to prove him wrong, you are there to close a sale. Allow them to let off steam.

By telling you what they don't want, they are communicating their desires by omission.

Decision

If you have successfully negotiated the objections and succeeded in creating real desire for your product, it's now time to close the deal. Everybody knows the close, whether they realise it or not. It's the point in the evening where you kiss the girl, make your final sprint for the finish line or pop an important question. You have your target, you have created favourable attention, interest and desire, now it is time to go in for the kill. This is the moment of truth. This is what you have worked towards. Do not be afraid to make a decision and ask for the order. This is where the Great Potential Salesperson fails – often because they feel self-conscious about asking for money.

It is entirely possible that the prospect may say no, and they may say no in different ways. Asking to think it over, to consult with others or to come back another time, are all common rejections. Although in other cases they may be legitimate formalities that your target has to observe.

You will naturally be disappointed but do not assume that this is the last word. Many successful salespeople work on the principle that the sale does not begin until the customer says no. It may be an exaggeration, but persistence pays off in a surprising number of cases. Most important, yet again, is that you must listen, ask questions and find out the reasons why. The prospect may be saying, 'No, I don't think so... ' rather than 'No, definitely not.' If you have been paying attention to the client and the signals they are emitting, you should be able to guess.

If a person really does not want to invest in your product, service, or you, there is no point in wasting any more time. If you stick around now, the target will begin to dislike you and that is death. They will never allow you into their office again, and even if you don't rely on repeat sales you don't want to build a poor reputation either.

Thank them for listening and try your luck elsewhere.

However, if you have reason at all to think that they may change their mind, do not give up and stay at it.

Sometimes it's Hobson's Choice. If you press too hard too soon, you may not get the decision you want and the prospect may move further away. However, if you leave it too late, you may miss the opportunity.

Most sales are not a simple yes or a no. To help you along in the process of closing the sale, I have outlined below a number different of closes adapted from *The Supersalesman's Handbook* by Bill Davis.

The Trial Close

You do not necessarily have to wait until the end of a presentation to try a close. You may make your move at any time if you get a positive response. You can ask, 'Which colour do you prefer?' or 'What style suits you best?' If the prospect says, 'The blue one', you immediately know a willingness to buy. If you ask when they need it by and the prospect replies, 'I need it by the 5th', then you know there and then that they are committed.

Assuming the Sale

This ploy works with timid people who find it hard to say yes or say no. You simply take it for granted that the client has decided to buy and start taking the order. The salesperson can ask, 'Will somebody be at your home Friday to receive the furniture?' Even though the prospect has not given their overt consent yet, if the reply is, 'Wednesday morning will be fine', then you know it's a done deal.

The Step-by-Step Technique

Many people find it hard to make major decisions, but will quite happily make minor ones. You might keep asking the prospect a series of small questions, which they will find comparatively easy to answer. Do you agree that this machine will cut costs and increase efficiency? Would you like it in black or green? Do you wish to take advantage of our easy credit terms? Step-by-step the rest of the decisions are gradually made until the entire transaction is completed.

Give it to them

If you cannot close the sale on the spot you could try giving them the product for a trial period. After that period, the prospect will have become so used to the benefits, they may sign the order. Similarly when I was selling sponsorship, I sometimes gave it to them on the understanding that they would not pay if they were unsatisfied. In this particular case, we wanted the long-term relationship with the customer so much that it was an acceptable risk.

Silence

Sometimes silence can be a powerful weapon. Not many people can stand silence for an extended period of time and they will feel compelled to say something – often something in your favour. If you have built the relationship properly in the earlier stages of the process, the prospects will be inclined to tell you what they know you want to hear.

Fear

This is perhaps the most powerful closing weapon of all, and there are many sources of fear in our lives. The fear that inflation will make the price go up. The fear that the prospect's competition will purchase, leaving the prospect looking inefficient and ill-equipped. The fear that the prospect may lose the friendship of the salesperson if they do not buy.

Remember that the further you go from emotional contact and relationship, the harder it is to close. As a salesperson, you are always working to manoeuvre the prospect into a position where it is more reasonable to say yes than no.

Action

Wow, you've just closed. Now shut up and start writing, take the order and go. If you act hugely relieved, the prospect may have second thoughts that will scupper the sale. Many do not know when to stop talking and continue to sell after the deal is made. If necessary, talk about anything else but the deal.

Once the salesperson has achieved the task, most good organisations have a system that kicks in and it's critical that you deliver everything you promised. Reinforce the deal with good service and maintain long-term relationships with the client. Your subsequent sales will be much easier.

If you keep to the five basic steps and be patient, you will become a good salesperson. Remember it's a process, but it always pays to brush up on it, even when you think you have it down to a tee. Whenever I am involved with a team, I make sure that I go through it with them over and over again, even though some of them start rolling their eyes to heaven.

I make no apology, although I sometimes get others in to say the same thing in a different way. The reality is that people and organisations constantly lose touch with the basics and for that reason managers, boring as it may be, must constantly relearn. In the Czech Republic, as in all countries, there were local variations to factor in. When dealing with dinosaur communist companies, we discovered that there was a two-part sales process. The first was the actual sale itself, where we convinced the client that, yes, they really did need our product. After they agreed to the sale, there was a second procedure to get the sale approved internally.

Remember the guy I mentioned who had the huge desk, boardroom and tiny expense account? When he decided that he wanted to buy our database (at a cost of $1,000, ten times what he could authorise), all he could do was give his theoretical approval for the purchase. Then our company had to chase up the other six managers in his bank required to sign off on the purchase before we could get paid. It was like that for all the post-soviet clients, and it was highly probable that at least one or two of the people needed to sign off were taking time off, having babies, on holiday, sick or something else. It took us months to get our sales approved.

Of course, the sale itself was the harder process because you had to fully live it, putting all of your confidence in your product for the client. Getting the payment authorised was just so much phone lifting.

In the end, in whatever you turn your mind to sell, its determination, self-confidence and belief in what you are doing that wins. That was why it was important for my team to share in the vision of the company, to firmly believe that they were offering a good product and that they were fulfilling a useful role. The best way to achieve this was for Aspekt to have a specific mission. With a new venture the entrepreneur is committed because they want to make money and be successful. But why should the people around them be motivated? They aren't owners; they're workers doing a job. They might as well be doing the same work for a large organisation for more money and more security.

Having a specific mission is the best way to bridge this mentality because it draws all of the different motivations together into one single agenda. When properly conceptualised, the mission gives a single common goal and contribution for the entire team to work towards, a goal that does not conflict with the necessary economics of making a profit.

The mission of Aspekt was to create openness and transparency in the Czech financial sector by facilitating the flow of information and allowing for internal development and communication.

This was a goal that we could all sign up to unambiguously. We all knew that it was a necessary service, a desired service and therefore would be a commercially successful service. My employees were good, but they still needed leadership and direction. Giving them a mission was just one way of doing that.

The real effort for me was working in a foreign country with a different culture. The fundamentals of business didn't change, but the execution had to be varied accordingly. Being unable to speak the language was a disadvantage, as you might imagine.

While I made intensive efforts to learn and study it, the Czech language like other Slavic tongues is very difficult. It's one of the top three hardest languages in Europe, coming after Hungarian and Finnish. I found it quite intimidating to arrive in the Czech Republic and to be surrounded by people I could not understand.

The practical result of my inability to speak Czech was that I had to work entirely through Petr. This was both good and bad. Normally, a small enterprise is very much hands on and front line, but I was forced to take a back seat because I could not conduct most of the necessary correspondence.

The first disadvantage was the obvious one. Invariably in translations, my counterpart would be nodding away politely as if he understood everything. In reality he was probably only taking in maybe eighty per cent of what was being said and I was sitting there completely ignorant of the fact.

In such cases, you think you are fully understood, but you are not. You have to be very precise in what you say. When you can't communicate directly it's frustrating, and you either have to learn the local language adequately, develop the skills to work through an interpreter, or both.

The second disadvantage was in lost opportunity. Every time you walk down the street you can see a business opportunity. Most of us don't consider it because we don't think like that. We have our minds on the next pay cheque, the bills that have to come out of it, picking the kids up after school or whatever.

Entrepreneurs think about these things as well, but they also are looking at the quality of services or products around them. Whenever there is a problem with those services or products, there's a business opportunity for the individual that can put it right.

Likewise business meetings are a constant source of opportunity but, because I couldn't converse in Czech, I was unable to avail of any of the information that might have come up in those early encounters.

But I turned the negative into a positive and devoted myself more fully to the essentials. If you start taking every opportunity, taking every lead, you can get bogged down and I avoided that. Like I said, while execution is different, the fundamentals stay the same – and I monitored those like a hawk.

It also meant that I didn't have to deal as much with the paranoid and insecure bureaucracy left over from the communist era.

What made it so bad was the fact that nobody trusted anybody else, hence the long, drawn-out getting-to-know-you routine that you had to suffer in business. Everybody knew that corruption was rife, so the government tried to curtail it with checks and balances – and endless, endless form filling. It was another method they used to keep control.

They had crazy systems of notaries and apostillisations – where you have signatories verifying other signatories. They just did not accept a signature from an organisation. You had to have a document from someone to prove that you had the authority to sign. Then you needed a document to prove that the person who gave you the authority to sign actually had the authority to give you the authority to sign.

It was super-legalisation for a system gone mad. There was no difference between a big bank and the government, they were all just big bureaucracies and it didn't matter to the people working with them. Go into a meeting and there were four people attending when one was sufficient.

It reminded me of the joke about Russian communist cops:

Why do Moscow police always patrol in threes? One who can read, one who can write and a third to watch the dangerous intellectuals...

Sometimes a deal would be lost along the way (which happens, it's just part of normal business) and I was never quite sure why it hadn't worked out. My mind would wander over that horrible bladder of checks and treble checks and wonder if our deal had slipped through a crack.

Of course, it was only a few years later that I discovered that we were not on the inside track so to speak. You were supposed to tip along the way, small bribes to grease our applications across all those desks.

During our start-up period, however, I was so innocent that I was totally unaware that bribes were expected. I would have refused on principle anyway – even if I had understood, I would not have known who to bribe or how much to give them, let alone how to phrase the transaction. Instead we kept ringing up and asking people 'Where's my form?' The worst part was not knowing what we were up against. If we had understood we would have devised some strategy to cope, instead we just made those phone calls again and again.

However, and partly because of our naivety and innocence, we ended up with a blue-chip reputation. It was one of the qualities of our product, we wore down the bureaucracy and won business without being compromised ethically, and contrary to popular belief that wins you a lot of respect. Today, we tend to get the bigger and the best deals, although it has taken a long time to get us to that position.

Naturally we had some advantages. Because of our size and sector, we didn't register with the mafia. For instance, if you opened a pub you were in the public eye and if you were successful everybody knew it. That was when the 'security people' called round to 'offer' you their protection. Refuse to pay it and you and your staff would probably get regular beatings or something equally unpleasant.

By comparison, we were a small operation in a specialised field, not something that would draw attention. To the outsider, we were just one more anonymous group of office workers.

Companies often bribe when they are desperate. Costs and time always run over expectation, and many enterprises undertake drastic action to stay above water. Some go on a second round of financing whereupon they get carved up by a new investor, assuming that they can find one, while others will consider giving backhanders to secure business and cash flow. When companies are weak they'll consider that last option. We never did, although Aspekt was getting into difficulties.

We were four months into our enterprise, and were close to producing our first copy of the magazine. However, for one reason or another, our final launch date kept getting pushed back. Despite the outsourcing and economising, I was running very short on cash.

I had two credit cards maxed out to the tune of £2,000 (about €2,540 then) with repayments overdue. My mortgage on the family home back in Dublin hadn't been paid in six months, and most of my other expenses were also outstanding, including personal overdrafts and bank facilities. I had spent about £60,000 on the project, including investor money, and I was closer to the edge than I had ever been before. I had come from a depressed economy and was in an alien market. It had to work. Though I had the confirmed orders for the magazine, and my calculations told me that the first edition would break even, there was no way I could get credit on the local market. Things were so bad I actually attempted to get a loan from an Irish bank again, but once again it was no-go without a guarantor.

Friends and family were now my last resort. Out of pride I could not ask all of them for credit, while others I asked simply refused. In the end only one good friend, John Killeen from Galway, agreed to go guarantor on a loan of £1,000. And the bank's second condition? Another £1,000 also had to be placed on deposit in the account. It was a ridiculous transaction and unfortunately, it didn't even look like it would arrive in time. In the end John just gave me the £2,000.

I also knew that I had to keep up morale in the team. Petr and the others knew that Aspekt was on the knife-edge. What they didn't know was just how much stress I was under. I was beginning to have doubts – big doubts – about our ability to survive as far as the cash-flow cycle.

Managing the morale became a balancing act. I had to be honest with the team because trust is what I operate on but, at the same time, I had to portray confidence and reassure them that things were going to work. It was a pure leadership role, although you as the entrepreneur are under the greatest stress of all, it is up to you to maintain the confidence of the group. You can never be seen to crack or give into the difficulties.

One thing that makes it easier is the fact that employees don't look as far ahead as the entrepreneur does. Mostly they simply think about getting their salary at the end of the month, and if they know you will deliver on that they will generally stick around. Payment of your employees is sacrosanct; it's your moral obligation and your commitment. Screw around with that and you aren't worth working for.

I took a gamble. Even though the magazine hadn't been printed, I stuck my neck out and invoiced all my advertisers in advance. About ten per cent of them paid up for a service they hadn't yet received, and the trickle of money was just enough to keep things ticking over. In addition to that, I had discovered about £1,000 left on my last credit card, and with that money I took all of the Aspekt team, about five employees, away to the mountains on a skiing weekend. They had worked very hard and I wanted to motivate them and keep the fun going, not least because it was critical to start work on the second issue to build cash flow.

Although it was the last ready cash available, I had no qualms about spending it. Shortly after the magazine was launched, the rest of the advertisers paid and the first issue broke even. As it turned out, the first copies of the magazine sold on the strength of the updated telephone records alone. Obviously we weren't the only people who were annoyed at Cesky Telecom. A few weeks later our software package was released and Aspekt Kilcullen was in full flow.

To crown out achievements, we subsequently won a contract with Reuters to supply them with their data, giving us guaranteed repeat business from a respectable firm. I was now the owner of my first successful Czech company.

Now that we were in a cash-flow cycle, we could evolve with the market and in time we used our position to leverage into other products and services. For a publications firm, events management is the natural avenue to take. We ran training seminars, conferences and exhibitions, got five or six sponsors to pay for the costs and invited all of our customers. A few of these events went on to become prestigious annual undertakings, such as the Signum Temporis Financial Industry Awards, which recognised the most transparent and open companies, and the Prague Stock Exchange Ball which was attended by up to 1,500 people.

I ended up going to one of these awards in a kilt borrowed from a Scots friend in the Czech Republic called Ed Gemmell. I needed Ed's kilt because I had broken my ankle shortly beforehand and could not wear my usual black tie outfit due to the plaster cast. Then as a dare I hobbled up on stage and asked the Czech Minister for Finance to autograph the cast...

Aspekt grew from three people to over fifty people. In retrospect, there were a lot of lessons in the experience. Even though I had used almost the same formula for *Afloat* magazine, I had also tried out new things in a new market.

The most obvious problem was lack of capital, and it's the item that many entrepreneurs face in their first few months. It's been said over and over again, but I might as well repeat it here.

Things take twice as long to do and cost twice as much.

I had some figures made out, but I was so enamoured with the belief that I could make it work that some kind of optimism must have crept into my sums. Of course, my plan did not have too much in the way of detail anyway and was completely unsophisticated. I just knew what I wanted to do and that the market was there. Of course, once you get going so many additional expenses crop up that your original plan almost disintegrates. When that happens you are forced to rely on your creativity to succeed. Sub-renting, outsourcing and speculative invoicing are tactics that can be used repeatedly to assist you in bridging the start-up-to-cash-flow gap. I thought that I was fine with £35,000 and that I would be up and running in three months. As it turned out I did extremely well to get things moving in under six.

After Aspekt was up and running I moved on to do other things, leaving the administration of the company to the management team that I had in place. However it lost some of the original creativity and the overheads on events management and publishing rendered it unprofitable. In 2000 we cut it back to a purely data business. We had to let go of twenty-five people, which was tough, but there was no other way. Since then we have renamed the company Aspekt Central Europe Group a.s. (a.s. is the Czech equivalent of plc) and the Kilcullen side split into Kilcullen Kapital Partners. Aspekt now concentrates purely on its original concept of data business.

So whatever happened to my wonderful team? Petr Kucera became the managing director of Aspekt and received a share-holding in the company. He and Daniela Kafkova later married while Ian Smith got a little burned out and returned to the UK. Ian remains a friend of mine and a friend of the company to this day, and later admitted that he had never worked so hard in his life.

Chapter fifteen

Setbacks

In July 1996, I became involved in a new venture. I was always keen to use Aspekt as leverage, and I saw the opportunity with an English language publication in the Czech Republic. *The Prague Post*, a good expatriate focused newspaper with general content, was already being published, but I wanted to start up a purely business publication for which there was a market.

A small but successful business newspaper called the *Central European Business Weekly* was in circulation covering five eastern European countries. It was written and published by another of my barfly contacts, Ian Brodie, and it was a textbook example of what can happen when you hire the wrong person.

To my mind, Ian Brodie was the classic expatriate. He was part of that anonymous crowd of British people who can be found hanging around in any Irish pub all over the world. In fact he was a Scot but he had worked abroad for a long time, earning his spurs as a journalist. One of his ventures was a publication in California for the expatriate English population. A witty and funny writer, Ian's stories were taken from the wire and gleaned from gossip and chat in the pubs. On a tiny budget and with low-quality paper he produced each week his *Central European Business Weekly*.

My reckoning went thus. If a journalist like Ian could already get the paper out every week, then I could pull in a few talented people, add a bit of spark, marketing flare, better quality printing and turn his one man show into a respectable business, while keeping costs under control. Ian would run it, making the best use of the extra staff, whilst I would remain a silent partner offering advice and strategic direction.

From his side and in addition to other benefits Brodie also saw more potential in revenue. The advertising for the *CEBW* was fragmented between the five different countries in which it was sold. Advertising budgets are driven on a market-by-market basis and there were not that many companies that advertised the same way in all five countries, so for him it would be better to have a handle on the advertising market in one country than odds and sods in five.

It looked as though the arrangement would suit us both fine. Ian could continue to work as a journalist, while I could devote myself to my core business, including some plans I had for expansion.

We decided to call our new paper the *Czech Business Journal*. Having examined the markets we decided that both papers could be produced in parallel because there were different focuses for each, so Ian would also keep his *CEBW* going and make it available in the Czech Republic.

We structured the funding through Aspekt. On behalf of Aspekt, I took a minority shareholding in Brodie's existing business, and then we each invested $40,000 for fifty per cent each of *Czech Business Journal*. Since Aspekt was my main business it was intended that Ian would run the *Czech Business Journal*.

The concept was right, the time was right, there was a market, the investment was agreed and the people were in place. I played my usual role of coaching the start-up through the first six months to the launch period. We had hired a very good editor, we hired good salespeople, held brainstorming and training sessions and kept our plans as secret as possible.

It looked fantastic. We had even pre-sold enough advertising to make the first issue profitable. It was to be a textbook launch.

Then it all went wrong.

The first problem seemed to be financial. On paper we were fine because there was a commitment to raise $80,000 between us. In reality we were completely undercapitalised because Brodie never put in his share and we were constantly struggling. When we found out it put us into something of a quandary. Not only had Brodie failed to find the money, as he'd agreed to do, it became obvious that he was unlikely to do so.

Since our business journal seemed to have everything else going for it, I decided that I would not be throwing good money after bad if I bailed him out. Eventually we agreed to a restructure and in return for another investment of $30,000 from Aspekt we took forty per cent of the combined publications. Brodie ran the company as the majority partner, which was fine with me. I had neither the time nor the inclination to go in and run the company as I was already tied down elsewhere.

Unfortunately, I was foolish to think that it was a simple matter of money. The real problem was Brodie. I didn't know it until much later but I had hired a conman who was later to serve prison time in the United Kingdom for fraud.

True to form, he turned out to be a terrible manager and he made mistake after mistake of the most elementary kind.

His first error was not registering the business name quickly enough. He agreed to organise the registration but gave it to a cheap, second-rate lawyer and never followed it up, causing problems for us later on.

On another occasion, we put in money for the *CBJ* payroll and some bills. Unfortunately the employees never received it and I don't know what happened to the cash.

Then, in October 1996, just one month before launch, Ian made a fundamental mistake that cost us the entire venture.

Now I've always been open and transparent, and oddly enough I learned from sport the advantage of this. One time I was in an international sailing regatta in Newport, Rhode Island, sailing a two-person dinghy as part of the Irish team. As well as us, there was an English team, a French team, a German team, a team from the Soviet Union and one from the United States. Before the race the Americans talked away enthusiastically, giving away virtually all their secrets. How they were going to race, what their plans were, what their strategy was, what they were doing to make the boat go fast. Everything.

The English guys were listening to the Americans but were being fairly tight-lipped.

The French were the same, and their knowledge of the English language was OK.

With the Soviets, you had no idea what they understood or felt because as far as we knew the only spoke Russian (personally I think that they could follow what was being said but didn't let on). The Germans were pretty much the same as the English and French.

So who went out and won the race?

The American team.

Why?

Because they reckoned that they were better, and they were. And not only that, they had also involved everyone else in their dialogue. By saying what they were doing, they managed to get a bit of a discussion going, and so the Americans learned and exchanged. Now maybe they kept a few fundamental things back, but overall their attitude boiled down to: 'We can tell you everything because we're better than you, and we don't have to worry. In fact, by telling you all this, we dare you to try and do it better!'

In contrast, the teams that remained silent were the ones that lacked confidence in their abilities, and so they lost.

Of course, it's debatable whether the American spin was born of intent, naivety or a combination of both. It's just the way their society operates, based on openness and the free exchange of ideas. You don't get, unless you give. Stay silent and you learn nothing.

Some people might consider my tactic of learning information in the pubs as being risky. Perhaps someone would steal my ideas, or tell a potential competitor.

Don't sweat.

The fact is that business ideas are two a penny, if you have an idea then you are guaranteed that twenty other people have had the same idea too. I get people sending me business plans now and they are absolutely paranoid. They think the whole world is going to go out and copy their idea. The reality is that the success of the venture is in the execution, and the resources for the execution. And that means the right people first of all, and the right money. The only way you'll get either is to open up and talk.

On the other hand, when you are ready to strike a blow you don't go and tell your opponent.

There was a company in Hungary running the *Budapest Business Journal* and they were planning to enter the Czech market with a similar publication to ours. They had seen the same opportunity as me, except they were ignorant of our existence and weren't planning on entering Prague for another six or twelve months. First in gets the market and we were poised to take it all.

Then Ian, because he had never made the transition from journalist to businessman and probably needed to fill a few column inches, wrote in his *Central European Business Review* about exactly what we were planning to do. Thanks to him our competitors became fully aware that they were about to lose their chance at the Czech market.

The Hungarian company moved with astonishing speed. We launched the *Czech Business Journal* at the beginning of December 1996 and two weeks later our Hungarian-based competitors launched the *Prague Business Journal*. We now had two papers competing in a limited market.

I had some difficult choices to make.

All things being equal, I felt I could have handled the competition and saved the paper, I had done it before and I could do it again. But things were not equal. I couldn't do it with Ian Brodie and the team below him, they just weren't capable of it. Replacing them with the very good management team from Aspekt was a possibility, but I didn't know if I dared divert them from the core business. We also needed more finance, but it would be very hard to find an investor when we were in a crisis situation. To round things off, our target market, small enough to begin with, would now have to be shared with a very aggressive competitor.

I pulled out in March 1997. The *Prague Business Journal* had won out after only six weeks and I had lost $70,000 with absolutely nothing to show for it. The loss of the *Czech Business Journal* goes down as one of my great failures.

Apart from the money, it was an emotional and psychological setback. It dented my confidence, but was also a dose of reality. What I learned essentially was that if you've got the wrong person, you've got the wrong person, and I should have left three months sooner.

The warning signs were there, principally in Ian's dishonesty and lack of ability, although I wasn't aware of the worst of it until after. What little I had known about I was prepared to overlook because he was running the paper as a lifestyle business.

That was a big mistake on my part.

While Ian Brodie was a genuinely pleasant man, he was a crook and one of the true rogues you encounter in emerging markets. Apparently he got early release just before Christmas 2001 and made an unexpected return to the *Dubliner* in Bratislava dressed up *incognito* as Santa Claus. It caused quite a stir and the last I heard the sixty-year-old had moved with his child to Croatia. No doubt he will show up again.

In February 2005, as I put the finishing touches to this book, I paid the final 130,000 Czech crowns (over €4,000) to clear the last debt relating to this venture. It was a moral payment in that I was not legally bound to do so since it had been Brodie's company that had gone bust. However entrepreneurs live and fall on reputation so I felt obliged to put it in order.

There was no point in getting mad with Ian and neither did I have any angry exchanges with him. By the time I knew the full extent of the mess he had made, he was gone. Besides that, I don't have a confrontational style. If you have a belligerent manner, you've got to be prepared to go in and take absolute control. I prefer to work through other people and, although I got burned on this occasion, I still choose this approach because it doesn't keep me tied down. That was very important to me because at the same time as the *Czech Business Journal*'s demise I was involved in two more new ventures as well as expanding Aspekt.

However, if the people aren't right, either change them or get out.

Speaking of the right people, I also had a severe lesson on the difference between European and American employee attitudes, thanks to the broad range of nationalities represented in our expat workforce.

One evening, I was sitting down with one of my key marketing people from the *Czech Business Journal*. Together we discussed plans and plotted our business strategy. The woman was very positive, loyal and told me that she was absolutely committed to the company.

Later that evening, she met our competitors in the *Prague Business Journal* who, sensing our weakness, offered her more money and greater prospects, whereupon she became very positive, loyal and absolutely committed to them.

I heard about her defection the next morning at our management meeting and I was actually quite shocked. However, with the highly competitive business we were facing, there was lot of this employee volatility, and a trend soon emerged.

It's a little unfair to generalise from a few examples, but what I saw was that the culture of European employees was less dollar-driven than their American counterparts. When you were low on money and the chips were down, you could count on the Europeans more. Now it's not that I'm anti-American, quite the reverse in fact, however you must understand that the American approach can be misleading for those in Europe, particularly eastern Europe.

Let's say Pavel from Prague meets Mike from Michigan. Pavel's natural state is dour. He doesn't smile or open up. Mike by contrast is super friendly and positive. He talks away to Pavel freely. Pavel is delighted and feels he has made a real friend – but he hasn't. Friendships do not come that easily between human beings. Mike has a friendly, familiar attitude, but when the push comes to shove, he is not Pavel's friend. He's merely another acquaintance.

For the likes of Pavel, this very disorientating and extremely disappointing because with the first wind-shift his 'friend' Mike has disappeared.

I'm not going to go delve into the reasons why Pavel and Mike are the way they are, although I would imagine that differing socio-economic conditions and culture explain most of it. What I do want to point out is that if you don't know and understand this difference in attitude, the confusion can cost you. In my experience, American loyalty is more dictated by dollars and the prospect thereof than anything else. Once you know and understand this, it's fine. It was a nasty revelation for me.

Mind you, in the end I actually prefer Mike's all-friendly approach to drab Pavel, Mike is just easier to digest.

Around the same time as my fling with the Czech Business Journal, I also decided to expand Aspekt outside of the Czech Republic.

Poland looked like a good choice, even better than the Czech Republic in certain respects. The fastest growth, a population of forty million, a dynamic emerging market and great change and development in the financial services industry, which was my primary interest. Of course, the reality was much less optimistic, with some estimates putting half of the population below the poverty line. Many Poles were, and still are, living on the land in a horse and cart lifestyle straight out of the 1800s.

Ironically the corporate strategic planners often put both the Polish and Czech markets together, but, although they are close geographically and the languages are seventy per cent similar, they are quite different culturally. The Czechs regard Polish people as boorish and aggressive, while the Poles consider the Czechs to be cowards. Polish Communist leader General Wojciech Jaruzelski recounts a popular joke in his memoirs. 'The Polish dog crosses south to eat, the Czechoslovak dog crosses north to bark!'

Another anecdote describes how two fighters, each from the Czech and Polish resistance, met up after the war with an American.

'And what did you do when you caught a Nazi,' the Pole was asked by the American.

'Ah! Every time we found one, we attacked him, cut him up and slit his throat!' he answered excitedly.

Then the Czech was asked the same question. 'Oh, we would have loved to have done this, but we weren't allowed!'

One of the comparisons to do the rounds referred to the first non-communist leaders of each country. It was said Czechoslovakia's Václav Haval is a poet and playwright, while Poland's Lech Walesa is only a shipyard electrician.

These are crude tales but on the whole they do expose the central character differences between each nation. I wasn't sure if I was so enamoured with the Polish culture, but it was worth a shot regardless.

It was 1996 before I could grapple with Poland, but when I did, I planned to use the exact same formula as before, built a round the best team I could assemble. The idea was to get started in the capital, Warsaw, and push our publication through intense high-level, one-to-one sales.

There were problems immediately.

Everything about the environment in Warsaw was different. For starters, I took an immediate dislike to the city itself. It's a bleak sprawl, ugly to look at and a cold town in winter. Completely destroyed by the Nazis, it was liberated by the soviets and rebuilt very badly. That's not a fault of the Poles of course, but Warsaw is still an eyesore. Polish people are very nice, but I found the Poles to be more creative than their Czech neighbours, especially when they were being devious.

Polish executives had to be micro-managed. The Czechs could be given a brief on a Monday morning and, when you came back on Friday, it would have been carried out exactly as you had asked. The Poles were different. When you left them a brief on Monday, you were guaranteed that by Friday either:

a) they had thought up a better way to do things and done that instead (a better way, that is, to their own way of thinking, which often ended in disaster); or

b) they hadn't thought of a better way, but still hadn't done it your way, again, generally leading to disaster.

The only way to combat this was to get your next-in-line to sit on them every day, Monday to Friday. You had to be very tough and frequently say, 'Do the job and you get paid. Don't do the job and you're gone.' That wasn't my style, but I found the workforce left me no choice.

Meeting Polish executives was also a difficulty. To help get Aspekt going, I hired Michael O'Brien as development director. Michael is a great salesman (and a great guy, the first to represent Ireland in fencing at the Olympics) but he was having a tough time getting meetings until we discovered why.

The president of a Polish company would very often only meet with people of equal status or above – in short other presidents. I had encountered the status relationship before, but I had never seen it so rigorously enforced. The same was even true for secretaries. The secretary of one president would be more inclined to talk with the secretary of another president, and so on down the line. It was the most status-ridden business culture I had ever worked in.

It's not that I'm big on titles or care about status as such, but I could see that it was a lot easier to get meetings when I called myself chairman and CEO. So the next day, we sent Michael off to get some new business cards, this time with the word 'president' printed on them. Michael was president of not a whole lot, but it helped to get him in front of decision-makers.

The other thing I under-estimated in Poland was the endemic corruption in the capital. 'Quickmoneyitis' had set in. While making money is something I both respect and encourage, I also adhere to some principles. In Poland in the mid-1990s, the reverse was the case. All of the advertising agencies wanted a bribe, and so did pretty much everybody else.

On one occasion we offered to sell our magazine title to a large and apparently reputable publishing firm for $100,000. After hours of negotiations in a smoke-filled room, the company's vice-president dropped a bombshell. He wanted a $30,000 backhander before he would allow the company to purchase the magazine. He even had a cash trail prepared to funnel the money.

We never sold that title.

I should say that I love the Polish people on an individual basis. They have big hearts, they make good friends and generally are very intelligent. However in my experience a person needed deep pockets to ride out the corruption of Poland.

In 1995 AIB purchased 16.3 per cent of a small Polish bank called Wielkopolski Bank Kredytowy, better known as WBK. This was considered a good bank in Poland, however I knew from a frustrated software salesman trying to sell technology solutions to the WBK that its IT people were driving expensive cars and living well despite being on relatively small salaries. This could have been perfectly innocent of course, although considering the practices in the Czech Republic, it was equally likely to be a symptom of the endemic corruption in the post-communist banking system. At the time of AIB's investment, the WBK branches could not even talk to each other electronically.

Then, shortly after the investment, WBK made an enormous profit, but it was nothing to do with their normal business.

By 1996, the Polish National Bank had mandated all banks to have government debt on their books, and while inflation was high this was counter-balanced with the government paper generating a twenty-five per cent plus return.

Then inflation was cut in half and the value of the government paper and bonds doubled, showing extraordinary profits in the value of the bond portfolio on WBK's balance sheet. Within AIB, Poland became the watchword and the place to invest. I later found myself at one of AIB's conferences where they extolled the virtues of investing in Poland. Foolishly I brought up some of the negatives and was promptly eaten alive for my trouble. But whereas I had hands-on experience of doing business in central Europe, the bankers in question were very far from the coalface of their investment, they did not speak Polish and it sounded to me as if their Polish partners were running rings around them.

To be successful, AIB needed market share in the retail bank sector. Subsequently, in 1999, AIB bought eighty per cent of another Polish bank, Bank Zachodni, in a move that was important to give them critical mass in the country. After four years of a presence in Poland, I'm sure that AIB have grown wise to the abuses within the system. With micro-management, tight control and the continuing enforcement of their own standards, not to mention recourse to their particularly deep pockets, the AIB's investment will eventually pay off. And it will do so in a solid financial fashion, as opposed to a flimsy paper value.

However, there is a world of difference between, on the one hand, a massive financial institution lumbering its way into a new market and, on the other hand, individual entrepreneurs operating off borrowed money and projected cash flows. You can tell the quality of a country by the ease in which the smaller operator can establish himself, and in my experience, Poland was not an easy place to become established. Poland for an out-of-towner, unless you have scale, is bad news. Stay away and apply your energy elsewhere.

In fact Poland cost me a lot, in more ways than one.

I have to like the people that I work with, and I have to like the environment. In Warsaw I didn't like either. I was now working out of three countries rather than two. One week in Dublin with my family, one in Prague and one in Warsaw. It was punishing, both physically and mentally, but I stuck with it for three years. Unfortunately, in retrospect, it damaged my family and I grew apart from my wife Suzanna.

During that time we built up a turnover and made it relatively successful, but the formula was just not coming together in the way I hoped.

To this day I don't exactly know why. Perhaps I was overstretched, perhaps I didn't suit the culture of the country, or perhaps on a subconscious level I simply couldn't stomach the place anymore. Maybe it was an unhealthy combination of all three. Whatever it was I had a hard look at the venture.

We had built up the Polish office, we had achieved a decent turnover and it was actually quite successful. But it had cost Aspekt approximately $200,000 over three years, and now it needed another significant investment. To do that, would put the entire Aspekt company at risk for the sake of the Polish operation alone.

The scale was bigger than the depth of my resources at the time, so I withdrew to the Czech Republic, which was a heavy blow to the morale. As it transpired the Internet was coming on stream and we could service the Polish market without needing a full office in Warsaw. We decreased it to a single researcher whose job was feeding information on the Polish financial sector into our existing database.

I regard the whole venture as another one of my great failures. To me Poland was three years of effort poured down the drain, and it was another severe blow to my confidence.

However, again, there was another lesson to be learned. Following my negative experience there, I concluded that I preferred to deal in smaller markets. I also decided that smaller entrepreneurs should be wary of Poland, although the country improves day by day.

Though there was a happy postscript to Poland.

Adopting the Internet-based business model turned out to be a successful measure. It enabled us to retain clients but shed the additional expenses, and we rolled out identical services across all of eastern Europe. Aspekt now gathers data from ten eastern European countries, including the Baltic states of Latvia, Lithuania and Estonia. In 1997, we took on a representative office in London, followed by another one in New York in 1998, though the move did not realise its full potential. The Czech economic miracle was soon to have a tough landing as things started to go wrong in their economy.

It was very strange for me to go back to New York. Ten years earlier I had been there for the Sail Ireland project. Now I was back, an Irishman promoting a Czech business on America's Wall Street. To celebrate, I hosted a reception with the Czech ambassador to the United Nations as an honorary guest. For fun, I also rounded up all my Irish friends, and we ended up with a big reception that had too many people at it.

Between the *Czech Business Journal* and my failure to get moving in Poland, I had to learn how to quit. It was a hard thing to do when you are not a natural quitter, but as an entrepreneur it's something you have to learn. You live, you try, you fail – and you move on.

So I cut my losses each time and started again.

I could handle the psychological stigma of failure, it does not bother me. The greatest spur for me was the pressure of succeeding on a purely financial level. I tend to like pressure and I put myself under pressure because that's when I respond best. It's a game of tennis, it's matcpoint and I'm behind. Everything depends on a comeback to win. Sweet.

I'm the last passenger for a flight. I'm late. There's ten seconds to spare before they close the door. Perfect.

Just getting the very, very last out of a situation. That's the adrenaline kick for me. Just because you quit, doesn't mean you give up.

The ABN Amro Signum Temporis Awards. As a result of a bet, I went onstage with Mr Kocarnik, the Czech Minister for Finance. My broken leg was in a plaster and I was wearing a kilt...

With two Presidents - Václav Havel and Mary McAleese (with husband Martin) in the James Joyce pub in Prague during a state visit. Not long after settling down in the pub over a pint, which Vaclav clearly relished, Mary decided it was time to leave when some of the crowd became boisterous. "When you hear the 'Yee Haas' its time to go," she said jokingly. Václav stayed on.

Sean Melly and myself at the rebranding of Globix Telecom into eTel in Prague. We established Globix with only €180,000 in 1997 as a Czech and central European telephone company – three years later, Sean sold 45% of the company for $55 million.

At the launch of the Czech Credit Bureau with the CEO's of all the large Czech banks (including Jack Stack [fifth from left] and our project team. This was one of the largest and toughest deals to close, but has since become very successful and has made a vital contribution to the development of the Czech economy.

Pride of Galway, a ninety-foot youth sail training vessel, which I ran with John Killeen for three years.

The Lord Rank - run by Ocean Youth Trust Ireland - brings challenge and adventure under sail to young people and offers far better prospects for rehabilitation that the system we currently use.

Being the first to jump is sometimes tough ....here I led the way first on a management company training weekend. Of thirty-five people at the training only a few dared jump – however the rest shared the challenge and talked about it for a long time after building the dynamic of the company.

Richard O'Donovan with the Kilcullen flag on the North Pole. We supported him in his marathon and personal quest to the pole which he used to raise money for a dogs and cats home...

With family on St Patricks Day 2009 in Spain. Suzanna, a wonderful person, has been a brilliant mother to our three daughters. We remain friends and I am eternally appreciative of the support she gave through difficult times.

The water-babies.... my three daughters Aisling, Roisin and Saoirse, each talented in their own different ways.

Pushing the boat out with my son Cormac and his mother Lucie Bukova.

Dressed in Arab gear, inspired by doing business in the United Arab Emirates and Dubai. An example of acting locally and thinking globally!

In Moscow – Russia remains fascinating, however it is an incredibly intimidating place to do business.

Brothers and sisters, left to right: Pauline, Mairead, Mona, Cormac, Eoin, myself, Annmarie and Frances.

On my bike in Prague's famous Old Town Square where Adolf Hitler once paraded, together with many other invaders through history. Most left the city intact in its glorious splendor – including the commercial invaders who came after the 'Iron Curtain' was brushed aside...

Sailing remains a passion and simple joy. On the waves on board the ***Green Dragon*** *with Nicola Mitchell.*

Chapter sixteen

'I am from Central' – The Czech and Slovak Credit Bureaux

I will never forget the day in 1995 that I stepped through the doors of a Czech bank to get money. Although I had been in the country for two years and was the owner of a Czech company, I had never been a major customer of any Czech bank. I did have an account in Komercni Banka, but I used it for nothing else other than paying my staff.

It was the right time to make myself known as a business customer and build a credit history. I had been there for two years and I had cash-flow issues. Money was coming in but it was erratic and irregular, and paying bills was occasionally difficult. I needed an overdraft.

I also wanted to build a personal relationship with my bank manager. Banks don't lend money, but bankers do. It's the human element of sales again, and I knew from past experience what a positive thing it is to be in with your local bank official.

With my first business, I developed a close relationship with the manager of my branch. I had tremendous respect for him because he risked his neck by extending credit for Afloat when I had sales orders but no capital. If I needed additional funds in a hurry it was possible to lift the phone and agree the facility verbally, while the paperwork would follow later. He trusted me and I trusted him.

In the 1980s in Ireland, it was an exceptional arrangement, although these days it's common enough. At the time of writing, that sort of client–customer relationship has yet to arrive in eastern Europe for the smaller enterprises, but I know that the first banks to provide it on a systematic basis will do well.

When you are dealing with finance, even when you have gone through all the rituals of cash flow, spreadsheets, contracts and legalities, you are still dealing with people.

Years later, I was endeavouring to build relationships in Prague. Having observed the formalities in Komercni Banka, we got down to business.

'We need a facility.'

'We want you as a customer.'

'Can you give me an overdraft?'

'No.'

My meeting came to a rapid conclusion. Komercni Banka couldn't give me an overdraft because they didn't have one to give. Banking products, which I had taken for granted in Ireland (and Ireland could be a little slow on the uptake), were not yet available in the Czech Republic. Of course this was now changing, and therein lay the opportunity.

A few months later, I returned and they offered me a 'credit', or a loan in our lingo. It wasn't a large loan but it was on a year term and quite expensive at fifteen per cent interest. I didn't need it by that stage, but I took it anyway to build a track record. I repaid it as agreed and the following year I went back to ask for twice as much. However, I asked at a different branch and discovered that I was back at square one. There was no centralised record of my credit history and the branches of Komercni Banka had no system for sharing information between banks, with the presumable exception of calling each other up.

Of course that was probably dependent on whether they had the updated telephone numbers from the Cesky Telecom exchange.

Having learned this, it came as no big surprise to discover that the entire Czech banking sector had no structure through which to share information. For all this branch of Komercni Banka knew, I might have had ten or twelve unpaid loans accruing interest right across the country. Nobody within Czech banks had any way of knowing how many chequebooks I had, or mortgages, or leases or financial agreements of any kind.

At roughly the same time of my dealings with Komercni Banka, I was contacted by a private investigator who specialised in worldwide financial investigation. He also had links to an Israeli private intelligence agency that was being run by former Mossad agents. Considering that Mossad is one of the most effective and ruthless intelligence organisations in the world, I wondered what this man could possibly want with me.

My investigator friend was interested in our eastern European operations because we were in the financial information business. It was still a relatively young market when he approached me and information was hard to come by for his clients, who were principally banks. What he wanted from Aspekt was access to the extensive databases we were building and the use of our research capabilities. Most of our information was open and public, so it was just a matter of input and software to process it all, which was our added value.

Like many other business opportunities, I explored the possibility of a partnership with him in the data-mining sector. In the end I turned it down, it just didn't fit with my vision. The investigator's contacts and targets also made me nervous. I had no desire to return to my family in a body bag, courtesy of some Russian Mafioso not keen on disclosure.

To be fair, he might have said the same in that my approach did not fit in with his. I'd like to pay him a compliment, however, he is a very private person, so this much will have to do.

However, it was this contact that opened me to the network of credit information companies that banks and financial institutions rely so heavily on. Unless there are issues regarding invasion of privacy, it is not something that's often in the public eye. But it remains a necessary, high-level, business-to-business function that can be extremely lucrative.

A system of sharing consumer credit is a fundamental part of any western economy, specifically for the financial institutions. You can have all the computers, you can have all the nice offices, you can have all the nice people in pristine branches in affluent areas, but without a system of risk management, you have no bank.

Banks especially are risk averse, for very good reasons. If they give out money to a company they can generally only get an interest rate of five or six per cent on what they lend. If the entrepreneur invests wisely, he can turn that loan into a business with revenues many times that of the original loan, whereupon the bank receives its original loan plus the interest payment. However, if the entrepreneur loses everything, then the bank gets neither the loan repaid nor the interest.

So with entrepreneurs, the bank is assuming all of the risk for very limited returns. This is OK if the entrepreneur is successful, perhaps the bank will be rewarded with large accounts and repeat business, but on a purely mathematical evaluation, the bank has more reasons to be stingy than generous. Added to this was all of the corruption in the Czech system putting the banks there in an even worse position.

Obviously there was room in the market for a consumer credit bureau. J.P. Morgan once said, 'Banking is not about money. It is about information.'

Although building the infrastructure of a credit information company can be complex in the extreme, once established you have guaranteed, repeat business from a blue-chip client base. In fact it's not much different to a vending machine. The database is the vending machine, and the banks and financial institutions the customers. For a fixed price, generally quite low, the electronic database will dispense the credit history of a single individual to the financial institution.

Unlike the vending machine, there is never a queue, there are no hard lads breaking into you every night after closing time, and instead of fifty or sixty uses per day there are more than 3,000, and that's for a small market. This was exactly the business model I admired most. It was taking raw data and adding value to it by refining and repackaging. And because it was an automated business, it would require the minimum of management after it was up and running.

It was another wonderful irony of business that in facing an obstacle – gaining access to low cost commercial finance from banks – I had been presented with another business opportunity. But that's the way it is. The Czech banks were in dire need of a service that I could provide. They needed information, and I had a business that sold information.

Of course it was by no means a perfect match. My company researched other companies, not consumer credit. The data Aspekt handled was also publicly available. Credit details are not.

This is not something with which I have an issue. Protection of the individual's right to privacy is becoming increasingly important as our reliance on computing power grows. However, even confidential data must be computerised if we are to have an efficient, knowledge-based society. Technology has led to an unprecedented level of service and freedom for the consumer, and I believe that, in time, commerce and society as we knew it in the latter part of the twentieth century will be completely transformed.

In 1995, however, I wasn't totally sure how credit information companies were structured, or how it might be possible to break into the sector. But again it was a matter of leverage and creative imagination. Aspekt had been built up from very little and I was sure that I could do the same again. I would just follow the formula.

For two years, I developed the concept of the credit bureau between the various banks. By kicking the idea around between the largest seven institutions, I hoped to learn exactly what they wanted and at the same time educate them into what was a completely new idea for them. It was necessary to have that many institutions involved from the beginning because the credit bureau couldn't be successful unless it had eighty per cent of the market.

It was somewhat similar to what I did when I set up Aspekt. You listen to the market and air the concept. When you get a feeling that there's something solid there, something worthwhile, you can harden it into a business plan and consider your next step forward. We already had a very good basis from which to tackle the credit bureau thanks to our reputation, client skills and technical ability, and eventually seven banks decided that they there were interested in taking it further.

Of course, bankers often make decisions out of fear and greed, and when they do it's in that order. There was a certain amount of carrot and stick work involved in selling the idea, but once one came, the rest followed.

Other outside factors also motivated the banks. There was a fear that the Czech National Bank would develop its own system, an unprecedented move that would have conferred huge power to the state. The was also the possibility that consumer credit would go the same way as corporate credit – where there was such competition that the banks lent money without really checking who was getting it.

That isn't to say that the bankers only had a herd mentality. Two years later, I discovered through someone's slip of the tongue that the president of the Bankers Association had personally rung the Czech ambassador in Dublin to check me out. Luckily for me, I was already known to the ambassador, who was a very nice guy, having contacted him years before when I was contemplating setting up in Prague. We had connections in other areas and it was an enjoyable meeting, but I didn't expect anything out of it since diplomats are not business people.

However, what makes diplomats important to business is that they are information people, and they like to know what's going on and who's in town. That contact, more social than anything else, was pivotal in the creation of the Czech Credit Bureau and I never knew until years later. It's strange how things can turn out.

Once we had the banks with us, it was time to find strategic partners. There was no point in us trying to make a complex deal even more difficult by trying to build our own infrastructure, the best idea was an international company that could offer both investment and expertise.

Thomas Denemark was a bright researcher with Aspekt, but I saw that he was going to leave unless he was given a challenge. Our proposed credit bureau needed to be a totally separate business from Aspekt, because Aspekt did not have the resources to fund it. I then gave Thomas the brief to research the project on a global basis.

He looked in Australia, the United States and all around Europe. Again it was an Irish company that first caught my eye. The Irish Credit Bureau, owned by Irish banks and leasing companies, was a very interesting model.

The ICB is the biggest credit-referencing agency in Ireland, and is owned and financed by its member institutions. Every time an Irish person applies for credit from one of these lenders, the lender accesses the person's credit file to find out about their reliability. The credit file gives a list of their bank accounts and loans, and whether the person has been missing payments, etc. Of course, most people aren't aware its being done, or at least the extent of the check.

The ICB was also quite profitable so I approached them with a view to a partnership. They were very open, very positive, but their brief was to run a business in Ireland for their members. They couldn't get their head around the idea of developing a business in central and eastern Europe. I don't think it was naive or negative of them to decline because an organisation is like a person, either they want to do something or they don't. Similarly if a business idea doesn't suit an entrepreneur, they shouldn't get involved.

Instead of the ICB, I found partners in a US company called Trans Union, a very large corporation with credit bureaux in over twenty countries. As one of the top three credit reporting companies in the US, Trans Union had grown out of a railcar leasing firm that had expanded into consumer information by acquiring the Credit Bureau of Cook County in 1969. Back then, the Credit Bureau was manually handling 3.6 million card files in 2,800 separate drawers. By 2001, Trans Union had files on 190 million adults in the US, and was receiving between 1.4 and 1.6 billion records per month from various lending firms.

That level of information management staggers the mind.

Larry Howell was the president for the Asian, Pacific and European regions of Trans Union, but I had a lot of difficulty tracking him down. He was out on the back of a yacht in the Mediterranean and he very rarely had his mobile phone with him. Eventually, I did manage to get a call through to him and Trans Union came on board for thirty per cent of the business with an investment of $500,000. I put in nothing other than time and energy. In fact I had little to put in, but managed to stay as the largest shareholder.

For strategic reasons, I also approached an Italian multinational called CRIF, which specialised in the design of consumer credit databases. They had a software system that was worth $2 million to us if we had to buy it for the Czech Business. In return for being paid on a per use basis, CRIF took another thirty per cent of the business, leaving my organisation with a forty per cent shareholding in a company that had $500,000 in it and the use of software worth four times that.

I was familiar with the American business culture, but this was the first time I dealt with Italians and I found that they are very much a relationship people, which is a good mix for Irish gregariousness, but were also somewhat confrontational. You had to be very tough and ready to stand your ground regardless of what was thrown at you. Only then could you start dealing on an equal level. If you went in to negotiations with a compromise attitude, you were doomed. They'd simply walk all over you.

With my first meeting with CRIF, I spoke with their managing director, Carlo Gherardi, and the personal dynamics were very good. 'I wasn't so sure about the business, but we really liked you,' Gherardi later said to me. 'We liked your attitude, we liked your approach and we took the risk with you.'

As the local partner, it was our responsibility to carry out the groundwork and get all of the Czech banks to share their customer's credit information.

We faced some competition in our bid – the most serious from a Czech firm called MUZO whose core business was the administration of credit card transactions. They were a pretty strong rival and already had large database systems in place for card purchase authorisation and processing, as well as strong links to the banks and leasing companies.

However MUZO's big mistake was believing that they could reinvent the wheel and build a credit bureau on their own. Probably they could have, but it would have taken them years. Our partners, on the other hand, had decades of experience between them and systems that were already tried and tested by the market.

After boardroom discussions, the seven founding institutions made a joint recommendation in our favour under the aegis of the Czech Banking Association and in 1999 our team was given the mandate to begin work on the Czech Credit Bureau.

The end product of our credit bureau was to be a credit report that could be generated per request for anybody seeking a loan or finance. This report would be based on fifty computer data fields that had to be equally centralised between all the banks. I didn't know it then but, with all of the politics and the complications, it was going to be the most complex and difficult deal I would ever put together.

The size of the respective bank teams was the first problem. Each bank had two or three middle management representatives from each department of the bank, be it legal, IT, commercial, risk management, or whatever. Jointly they amounted to a combined team of around thirty people. It was our job to get each of these teams, and each member of the team, to communicate with their counterparts and get them working in unison.

And what a painful process it turned into.

I have nightmarish memories of going into large, smoky meeting rooms filled with senior managers to make presentations. Sometimes I would be on my own presenting, or perhaps just with an interpreter. After a series of meetings I would run out of business cards – their regular distribution more akin to dealing a pack of cards than a personalised introduction. Everybody would say this is a wonderful idea, a great thing to do, and so on – but nobody would ever make a decision. Their knee jerk reaction from each of the teams was 'I will if you will', and none would be the first to get the ball rolling.

The senior team executives met every second Tuesday in the palatial boardroom of the Bankers Association in Prague. Massive wooden furniture, oak-panelled walls, crystal chandeliers. Everything that one would associate with the uppermost echelons of the industry. The agenda for these meeting was contained in the master framework agreement. This document was divided into a list of thirty objectives that had to be met before a workable information exchange could take place. We wanted a big bang situation where all the banks would just give up all their data without preconditions but instead, because the data was wound up between each section of each team, it had to go along in a piecemeal fashion. We moved painfully along the agenda, point by point. Unfortunately, the framework agreement was a document in flux and when we cleared one point another two or three would sprout in their place.

It was like chopping the heads off the Hydra. Except it was boring.

One day in early December 1999, I met with the senior risk managers in the chambers of the Bankers Association. At this stage we had been discussing our credit bureau project for over a year and the decision to go with it was virtually made. Things were looking positive and I decided that I could take a little time out and let the teams work away on their own for a while. I'd been away from my family too much and I wanted to take my wife and children away for a few months to ring in the millennium in style.

We rented a boat in the Caribbean and sailed it around the warm waters together. We had a great time and I relaxed and stopped worrying so much about the ongoing process. I knew that in my absence, there would be several meetings and progress was assured.

The following April, I was back in the boardroom of the Bankers Association. Same room, mostly the same people, same agenda. Still going slowly. They had moved a few points along, but other things had cropped up and were causing concern all round. Of course, the real problem wasn't in the agreement, it was in the culture. There had been changes of personnel in the teams and people didn't trust each other. The old communist attitudes were still dominating. The biggest giveaway was their continuing fixation with long, formal titles that were as grand and useless as those big desks they all had. 'May I ask Mr Dr Kafka a question,' etc.

It was the same la-di-da waffle. They were all agreeing in principle, but only in principle. Nobody was actually *doing* anything. It was ridiculous because they needed to share that customer information to help each other – it was the one area where they had a clearly common interest.

All I could do at the meeting was stew away in my own impatience while hours were spent discussing a minor detail. A minor detail that could have been resolved by a few quick phone calls months before. Perhaps a change of tack would help.

Near the end of the meeting, I took out all of my holiday snaps and tossed them on the table. Beautiful shots of me and my family in the sunny climes of the Caribbean for New Year's Eve 1999 spilled across the dull oak. 'Lookit, if you could all get agreement on this you could take holidays for three months. You could be doing what I was doing instead of spending all your time here.' I was bragging, but at the same time sending them a deliberate message, bluntly that the bureau was going nowhere and unless we kicked ass it would continue going nowhere.

'Yes, yes, we agree,' chuckled the collective Mr Doctors of the Czech banking industry. 'Good point.'

Of course, had I been a Czech person and pulled a stunt like that security would have shown me the door. Waving your holiday snaps to make a point to conservative financial types is not the done thing as you can imagine.

I could get away with it because I was a foreigner. Sometimes it's the outsider that brings change because insiders are too caught up in things to distinguish the wood from the trees. Of course, it was equally likely there were local people who were better qualified and knew more than me, but weren't listened to. Often we assume that the foreigner, because he comes from a foreign shore, knows more. Very often he doesn't. It's the old tale of familiarity and contempt again.

The reality was that I was no real expert on banking or credit businesses. All I was trying to do was get them to share data.

This didn't necessarily mean that things happened any faster for me. The risk managers had laughed politely at my cheek but they all went back to doing things their own way. The discussions with that committee went on for another full year.

In the middle of all this, a new data protection act was being formulated in the Czech Republic. It attempted to make an accommodation between the rights of the citizen to have their personal data protected and the privilege of the bank to suspend some of those rights if it was going to lend money to the citizen. The new act delayed and complicated things, but then everything was a delay at that stage. We worked in parallel with the incoming law as best we could.

Over the previous years, seismic changes had occurred in the Czech banking establishment. Of our original seven banks, one had gone bankrupt while another had been taken over. The five remaining were Bank Austria Creditanstalt, GE Capital Bank, Ceská Sporitelna, CSOB and Komercni Banka.

As part of a process of foreign acquisitions and normalisation, a lot of international staff had entered Czech banks at very high levels. Although we might have relied on them to support the idea of a Czech credit bureau, the truth of the matter was that they had bigger fish to fry. Together with their new Czech colleagues, the foreign executives had to deal with huge deficits on their balance sheets, a hangover of years of corrupt banking. The quarter per cent or so reduction in rates that our bureau would contribute was irrelevant compared to the billion-dollar losses suffered by the Czech banks during the transition period. It was only as the banking market stabilised that a credit bureau became necessary.

However, by May 2000, things began to come together. The Czechs passed their Data Protection Act and later in the same year, we managed to get all of the bank CEOs, who had been working at too high a level to get too much involved, together for an informal breakfast. I made a connection with one of the bank's chief executives called Jack Stack. He was an Irish-American banker in his fifties, with an Irish passport with a Kerry address, who was responsible for the largest savings bank in the country. When he took over the job of chief executive of Ceská Sporitelna, the bank had 15,000 people working for it and held accounts for one-third of the Czech population. They were very good people and very talented, but the bank had been government owned and run in the communist fashion, and so had all of the problems associated with that.

It's mode of service and operation was also completely outdated. When Jack took over the running of the bank in the mid-1990s, it was ten years behind its western counterparts.

What do you do to make a difference in a suffocated environment like that? How does one guy create change in such a committee culture?

Many people who tried, failed. A lot of managers hired in the decade after the fall of communism tended to be people who looked good on paper. They worked with consultants, had lots of qualifications or had the right connections, but they weren't necessarily people who knew a lot about banking in the socialist environment, or about the people who worked in it.

Jack was different. He was a professional banker through and through and because it was instantly clear that he knew what he was talking about, he commanded respect. But more than that, Jack understood the personal dynamic of the organisation he was responsible for. Without that ability, it's unlikely that Ceská Sporitelna would have been turned around from an inefficient dinosaur to robust financial institution in such a short period.

Let me tall you a story about Jack.

Traditionally, all the managers of this bank would get together for an annual meeting. All in their business suits, they'd meet in an auditorium and present the strategy for the coming year. Over one hundred managers gathered in one room, discussing revenues and forecasts and other dry stuff. Jack was there, but he had only been on the job for a month or so and was still the new guy. After his number two had finished presenting his plan, it was Jack's turn.

He started normally, more humdrum stuff. Then he began to get a little animated and took of his jacket. Only a few people in the front really noticed because the rest are all dozing.

Then the tie came off, and a few more bankers woke up. Jack is still talking about the plan and what they're going to do in the coming year. Next thing, his shirt sailed through the air, and suddenly the bankers are all awake because under Jack's shirt is a T-shirt with the logo of Komercni Banka – their biggest competitor.

In front of his aghast audience, Jack ripped off – and I don't mean he took it off quickly, I mean he *ripped* off – the T-shirt and reveals a different logo. This time it's CSOB, another big competitor. The bankers were horrified, here's their own CEO wearing the colours of the competition. What the hell was going on?

But Jack wasn't done yet. CSOB disappeared and now it's Bank Austria Creditanstalt. Gesticulating wildly, Jack jabbered on about the plan. The plan to deal with the other banks. The other banks whose T-shirts he was wearing. Now it's GE Capital Bank, and the audience were going wild.

GE Capital is flung away to reveal his fifth T-shirt, Ceská Sporitelna. Still spluttering away about the plan, although nobody was really listening to it anymore, Jack jumped up on to the table and dropped his trousers. The bankers gasped. Now in a pair of boxing shorts, he punched the air furiously and finished the presentation by shouting, 'This is what we're going to do! We're going to beat the hell out of the competition!'

Jack's stunt was gimmicky, but you can be pretty sure that within two days eighty per cent of those 15,000 people knew about it. It was instant pay off. How else could the CEO interface with all of his employees in such a short period of time? It was an extreme example of how one person can be a catalyst for change.

This is an example of the entrepreneurial art in action. Although Jack was put in by Austrian Erste Bank, which had purchased fifty per cent of Ceská Sporitelna, it was the Czech bank that became the more dynamic of the two. Like a good entrepreneur, Jack invested heavily in his first asset – the bank's own employees. Very soon after his arrival, he had tripled the staff training budget and introduced incentive schemes for both employees and individual branches, rewarding them for performance rather than the old system where they got paid for just showing up. He also brought customer services and the bank's products up to scratch and, within two years, Ceská Sporitelna was on a par with any western consumer bank.

Jack became a good friend and we played tennis together. As foreigners doing business there was a good rapport, even though we operated at totally different ends. He understood what we were trying to do and was very supportive. That rattled the middle management. Once they saw their bosses taking an interest they became a lot more enthusiastic. Finally, in March 2001, the banks signed an agreement that authorised data sharing for all the required fields. All we had to do then was finalise the infrastructure and by 2002 the Czech Credit Bureau was in full flow.

It had taken seven years, but we did it.

However, there was one unfortunate incident. In 2001, I undertook an internal restructuring of my various enterprises, which naturally involved the transfer of shareholdings, including my shares in the Czech Credit Bureau, to the Kilcullen Mozart Group.

There was a facility in the bureau's shareholder agreement where any party could transfer ownership as long as it went to a company that was at least fifty per cent owned by the party in question. What I did was legal and above board and there was no attempts at subterfuge. I followed the procedure, advised the board of directors as a matter of courtesy and the restructuring took place without a hitch.

Six months later, the lawyer in CRIF discovered this and failed to understand what had taken place. Whether she thought I was trying to offload the shares or create a totally new entity or something similar I don't know. In fact, to this day I'm not sure what she thought was happening, but she didn't like it anyway.

CRIF's legal department fired a broadside at us and threatened legal action which, if successful, would have made it difficult for us to sell our shareholdings. That would have anchored me to the bureau permanently, and while I would make money from it each year, it would not fit my style of entrepreneurship. I wanted to create a new entity, give it value, sell it and move on.

At the beginning, I tried to fight it on my own because I didn't want to incur legal fees over what was simply a misunderstanding. However, it soon became obvious that the Italian lawyer had got her teeth into it and wasn't going to let go.

The whole incident came at a really bad time because I was in the middle of a cutback of Aspekt's event management and publishing enterprises. In order for the company to survive I had to layoff two-thirds of the staff which was unpleasant but vital. After six months the lawyer in question actually came to Prague and after we talked and explained everything, she realised that nothing illegal had taken place at all.

Unfortunately for the sake of saving face, the Italians still refused to back down and I was faced with a stupid but seemingly inevitable legal action. The situation had deteriorated so much that Trans Union's lawyers in Chicago were also pulled in to make a three-way split.

I sought advice from another Prague-based lawyer who dealt with Italians frequently and she told me bluntly that I now had to fight fire with fire. With no other option I hired David Beattie, the best lawyer I knew, to put together the most aggressive riposte possible. We assembled a list of points and hurled it back at CRIF, hoping to force the issue.

As soon as CRIF's lawyer received it she caved in.

The whole thing had taken one year, cost $50,000 between our combined legal fees and hadn't changed anything at all. It was a complete waste of time and effort.

Of course the art of succeeding in this type of situation is not to make the adversary look bad, you have to allow them to save face. It was entirely the fault of CRIF's lawyer for persisting with a legal action that had no basis in reality, but that was a feature of Italian culture. Italians are a great people that I love doing business with, but they will try to bully if they think it will work.

The other lesson that I learned from this was the danger of remote communication. Email is completely one-dimensional and although it is perfect for ninety per cent of business dialogue, the other ten per cent requires body language and emotional depth. As in sales, crisis management also requires the bedrock of trust to be established and it's very hard to trust someone when you haven't had a personal meeting. With a face-to-face encounter, it's much easier to get a feel for things. We should have met with the Italian laywer immediately, but it never happened.

By the standards of the industry in the Czech Republic, we struck while the iron was hot. We were the first in, we had developed a relationship with the banks, approached the right strategic partners and then implemented the project in a country that was way behind the norms of western banking. I'll stick with the venture for another few years adding value wherever possible and then I'll sell it on.

Right now it's a good business, we get paid €1.50 per enquiry and at the time of writing we were looking at one million enquiries per year. Soon it will be three million enquiries, and it will continue to rise as more and more credit facilities are offered to the average Czech. It also gives a strong basis for credit scoring, decision analysis and a range of software and solutions we can sell to other banks.

Of course, with more information available on borrowers, the lenders are more secure and can lower rates, which in turn makes credit more accessible to the Czech people, making more business for our bureau. It's a beautiful cycle, and now we have the go ahead for the Slovak Credit Bureau. Same partners, same shareholdings. As for Thomas Denemark, he went from researcher to managing director. Eventually he resigned from the position, which was sad as he had given it his all for five years. However he was young and as the organisation got bigger, he was outgrown to a degree.

Getting more involved with the financial sector has also had attractive spin-offs. We've built up a very strong record with the Czech banks and that has helped with our subsequent property investments. When we put in a bid for the Prague Stock Exchange Building, five banks offered to lend us over €14.5 million. We then managed to pull in €5 million of equity investment to buy the building for €19.5 million and little over a year later we sold it for over €25 million – repaying the banks and doubling our investors money.

Not bad for the Irishman who couldn't even get an overdraft.

The successful formation of the Czech Credit Bureau, which we will roll out into other countries, is one that I am very proud of and as a matter of fact, it's actually my all-time favourite project. On 1 October 2004 it went live in Slovakia.

It was tough, complex and a great apprenticeship into the inner workings of banks and financial systems. It was wealth creation based on pure, creative entrepreneurship and, other than some time and expenses at the early stage, there was little investment.

Now that's how you create value. It's amazing how lucky you become the more things you try and the harder you work.

Chapter seventeen

Globix Telecom and eTel

Starting a telephone company was not something I had ever contemplated during chats with my career guidance teacher at school. While barriers to entry have now dropped dramatically in this business thanks to wide scale deregulation, back in 1996 it was a fairly brazen thing to attempt in a monopolistic market.

I was also getting a little tired of being overcharged by Cesky Telecom. They held a monopoly of the Czech market and were charging nearly $2 a minute to dial New York and a similarly exorbitant rate for other international calls. Because we made a lot of overseas calls (I'm a phoneaholic) it was hurting us, not critically, but enough to make me start thinking. I then learned I could buy a minute from London to New York for about ten cents and perhaps another ten cents from Prague to London, and it got me thinking.

At the same time there was a buzz in the world of telecommunications. I had been reading the international business magazines and it was clear that this was to be the next big thing. Deregulation of monopolies worldwide was throwing up all types of opportunities at just the time when I was looking for a new one.

I had plenty of other pots on the boil, but once I get really interested in something, I find it hard to ignore it. The challenge of starting a telephone company was an exciting, technology-driven, fast-moving, high-revenue business, which worked for you twenty-four hours a day, seven days a week. It attracted me for all the same reasons that the Credit Bureau concept did. But, unlike the Credit Bureau, it had a real personal dynamic.

I called up the chief executive of a major telco in London one morning to ask whether I could meet on Wednesday. 'Sure. No problem,' he said.

Turning up on the Wednesday, I apologised for giving such short notice, to which the answer was: 'What do you mean short notice? You gave me two days notice!'

Two days was a long time in the telecoms sector. In the banking world, you had to have an appointment anything between three weeks or three months in advance, sometimes even longer.

From what I could see, the telecoms business fitted perfectly with my philosophy that the same effort in economic sectors of high growth for entrepreneurs will give a better return. Likewise if you are in a mature market and you want the fastest growth and capital appreciation, leave. Go to where change is greatest, such as in a transition economy or relatively virgin market for that product or service.

Another element of the gut feeling was the clear sense of purpose and a clear mission. Myself and my merry men – who ever else was going to come on board – would take on the monopoly provider and save the downtrodden Czechs a pile of cash on their phone bill.

The time to rob from the rich and give to the poor was at hand. Already I could see that the advent of the Internet was going to lead to a decline in traditional publishing. New competition had come in and revenues were going to be squeezed. I was still very much committed to expanding Aspekt by adding new product lines and branching out into new countries, and I was devoting the major part of my time to that.

However, the telecoms industry still beckoned. The appeal was similar to that which the transition countries held for me in the early 1990s – state-run behemoths being split up and privatised. Except this time, it wasn't a socio-political transition, it was a technological one, and from what I was reading it looked like the exponential potential that I had been looking for.

There was a mystique surrounding a telephone company. I mean, Jesus, how do you set one of those things up? Did you have to be like a modern day railroad tycoon? Getting thousands of people out laying networks and installing phones and basically creating a huge infrastructure before a single customer could be signed up?

I read about the area as much as possible and talked to anybody who knew anything about it. As with many things, once I began to do the research, the mystique evaporated. The smaller operators were buying phone-time in bulk and selling it cheap. They were basically middlemen, riding off the infrastructure that was already there. It was a basic business technique being applied to a different sector. The best revenues were in long-distance or international calls, and as far as I could see there appeared to be two ways of doing it: prepaid cards or accounts.

Low-cost call cards were making good money, but they were in the cheap end of the market for students, tourists, immigrants, and the like.

What was the point of doing that? In my own experience, a business customer was forking out the equivalent of €5,000 a month on the telephone. That customer would be worth the same as fifty customers who were spending €100 each time. The lower end of the market needed high volume and harder work for the same money.

With this logic, I assembled the concept of a central European telecoms company – a multinational firm that would service business customers across the post-Soviet states.

The Czech Republic could be the test case.

I was committed to high-end selling and to the business-to-business arena. It looked like I was going to need it too. By 1997, the Czech financial dream had started south. Their privatisation and grand stock exchange of 2,000 companies had not solved the inherent problems of inefficiency and corruption. They had succeeded in transferring ownership to individuals, but those individuals had not succeeded in restructuring the companies. My core business had reached saturation point in the Czech Republic, the roll-out in Poland was problematic to say the least, while the *Czech Business Journal* had been an expensive flop.

It was time for something new. I could see from the international media that others were doing well with their entry-level telecoms operations. So would I.

First I needed a local Czech partner prepared to take on the status quo, and that person had to have a strong entrepreneurial drive. Most Czechs are organisation people, even more so than average because organisation and committee is what the communists did best – or worst, if you take my view.

In essence, we had to take on the monopoly long-distance company, to go against state officials, take on cosy cartels and a telecommunications law that was totally out of date. I was going to be tied down looking after Aspekt, so I wouldn't be able to take the helm for most of the time, nor would I be able to delegate the work. You don't brief an employee to set up a telecoms firm…

I was drinking socially in Prague one evening with a friend called Matt Starr. Matt was an investment banker and both of us were studying Czech together. Over our pints, Matt introduced me to Radek Brnak, a charismatic Czech who had worked as a bond trader for an Austrian bank and had excellent English. What he did not have was an apartment, due to a problem stemming from a transition hangover between public and private property. Czechs were subletting apartments illegally, but they wouldn't rent to other Czechs. Apartments were still owned by the government but were being privatised, and so if another Czech got into the apartment he or she might claim possession, even if they were only there as tenants. With foreigners you could charge a rental and still get them out.

I offered to let Radek share my apartment and while we both lived an 'Odd Couple' existence, I discovered that he was very independent, a natural leader and someone whom I considered to be a natural entrepreneur.

Obliged to do his national service, Radek had reluctantly finished his job as a bond trader and enrolled as a conscript with the Czech army. Like me, he had low respect for the military culture and was a bit rebellious. Unfortunately for him, the Czech army were not indulgent. Having fallen asleep during sentry duty – a shooting offence during wartime – he was given a stint in a military prison.

Since then the Czechs have dropped conscription and changed to a professional army, which is just as well. All the conscripts were learning was laziness, how to dodge work and how to fool the system. With a voluntary force the army will attract people who are actually motivated by a military career.

All in all, Radek was definitely not the establishment type, which meant he was perfect for what I had in mind. Here was someone who was prepared to challenge the system and was a Czech as well.

On getting out of the army Radek was looking around for new things to try out, so I planted a few ideas with him but as I couldn't afford to wait for a year, like John Bourke did with one of his people, I needed Radek to come to the project himself. He had to have ownership because he was a rebel and entrepreneur, not a worker. I didn't want a person to approach it with a 'job' mentality, because that is the antithesis of entrepreneurial thinking.

Radek was strong-willed and intelligent and had looked at many ideas. Then it came. 'Enda, this is what I want to do,' he said – almost as soon as the words were out of his mouth, I was attacking the dial pad on the phone. I knew exactly who to call to get the entrepreneurial loop in progress and bring together the necessary industry knowledge, expertise and investment.

During my research of the telecoms industry, I had not only been learning about the general industry and its dynamic, I had also been searching for viable business formulas to emulate. I had originally shortlisted five potentials in the UK, Holland and Ireland. Each of the CEOs I had met had asked similar questions and all liked the idea. Not only that, they offered to invest on the spot, and when you hear that you know you're on to something good. My gut reaction for this venture was extremely positive.

After further investigation (I also had to flesh out a business plan) it looked like it was going to be a toss up between the Irish firms Stentor and TCL. Both had been set up to provide international and long-distance telecommunications services to the corporate market in competition with Telecom Éireann, an almost perfect alignment with what I wanted to do with my Czech telco.

Stentor had been set up by twenty-nine year old Patrick Cruise O'Brien, adopted son of the venerable Conor Cruise O'Brien, in 1996 and, at its official inauguration, Stentor was announced as the largest Irish telecoms firm after Telecom Éireann and Esat. The surrounding hype made the company appear quite attractive, but I just didn't take to it.

Stentor felt strange. There was no other way to put it. The company looked and acted the part of a good telecoms firm on the make, but there was something bothering me that I just couldn't identify. Even though Stentor looked the easiest to deal with because they had a lot of money at the time I approached, my gut feeling said otherwise.

I didn't commit. Not long after Stentor got into financial difficulties.

Seán Melly's TCL was different. Seán worked with Dermot Desmond's R&J Emmet liqueur company in 1990, but after two years wanted to move on. Legal complications arose regarding his contract, but it was reported that Desmond himself intervened – leading to a hefty compensation package for Seán.

Some of that money, along with a $100,000 investment from Bernard Sommers, was used to start up TCL Telecom in 1994 and from there the company grew rapidly. In 1996, Seán sold thirty per cent of TCL to WorldCom for $1,000,000 and, in 1997, the newly formed MCI WorldCom acquired the remaining shares for $20 million.

The moment Radek committed, I was on the phone to Seán to get our Czech telco up and running. Of all the potential partners I had looked at, Seán seemed the best. He had a reputation for being a sharp operator who didn't take prisoners. That suited me because I would not be able to devote myself full-time to the operation, and it needed a strong team at the top.

I was also familiar with the American corporate culture that Seán started in, and was used to dealing with characters like him. That said, I knew that under different circumstances our management styles would ultimately clash. True to his reputation, Seán was tough to negotiate and do business with, but most importantly of all when he gave his commitments, he honoured them.

With Seán came Bernard Sommers, an accountant with a totally different style of entrepreneurship. A former director of the Central Bank of Ireland as well as Independent News and Media Plc, Bernard became a man of repute in the 1980s when he worked as a company liquidator in very tough times. Himself and Seán were a diametrically opposed but well-balanced pair. 'Oh, you're dealing with the Irish Murphia', said WorldCom's David Hardwicke when he learned of our involvement.

With the team assembled, it was time to grapple with shareholdings and investment.

I needed some more cash at the time, so I raised another €120,000 with a mortgage on my house. I put up €25,000 for twenty-five per cent and was the company chairman, while Aspekt swallowed another €95,000. Seán put in €63,500 for thirty per cent and brought his expertise, while Bernard Sommers came in as a silent, €90,000 investor for twenty per cent.

All Radek could raise was €5,000, but for that he received twenty-five per cent which was a very good deal. In reality the €5,000 was a token contribution, but it was important as proof of Radek's commitment because it meant that he had something on the line like the rest of us.

While I had more money to put in than Radek, I knew that Radek would have to receive a share equal to mine. Otherwise there was a risk of him seeing himself as a worker and walking away. But in return for that cheap share, Radek was going to contribute sweat equity in a very real sense of the phrase. My idea at the time was to get our business model working in the Czech market and then to expand it to central Europe

Pistols at the ready it was time to put a flash name on our band of outlaws. Globix was suitably corporate so we went with that.

Over the horizon, we could see deregulation approaching the Czech market, and behind every foreign telecoms company that wanted to get a slice of the market. They would arrive on 1 January 2001. Meanwhile Cesky Telecom continued with their exorbitant tariffs.

However, our reconnaissance showed up a few interesting weaknesses in the state provider's position. First their monopoly was against the constitution as it was in breach of competition law. However, this had never been tested.

Second while we couldn't get a licence to sell voice real-time long-distance (only CT were permitted to do that), we could get a data licence. That opened up an interesting possibility. If we sold long distance time but delayed it for a millisecond, would that still constitute voice real-time, or could the delayed voice now be considered data? Again this had not been tested.

We concluded, based on the experience of other entrepreneurs who had done the same in other countries, that an immediate strike was best. For a relatively small capital investment, we could start selling lucrative long-distance time right under the nose of CT. It was also important that we got in before the larger competitors, who would be able to use their tremendous wealth to overbid and undersell us. Our only chance was to operate on a dubious legal basis and be somewhat established before they arrived.

It was a 'what if' scenario. If CT tried to close us down, we'd appeal it in court, which would tie up the matter for three years or more whereupon the law would be changed anyway. Besides, we weren't even blips on the radar screen. We had little money to our name and if CT did prevail in court, we probably wouldn't have much funds to pay compensation. We'd just declare bankruptcy instead.

Starting a legal action might be worthwhile if we were a huge multinational with pockets to match, but we weren't, and that made us feel safe.

With our investment, we set up the company and rented an office in the centre of Prague.. Getting telephone lines in Prague was very difficult, as difficult as it had been in Ireland twenty years before. The Czechs were playing catch up, and the poor service and congestion on their telephone exchange was only part of the problem. I took six months to get a phone line and buildings with extra phone lines were as rare as hen's teeth. But there was one place that I knew of.

Beside the Stock Exchange Building, there was a building with a very grim history behind it. Owned by two Jewish families who were exterminated in Nazi death camps, the Gestapo had later quartered themselves there and used it as a torture chamber. Between the war and the time it came to the commercial market, the Czechs had used it as a police station.

Despite the tragedies that had taken place there, it was perfect for us. Because it was also adjacent to one of the local switches of Cesky Telecom the area had also been wired for fibre optic networking. Available for very small money, we rented the location and refurbished it for Radek to move into with the employees.

In fact, the basement area was quite big and a lot of young Czech people worked in it. Radek himself was only in his twenties and so were his employees. They worked hard, partied all night and worked hard again. (They were quite a sociable group who often ended up sleeping there as well as with each other. It was a sort of new age hippy telephone company). They had their mission, to save Czechs money on their telephone bills, and a high level of customer service was paramount. But after that, they could do what they liked as long as they didn't wreck the place. That was the culture and it was a lot of fun for them.

Who knows, maybe it even cleared out some of the old ghosts of the past.

Time to clear up the mystery of how young telephone companies get started. In every large office building, there's something called a PABX, basically a phone switch, which cost about €30,000. We set that up to enable us to redirect our customers' calls.

Then we rented time on a cable to London, which then cost us about £60,000 per month (now you can buy the same for about ten per cent of this or less). London was an international exchange, so from there the circuits broke out all over the world. In London, we had a line to New York for about 10 cents a minute, and it was costing us on average (depending on the traffic on our lines) about ten cents a minute from Prague to London – a total of twenty cents per minute.

CT was charging $2 per minute for the same.

Of course, we couldn't just bypass CT's infrastructure completely. Instead we put some software into the customer's switch. Then, whenever the customers dialled '00' for an international number, their call went over the public lines to our PABX and from there to London. We still used the local loop, the bunch of cables that belonged to CT which connected our PABX with the rest of the system, but by piggybacking there was no way they could stop us.

Bluntly speaking, we were freeloading off the Czech infrastructure, but to our credit most of the problem lay with CT. In a deregulated market, we could have paid them a fee for the use of the local loop. Under the existing monopoly, there was no mechanism to make such payments, because nobody else was supposed to be providing the service.

As a result of their greed, CT was losing all the revenues from their international business calls in exchange for the minuscule cost of a local call, which is what the customer would pay to get onto our system.

We were even connecting up the customers for free.

Then we got a company in London who agreed to split the cost of the London cable with us in return for half of the revenues. Three months before we went live, we pre-sold capacity to achieve cash flow.

That €180,000 – no more than the cost of a fairly modest flat in Dublin city by the late 1990s – was just enough to cover two months' rental on the British cable and a few other costs, but it was enough to put Globix in operation as a telecoms provider. It's amazing what can be made from a relatively small amount of money when you know what to do with it.

People think that you have to invest millions and millions to get alongside traditional big business, but often you don't.

We were just a small agile operator and used some of the tactics developed by big business. One practice, used by supermarkets, was to sell their supplier's goods, then sit on the money for six months and allow it to accrue interest before paying the supplier. Unfortunately, this caused major cash-flow problems for smaller operators, and occasionally the supplier went bankrupt waiting for the payment. The practice was curtailed in Ireland but we decided it was perfect for us. We were not buying from vulnerable suppliers, we were buying from the massive international companies who owned the existing global networks.

Because we were trading as a telephone company, it was assumed we had scale and were low risk. We used this in our negotiations with the international companies and got a lot of credit, at one stage up to €2 million worth, and we used that in the cash flow of the business too. We could also negotiate very competitive contracts because we weren't locked in long-term relationships, while the monopoly provider CT was stuck with contracts with years to run on them before they could renegotiate. It was a real David and Goliath fight.

Because I had a good Czech partner, I could devote my available time to the strategy and development of the business. My voracious reading into the subject matter hadn't abated either, and I had graduated from financial newspapers and magazines to trade and technical publications. Price and service were the most important elements to business customers (in service, consider the human element of care and attention) and we exploited the huge gap between what we could offer as opposed to what Cesky Telecom did.

Simply put the sales pitch went like this, 'We'll save you forty per cent on your telephone bill and what's more the quality will be superb.'

The business just took off. At a Prague conference on deregulation in the Czech market in 1998 I had Radek, the MD of a company of twelve employees, up on the same platform as CT's managing director, presiding at that time over a workforce of 20,000. It said a lot about the potential of our company and it did a lot for our brand recognition and credibility.

Of course it also helped to have the events management arm of Aspekt organising the event and getting CT to sponsor it!

By March 1998, Globix had a very healthy cash-flow cycle, but now competition was beginning to surface as the market was being rebalanced. Finally, Cesky Telecom had brought in an arrangement through which new operators could pay a fee for use of the local loop (we were happy to oblige), and they also began to charge less for a long distance call and more for the local call.

Technology was developing rapidly. We had originally rented a two-megabyte circuit to London for £60,000, which enabled us to cope with thirty-two simultaneous long-distance calls. Our business had done so well that our limit was continuously breached and so we kept renting more capacity. Fibre technology was now available and capacity increased exponentially. What cost us £60,000 in 1997, cost £15,000 by 1999, and the price still dropped.

These changes meant that it was cheaper and easier for competitors to enter the market and they were coming to set up for themselves or to buy a company like ours. Deregulation was coming closer and with it loomed the large telcos.

In this time, Globix had done fantastically and now had sales of millions per annum. My partners in Ireland couldn't believe how successful it was, and questions were being asked about where the company was going. I had originally conceived it as a central European telephone company, and going by the Czech experience that goal was certainly attainable. Likewise Seán Melly and Bernard Sommers saw the possibilities and knew that the company had to go to the next stage. We had probably reached the limit of our small capital base and I was happy to be a smaller part of something much bigger, considering that I had other interests to take care of.

Radek, however, saw things slightly differently.

In reality, the business had grown too big for our Czech partner and there was a conflict of interest. It had to go to the next level, and Radek was not yet ready for that transition. In some ways, it was similar to my experience with the Sail Ireland project. Just as I wasn't ready to handle the politics of a £4 million project at that stage of my life, neither had Radek the experience to bring what had been a tremendously fun venture to a serious multinational stage. As chairman, I had the questionable honour of acting as intermediary between him and Seán.

But in business it's lead, follow or get out of the way.

Seán Melly was a very strong personality and Radek Brnak was a very strong personality. When Seán had one view, Radek had another. Every time fundamental decisions had to be made for the company, the disaffection manifested itself. They both held opposing strategic visions. In keeping with his American corporate culture, Melly had the bigger view. He wanted to go in with the Rolls Royce and find large investors and large partners. He wanted to incorporate the latest software and technology for billing and customer relations' management. He wanted to roll out the

Globix model in Poland, Slovakia, Slovenia and right across the rest of central Europe. And he wanted to do it his way – without Radek Brnak.

Radek had a similar vision of growing the company, but it was different in scale and feasibility. The deciding factor was that Melly had the ability and reputation to raise the type of funding required to make a central European phone company. Radek didn't.

In the friction that occurred between them, the momentum that Globix had built up was being lost and morale within the operation suffered. I tried my best to relieve tensions as they arose, and sometimes I succeeded, but it was taking a lot out of me.

This was a part-time job, a separate business, and it was becoming extremely trying.

A buyout was the only option, and shareholding valuations immediately caused more difficulty. The company had to be ready for the next level of expansion by deregulation and that made for an interesting standoff.

Seán Melly had a vision, and in his reckoning a central European phone company would be worth about $150 million, a price that was in line with the dot-com and telecoms boom valuations of the day.

However, this value was not based on the actual business of Globix, but on the potential business of a central European operation. Therefore, the investors would be buying into the vision of the expanded company, not the company as it existed. And since it was Seán's vision, a good deal of the investment was buying into Seán's ability to produce a viable central European operation.

What it meant for myself and Radek was that Seán was not going to value Globix, as it currently stood, at anything close to $150 million, and so had no intention of paying out $75 million for our combined fifty per cent of Globix.

I could understand Seán's rationale. As an investor you generally buy into the entrepreneur or team before the concept (unless it's technology you can patent), and therefore what Seán was asking for was reasonable, although hard bargaining ensued. The investors who were going to give him the financing for the next level of expansion would do so on the basis of their belief in Seán and Seán's vision.

Unfortunately, there wasn't much room in that vision for myself and none for Radek.

However, Radek wanted the same valuation and couldn't see, or didn't want to see, that the valuation that Seán was seeking for the larger company would be conditional upon having only one pair of hands on the steering wheel, and that only Seán could be that driver.

Globix had only ever been a sideline diversion for me, and Radek simply did not have the weight to bring in over $100 million in funding. To get from being a fledgling Czech telco to a central European multinational, it was time for Seán to lead, for me to follow, perhaps, and for Radek to get out of the way.

To do this, Seán wanted to restructure the organisation by making an umbrella company, called eTel, which would span Globix and the other incoming central European operations. For this to be successful, Seán had to own all of the shares in Globix because for the moment Globix and eTel were practically one and the same.

In 2000, a group of venture capital firms, Dresdner Kleinwort Benson Private Equity, Argus Capital Partners, Greenhill Capital Partners and Intel Capital, purchased forty-five per cent of e Tel for $55 million, giving Seán a valuation in the region of $110 million for the central European company. Although it was $40 million short of what he wanted, it still remained a tremendous achievement to raise that type of money for a multinational that had no business outside the Czech Republic.

Gradually, the transfer of ownership from myself and Radek to Seán began. It took three months to negotiate and another three months for the process of due diligence. Unfortunately, the dispute between the shareholders continued, despite the fact that our business was growing all the time and was now in the middle of a transferral.

Thanks to Radek's attitude, the deal almost unravelled. Part of it was his natural independence, the very quality that made him such a superb entrepreneur, part of it was a desire for more money. I was either the peacekeeper, or the 'meat in the sandwich' depending on how you look at it. We were right in the middle of the heady days of dot-com, telecoms boom. Stratospheric valuations were being made for the most insubstantial companies. Even our own sales tag could have been examined more closely – here was a company being valued at over €100 million that had begun from an investment of €180,000.

At the pinnacle of the technology trading, a dose of reality began to creep back in. The huge sums placed on the companies were questioned, confidence started to slip and the markets began to get shaky.

The venture capitalists and investors who had decided on the value of eTel decided that they wanted out. The deal was agreed, but the money had not been paid over. Radek Brnak was still being irrational, and that made everybody nervous. He was in a position to scupper everything, and he was quite capable of doing it. Three years previously, I wanted him to buy a mobile phone, but he refused to even do that. He thought they were just for stupid yuppies. The fact that he was the managing director of a phone company didn't seem to intrude on his logic.

While he was a very smart guy, and the project wouldn't have worked without him, he had an experience gap that was now becoming critical. He didn't really understand the difference between having money in the bank and only having it on paper. As an entrepreneur with two decades of experience – and with most of my wealth tied up in companies – I did, and I knew that now was the time to cash in and get out.

Ironically, it was Radek's unpredictability that eventually clinched the deal. The investors had got scared and wanted to be shot of him. By November 2000, all the documents had gone through and the cash released. With the $50 million Seán received for the sale of forty-five per cent of eTel, he bought out Globix for $35 million. Radek and I each got a large chunk of cash and shares in eTel.

While Globix had been sold for a very generous amount, there were much crazier valuations in the market. Austria Telecom paid €200 million for a company that only had revenue of €3 million. Globix had sales of €6 million, so did that make us worth $400 million? I think that would have been excessive to say the least, but had it been offered we would have jumped on it.

Unfortunately, the conflict between Seán and Radek decided otherwise and so when Austria Telecom expressed an interest in acquiring us earlier in the year, Globix was not in a position to respond. Perhaps we wouldn't have received $400 million, but we would have received more than $35 million.

However, I don't feel any sense of loss. Equally, we could have received three times less if the market hadn't held for as long as it did. Everybody involved with the Globix company came out just fine, although at the time it looked as though we were selling cheap.

During the transferral, Seán also offered me a deal whereby I would have a greater shareholding in eTel, and would become more involved in the regional companies. I turned it down for two reasons. While eTel's plans in Poland were very important, I'd had enough of Warsaw and wasn't keen on returning.

I could also see a downturn coming on the market. It's easy to be an expert after the event, but I could never understand where the revenue was coming from for many of the technology firms. It reminded me of one person I knew back home who told me about all of the companies he was going to set up.

'Sure I'll set up this because the government grant is...' he said for about four or five completely different things.

'But where's the revenue?' I asked.

'Sure I'll be gettin' grants for this and that,' and he reeled off the enterprises a second time.

'But where's the revenue?' I asked again.

I dropped it soon after because he got angry with me. All he could see was the money from the state grants and he didn't want his pet ideas to be challenged. He had confused an availability of money with good business, and it was the same for the telcos. Just because huge cash was being circulated in the area didn't mean that the companies were a good investment.

With eTel, Seán pursued the central European telecoms market and made excellent progress. By 2004, it had expanded to four more countries, had 43,000 customers and annual revenues of €100 million. Just to prove that the fundamentals of business don't change, the company still operates on the principals of lower cost, higher quality services.

For me, the personal feeling of accomplishment was great. It was like winning the lottery a couple of times in a row. I did not splash out as such because it had been a long process, and I was moving quickly through a lot of other responsibilities. But I had a tremendous inner feeling.

By contrast, there are many I know who work all their lives in careers and never get a breakthrough like that. This is what the art of being an entrepreneur is all about. It was not an accident that we succeeded, we had chosen a high-growth sector in a virgin market and, with a very low investment, created fantastic wealth. We could have lost the money just as easily if things had gone wrong, a good investment is a good investment, but it can still go wrong. A bad investment is the one where you regret committing your money in hindsight. Even if I had lost my money in Globix, I never would have regretted giving it a go because everything about it felt right.

For the first time ever, I had significant amounts of available cash. It was a turning point that was to take me to the next level of entrepreneurship.

Chapter eighteen

Investor and Entrepreneur

Globix Telecom and eTel were almost a sideline. However, while I had shareholdings in several enterprises that had grown in value, the wealth remained on paper only. The proceeds from Globix and eTel were my first real 'pot' of money, making me a true millionaire.

In retrospect, I should have taken stock. I'd read about other people's experiences in similar situations and the conclusion was to take time out. Friends and acquaintances were advising the same thing. Having made money, the next challenge ahead was to invest it and make even more, or lose it trying. Such is the risk.

But I was on a roll. For years I had been starved of capital and now I was keen to go to the next stage. For the first time as an entrepreneur, I had the resources to follow my own ideas. The plan was not to lead, but to continue working through other entrepreneurs and build a network of shareholdings where I, or an organisation that I would create, would add value without being compromised by the hassle of the day-to-day running of a business. In short, I wanted to become a venture capitalist.

I'd been successful in making money for myself so I concluded that I could make money for other people – But this time I would work at a higher level and on bigger deals. Hence the birth of Mozart Ventures Ltd and management company Kilcullen Kapital Partners in 2001.

Rather than working alone I invited Yorkshireman Ewan Gibb in as a partner. Ewan served in the British army and then worked in the City of London in finance with several top-level companies. His financial and analytical skills compliment my deal-making and business development skills and we make a natural team.

The bigger the scale, the higher the standard, the greater the reward.

Kilcullen Kapital Partners is my new driving enterprise and, touch wood, when this business is fully developed I'm going to start making a real contribution to improving the world we live in, give something back and go sailing again.

I originally decided to go fifty per cent on early stage, high risk venture capital and fifty per cent on property. However, property at best is slow moving and the venture capital side expanded more quickly. For this reason over eighty-five per cent of the initial portfolio ended up in venture capital.

This was expensive. When you invest in a company it needs more money even when it's successful because expansion is always costly. Of course, if it is not successful, it will also need more money. Therefore you can lose either way unless you're very careful. Fortunately, after a difficult start that cost more than we expected, things are looking well. We are now moving from venture capital into investment management, property and deal making. There is over €150 million under management and we plan to grow this figure to €1 billion and more.

For me, Kilcullen was the logical progression upwards. It offered a way to pull together different enterprises, restructure and develop. Kilcullen was designed as a 'boutique' or mini-investment bank into which I put all of my spare cash, while I transferred all the shareholdings of my various enterprises into the Mozart fund.

For most people, the idea of setting up an asset management, venture capital, corporate finance, real estate and investment bank company is a bizarre and seemingly impossible concept, but this is exactly what I set out to do.

I had been toying with the concept of Kilcullen since 1999, but had neither the time nor financial freedom to put it together. However, after the Globix deal, I finally turned it all into a classic venture capital structure, creating the platform for the fund and putting together the management team to run it. By putting my own money on the line, I convinced many other strong individuals to come on board.

However, this was the time that I should have relaxed and listened to those who'd advised me and whose experiences I'd read about. ('Time was invented so that everything does not happen at once,' said Einstein – and you better believe it.) While the structures were sound, I made the one mistake of putting it together too quickly. Even if you have a lot of cash, building an enterprise from scratch takes time and having too much spare cash, especially when you've been starved of it, can be a bad thing.

Within a few months I hired a lot of good people on large salaries to administer the fund and manage the interests in existing businesses. As I said, I have always believed that if you get the right people then the rest will take care of itself. However, while the people I hired were good, they were not the right people. They had the skills, they had the commitment, but they lacked the flair and the ability to start something. Essentially, they were workers.

Sure, when the enterprise was up and running, they probably could have developed it, however, getting starting is the toughest task of all and it's the burden of the entrepreneur and the entrepreneur only. There's a huge amount of difference in performance when you give someone a salary of €80,000 a year as opposed to a shareholding which locks pay into performance.

It's the difference between *hiring* a worker and *harnessing* an entrepreneur.

It's a tricky thing to hold an entrepreneurial mindset within an organisational environment. The most natural attitude for the entrepreneur is 'Why should I stick around and make money for you when I can do it for myself?' which is entirely the right question to be asking – but it left me with a practical problem all the same. I had moved too fast and it wasted a lot of money. What I had put together in a few months should have taken a year. I also went through a low period because I was doing too much and had become involved in too many things.

One gentleman I hired – and he was a lovely guy with great integrity and work ethic – had been the head of corporate finance in the local branch of a large Austrian bank.

One would have thought that he knew something about corporate finance, certainly that if he could do deals and make money for the bank he could surely do it for our start-up enterprise.

However it was much later – €100,000 later in fact – that I realised that while he'd been the head of corporate finance he'd never fully undertaken a proper corporate finance deal before. It was a learning curve, but at least I lost my own money rather than an investor's, which was good comfort because it didn't damage confidence at a critical time.

Today my approach is a little different. Managing other people's money brings a new level of responsibility. Instead of just dispensing the money from on high, I now bring whatever entrepreneurial flair and grey hairs I can to the project. Some of the projects haven't worked out, others have, our risk is spread and it's just a matter of staying the course. With Kilcullen Kapital Partners I now have a vehicle that simultaneously manages my wealth and the wealth of others who contribute to the fund. The combination of each has given me access to even larger deals than were previously possible and has turned me – through the discipline of a much more professional approach – into a full-time investor.

As an investor, I've learned two key things. First if you go into an enterprise, it always costs you much more than you expect. Second if you've made money, and you want to hang on to it, you invest in property.

It's a sad reality that you can always borrow and leverage on property. If you have €200,000 to invest, you can invest it in a business or you can go to the bank and let the bank give you another €600,000 and invest €800,000 in property.

If the property goes up ten per cent, you're going to get €880,000 for it, paying back the bank their €600,000 plus interest, leaving you with the guts of €80,000 for an investment of €200,000. You've made more than forty per cent profit on a ten per cent price increase.

It's probably one of the best examples of getting close to the big deal. Of course it's lucrative and secure, but the reason I don't like it is because you aren't really adding much value. It's just a building sitting there that people need to use and nothing about the deal has required much creative thinking or imagination. Plus with property, you generally need to have the finances to begin with.

But if you're an entrepreneur and you've made money, property is the easiest way to hold on to it and make more. As I'm responsible for more money than just my own, I balance the fund portfolio between property and venture capital.

So Tim Gunning and I founded Timeen Developments as a property development company. Tim is an imposing character, not least for his height. Standing well over six feet, Tim was almost that height at age fifteen when I first met him, and well able to look after himself. A mugger once attacked him with a knife, and got much more than he bargained for when Tim kicked him in the leg.

'I lashed out,' Tim told me one day, ' and I heard a bone crack...'

Fearful that the mugger might try and sue him for breaking his leg, Tim then wisely did a runner.

A fellow sailing enthusiast, Tim started business on virtually nothing and has built up a good portfolio of activities inside and outside our partnership. Besides becoming a close personal friend, he has all the features of a good entrepreneur; practical, streetwise, hardworking and driven. Timeen Developments is doing well and he currently has several good projects underway, including interests in Prague where he has a partnership with a real estate agency founded by Lucie Bukova, a personal friend of mine. She runs the agency with Johan Huurman, the son of my sister Mairead, so as you can see it's become a sort of family affair.

Of course it's the venture capital that really sparks my interest. What I admire most is the person who builds something from nothing at all because in business that's the ultimate challenge. I have one thousand times the respect for someone who starts with nothing and makes a million, rather than the person who starts with a million and makes a billion.

But the problem is that the venture capital projects cost you a lot more, no matter what figures you've been given. By their nature, they are fundamentally riskier, and even if the project is successful, it requires more and more money. Really what you're aiming for is someone to come and buy it from you at a considerable capital gain, making for a good deal all round.

So today I confess that I look upon investors with more sympathy than I might have done when I was the one in search of cash. Having said that, I find nothing more personally satisfying that giving the leg up to someone else when I believe they're capable of going the rest of the way on their own. If they make money, I make money.

It's still very hard work and it's quite hard-nosed. The risk is only one part – every new venture brings its own set of complications, good times and bad times, management and personnel issues, but it's a challenge I happen to like and a challenge I understand and respect.

Becoming a venture capitalist also carries its own irony. I usually didn't like dealing with venture capitalists and the really good ones were as rare as hen's teeth. It brings me back to the same concept that I mentioned earlier in the book – those who can't do, teach.

Most people who teach entrepreneurship and economics are invariably useless at it in practice. The same logic can be applied to many venture capitalists, especially those active in central Europe, my principle area of operation.

Most of them have all the right credentials, backgrounds in finance and investment and impressive curriculum vitae. What they don't have is that inner spark, that entrepreneurial spirit that so invigorates someone that they are prepared to gamble everything they have on one idea.

That spark is the essential gap between theory and practice, the leap of faith between logic and the abstract. It's the creative art. And because they don't have that spark, they don't recognise it – or understand it – in others. Instead they are getting paid large salaries to allocate other people's money under conditions that are far less risky for them. This combined with the fact that each month they have twenty times more plans than they can handle means that there can be a certain amount of arrogance towards the entrepreneur.

In some ways, it's similar to the snooty waiter in a high-class restaurant. The waiter is without doubt an expert in the etiquette of eating out, but does he have the right to look down on the diner who doesn't start with the right cutlery? Or doesn't place their knife and fork side by side on the plate when they're finished eating?

Not in my opinion. While a certain amount of decorum has to be observed, the waiter at the end of the day only serves the food. While that might be done with a certain amount of style, it is the chef's creative work that the paying customer has really come for.

In the same way, when the would-be entrepreneur approaches the fund for access to cash generated by other entrepreneurs, they have to deal with intermediaries who themselves are not entrepreneurs.

Take the following story as an example.

I was once assisting a fellow entrepreneur to raise finance for a project and we subsequently had dealings with an individual who ran a venture capital fund. He actually liked the project and was enthusiastic about it, so we submitted the plan to his firm, thinking it would get the rubber stamp based on his positive reaction.

Then the plan went to his investment committee. The committee members were totally disconnected from the entrepreneur in question and began to question the viability of the plan. One of the committee members disapproved and because of a requirement for unanimity funding was withheld. When we heard the reasons attached to the rejection, it was clear that the lone dissenter had a prejudice against the entire sector of industry in which the project was based.

Although the project in question was ultimately successful in its quest for finance, I found the affair very frustrating. We thought we had been dealing with the decision-maker, but we weren't, and when we dealt with the committee, it was obstructed because of one person's bias.

Having said all of that, middlemen are often indispensable. The chef does not have the time to serve the customers and the financier does not have the time to read all the business plans. Whereas I admire passionately the person who comes up with an idea, puts a business plan together and tries to raise money, the fact of the matter is that their business plan will still have to be scrutinised objectively. The entrepreneur may have the best will in the world, but if his or her plan does not come up to scratch regarding it's concept, market and execution, then it just won't go anywhere. Much as I would love to, I cannot investigate all of the business plans that come for my attention and the Kilcullen management team have to thin out the pile.

Those that survive the vetting process then come to me, and if I like them I meet the entrepreneur.

What am I looking for?

Well, a prospective investment will be made up of two indivisible elements. A good business concept and the right person to execute it. One won't work without the other.

If you have the most brilliant idea and you've got the wrong person to deliver it, it will fail. If you have a brilliant person with the wrong idea, it will fail. It's a fundamental of business and investment. But if both elements are present, the rest will take care of itself.

The first point of contact is of course the business plan. If you can make personal contact with someone who is in a position to help you, great. If not, chances are you'll be have to send a business plan in on spec at some stage. Regardless, you'll need to have some kind of figures worked out and some amount of research done. The business plan is simply a way to put those things down on paper.

The best business plans are the ones whose entire content can be summed up in two pages. I've seen the most elaborate plans with most elaborate models and most elaborate projections. Result? A load of crock. An over reliance on statistics suggests to me that the candidate hasn't really got a feel for the idea and is just hiding behind figures. If you have a really strong gut feeling for something it will come across and convince the investor.

Good business plans lay out five critical aspects:

- What the product or service is?
- Who the customer is and what they want?
- What it costs to supply and sell?
- What the market conditions are like?
- How much money can be made?

Simple as that. There might be other, additional, information to be included which will benefit the overall picture, but if any of the five core aspects are missing then the plan is incomplete.

I've actually seen a correlation between the quality of the business plan and the quality of the entrepreneur. The people who do exceptionally detailed business plans are often poor entrepreneurs, the very type who hide behind their figures and don't exhibit the necessary charisma. Then there are others who have terrible numbers but are larger than life characters, people who are so confident that they step out in front of their shoddy business plans as if to say, 'Look, forget the accountancy. Trust me because I know this will work.'

The latter types get my vote any day. I've seen so much of that textbook-type business plan carried by people with all of the credentials, all the years of finance and marketing experience, but they just don't have that spark of creativity.

That spark is what you need to see because without it there is no chance of a successful business. It's that creative art that makes the enterprise or idea an ongoing commercial reality. A truncated business plan that answers the basic questions of viability and profitability is a good enough starting point when carried by the right person.

The other thing is to research, research, research in every way possible.

Denis O'Brien once recommended that no one should spend more than two weeks at a business plan in case the market conditions changed and the opportunity passed you by. However, if you are not dealing with a sector of business as fast moving and fluid as O'Brien's at the time, then you are better off not rushing it. Get whatever information you need to know. If you have a good feeling about something, you should investigate it thoroughly. Often the more you research, the bigger the opportunity will appear and the more confidence it will build for you.

However, when you get that information, move. Don't analyse it to death. If you have a fundamentally good idea, no amount of analysis in the world will alter it. You've just got to decide quickly whether you're going to do it or whether you're going to get out and do something else.

Whatever you do, don't over promise and don't tell people what they want to hear just to get the deal over the line. If you have to lie about it, chances are it won't work anyway.

Also, don't go in with a begging bowl attitude. The begging bowl gets nothing in business. You're going to sell benefits, what you're going to make for the investor. It might be a cliché, but the line 'I've got an idea that can make you a load of money', is pretty much what the investor wants to hear.

If not exactly in those words...

You don't have to know everything about the business, certain expertise can always be hired, but what you must know intimately is the overall concept and strategy of the venture. What is the opportunity? How will you exploit it? If you don't know these things, you cannot fulfil the entrepreneurial role because it's here that the creative art is necessary. Market conditions change and the entrepreneur must be able to ride with those changes, adapting and altering direction in order to find profits wherever they may be hiding.

It's the essential difference between the worker and entrepreneur. The worker, no matter how skilled, effectively carries out repetitive and routine tasks for steady wages. The entrepreneur is a creative force who starts with only an idea and makes that abstract thought a reality by drawing together all of necessary elements to make it work.

The investor will go for the entrepreneur, never the worker.

No two entrepreneurs are the same, nor do they always succeed as I have found to my cost, but they always have the creative spirit in common.

Of all the ventures I outline here, it's appropriate and humbling to start with an unsuccessful one. Working with a second partner, Kilcullen invested a large amount of cash in a project that we never thought would go so wrong – but it did and it was a total write-off. And while I accept the responsibility for supporting the investment decision, it is a good example of a mistake I made in giving too much trust at too early a stage.

AlbumCity

In 2000, Jack Schrantz made contact with us looking for an investment in his Internet company. A former investor with the Austrian Raiffeisen Bank in Prague, Jack was in his early thirties and had a reputation for being a very intelligent individual. I had also met him socially and he was a good person to be with for a beer and some craic.

One example of Jack's reputation had come from a little addition and subtraction he did for Komercni Banka in 1998. He had put all of the bank's assets onto one giant spreadsheet and concluded that KB wasn't actually worth anything. He then won a stock picker's award because of this and ended up on the front cover of an influential Czech magazine.

Of greater interest to us was his Internet retail venture AlbumCity that he had started in 1999. AlbumCity was something of an eastern European Amazon.com, except that it just sold CDs and DVDs. Retailing was still somewhat inefficient and fragmented in the ex-communist bloc and there were no music stores that could supply the same selection that Jack could at as low a price.

Despite this, investors were wary of supporting online business-to-customer initiatives because of the lack of Internet access and scarcity of credit cards in the Czech market. However, Jack was succeeding for two reasons. First most of his customers were going online in their workplace or in college and second they didn't need a credit card because he operated a cash-on-delivery system instead.

It was a classic example of how market statistics belied the latent opportunity.

When Jack approached us, he needed money to expand his business into other eastern and central European countries. By then the company had been running for eighteen months and was already profitable, making it an instantly attractive proposal.

True to his reputation, Jack was a very clever guy, who was also very opinionated. Extremely intense, he was a chain smoking, caffeine addicted workaholic who was up all night, seven days a week. Unfortunately, he tended not to delegate and did not listen to other people.

Though the *I*nternet bubble had not quite burst, I was very wary of having anything to do with this space. However, we invested in the business because his company was presented to us as being cash-flow positive and profitable. It was just a plain, old-fashioned mail order business that was using the Internet, but it worked in the eastern European market and was ready to expand and do the same thing in multiple languages. If it worked, Jack would be able to make use of the greater purchasing volume (he was buying in bulk from the US) to reduce prices and increase profits at the same time.

We put in our money – and we watched it all go downhill.

First Jack's advisers, and Kilcullen's then American investment executive, got involved in a structuring that cost another $40,000 and was almost completely premature. They designed it like a multimillion dollar corporation with warrants, different share classes, and a Delaware US offshore structure to beat the band, causing huge delays and distractions.

It took several months and instead of expanding the actual business, the money was blown on lawyers and registration fees. It was almost fraud insofar as the money went to pay off debts and closing down an office in Poland and not into developing the enterprise from a commercial point of view, as had been intended. In short, much of our finance was completely wasted with nothing to show for it, and we didn't know about it until after.

However, the fatal mistake was Jack's decision to close down the Czech AlbumCity site while his expanded international site was still being developed. In terms of business survivability, he might as well have got into a warm bath and opened his veins because, at one stroke, he lost the cash flow and customers required to keep the venture ticking over.

He made this decision without consulting us. Had we known his intentions, we never would have allowed it.

To cap it all, the international site never worked properly and while we were hanging on and hanging on for it to get up and running, the business ran out of cash. More investors came in after us, also believing in the business, and sadly also lost everything. In the end, another investor was supposed to come in but never materialised and, faced with Jack's idiosyncratic business style, we decided to pull the plug on our involvement.

The concept of AlbumCity was right, but Jack's intensity combined with his unwillingness to listen to advice made him the wrong choice to manage it. Because he wouldn't delegate, it was impossible to build up a good management team around him, subsequently making the entire operation dependent on one man. Jack would smoke, drink coffee and work all night – and sometimes all day such was his commitment – but he got so absorbed in his idea that he became a know-all and impossible to work with.

As stated before, you back the entrepreneur – but the entrepreneur also has to respect the person who provides the finance, and to a certain extent we felt that Jack had betrayed our trust. Not deliberately, he didn't abuse or steal from the company or anything of that nature, but he got so buried down in detail that the rest of the world passed him by.

Unfortunately, when trust is breached in business, it's time to get up and get out because at this level investing becomes very personal. While Jack gave it his all and more, there was etiquette to be observed. A polite communication along the lines of 'Sorry Enda, we lost all your money but did our best', would have gone a long way.

Key 6 Business Solutions

After starting with a bad one, I'll move on to a good one. Key 6 is a success story. To date, it operates in two countries and enjoys success principally through the commitment of managing director James McCollum. A Bangor man in his mid-thirties, James and I first met socially and subsequently found ourselves with mutually beneficial goals. I was looking for a serious focus for an odds and sods entity called Key 6, while James wanted to run his own recruitment agency.

Key 6 had not begun as a recruitment firm. In fact it had been formed to take on bits and pieces of activity that no longer fit into any of my other companies after the restructure. This left it with an eclectic mix, amongst which were an agency for telecoms' billing software, a rock concert and market research, support and incubation for new companies entering the Czech market.

Probably the strongest focus of Key 6 was the name under which it operated. Key 6 had been manufactured from a desire to create a logo using 'strong' letters and symbols. The inspiration had been Kodak, a word that was created purely to use the strong 'K'. Kodak itself meant nothing, although now it is one of the most identifiable brands worldwide.

In Key 6, we had the strong K followed by a numeral phonetically similar to 'sex', which gave added impact (X is also a strong letter). Branding was also a consideration in the logo development as the domain Key6.com was available while K6.com was not.

Well for an eclectic mix, you need a capable personality, and Key 6 was managed by the uniquely entrepreneurial Hana Svehlakova, a Czech lady with a wonderful spark to her. Hana and I first met when she was a waitress in the Barok Café and I instantly knew that she was somebody above the ordinary. As it transpired, the waitressing was a money job she'd taken to pay off debts from a business that had gone wrong (her partners had jumped ship and left her 'holding the baby' so to speak). Prior to that she lived in Belfast where she'd worked briefly as an au pair amongst other things.

The undisputed highlight of Hana's tenure at Key 6 was the organisation of the Saw Doctors concert in Prague, a project done on a budget of about €35,000 and undertaken to please a very important client of Aspekt and Globix. The client was Klaus Tebbe, a very clever and hard-working German who set up the Czech Republic's second mobile phone company Paegas, now called T-Mobil. Klaus was sponsoring important marketing events and opportunities that we put his way, but rarely came to Prague so we were having trouble building a proper relationship with him.

That was until we talked about Galway and the Saw Doctors.

His eyes lit up. 'Enda, the Saw Doctors? Get them here and I vil pay!'

Klaus loved them. The Saw Doctors had been a big hit in Ireland when he visited in the early 1990s and their music brought back fond memories. We organised their gig and about 350 people came to it, including a busload of Germans. From the publicity viewpoint, it was a great success. T-Mobil got a lot of television exposure, including a spot on the Nova breakfast television channel and a prime-time chat show in the evening.

However, despite the fun of hosting so many diverse events, it had become necessary to give Key 6 a more definite role if it was going to last as a viable commercial entity. A strong brand was undoubtedly useful but a sustainable business exists through the provision of a primary product and/or service. Key 6 had neither.

When James McCollum came in for thirty per cent of the business, he focused Key 6 sharply as a recruitment firm with a complimentary list of other HR services, a concept that meshed well with the company's previous market activities. Furthermore, he developed the existing brand to encompass the new focus. The Key 6 logo now defines the six key secrets to successful recruitment for both companies and prospective employees.

Key 6's clients are now high-end companies in the financial services sector, often multinationals based in central Europe. Although James wasn't the first to the market, what was attractive about his firm was his unique approach to the business. He developed a more analytical selection procedure, which contrasted favourably with the more regular business models.

Many recruitment companies place people on a success basis, while others operate as head hunters who get a fee and are paid in stages. The problem is that when someone is hiring they get the right candidate fifty-seven per cent of the time, which is not much better than tossing a coin. That's a disturbing thought when you consider how much damage the wrong employee can do in the wrong place, and an unacceptable one when there are now so many methods for screening and testing candidates.

For these reasons, James' plans for Key 6 made the initiative instantly attractive. In addition, our impressions of James were very good. He combined local and international knowledge in a 'think local/act global' style that instantly found favour with me. He knew the recruitment business, was a dedicated professional, was a good manager of people and had a focus on training and quality of service.

Most importantly, James was an entrepreneur who had a firm grasp of what the business should be and where it should go. There was no ambiguity in what had to be done, or how.

Subsequently, we put in an investment of €100,000, being €60,000 in cash and the remainder in kind, such as office space and the like. The business is relatively small but very successful, and at the time of writing is generating profits and expanding.

Although our investment was relatively modest, I believe that Key 6 is going to do millions of euro in business relatively soon. James has great ambitions to expand the empire and I firmly believe he will do so. Needless to say, as chairman of the board I'm very comfortable with that.

Simply

Our mortgage business, led by Jan Urban, was a venture that happened by osmosis rather than any straightforward contacts, but again it was an investment based on the right plan/ right person scenario.

One spin-off from the creation of the Czech Credit Bureau was making contact with Jan Urban, then an executive with the Czech company Profira. Ironically, Profira were in competition with us to secure the agreement of the Czech banks, but if they had realised how advanced we were in the game they never would have gone against us. Unfortunately for them, we hadn't generated much publicity, but we were already well in with the Czech banks and there was only room for one operator.

Jan was one of the three founders of Profira and had a sizeable share ownership in the business. A young, ambitious, well-educated Czech, he had put himself through Harvard University and qualified as a lawyer, and was trained by White and Case and then McKinsey. He had an excellent attitude and personality and when Profira finished, I reckoned he was looking for something to do.

As it was, I had an idea ready which had come from three separate incidents. First I'd read an article about a mortgage broking business being sold for £100 million in the UK, which got me thinking, 'I'll have one of those, please!'

Shortly after I was listening to a talk by Ceská Sporitelna's own Jack Stack. Jack mentioned that for every €10 they had on deposit there was only €3 on loan, which was something they needed to change. The banks wanted to lend – they needed to lend because that was their business – but were very inefficient at doing it.

The third incident occurred when one of my managing directors was told that he needed to take ten days holidays to organise his mortgage. Between those three things it was clear that an opportunity was waiting for whoever wanted it.

I've been most successful by having ideas with other people, sharing the ownership and helping them to execute the plans, and for this business I immediately thought of Jan. In 2001 we met and had a brainstorming session on how a mortgage business could be put together and when we finished we were both committed to the project.

Since we didn't have an in-depth knowledge of the mortgage business, we cast our net for somebody who did. Naturally there were lots of mortgage and mortgage-broking companies in the UK and Germany, but because they were large organisations, it was difficult for smaller operators such as ourselves to approach them and be taken seriously.

Luckily, through David Beattie, I already knew an excellent broker called Peter Bastable.

In 1998 I was trying to buy a large Georgian house that I intended to convert into offices. I already had a tenant who was willing to use it as a business premises while we waited for our planning permission (only a matter of time since the area was already zoned for commercial use) and whose payments would comfortably cover the mortgage. Unfortunately, I had no spare cash at the time and my bank turned me down.

However, by presenting the same information in a different way and talking to risk managers in a different way, in addition to leveraging other assets that were available, Peter got me 100 per cent finance. With that finance I bought the building for €580,000. Seven years later, it was worth over €1,250,000 and had cost me nothing.

Peter Bastable made this happen, so when I looked around to get some expertise in starting a mortgage company, he was the obvious choice.

While Peter had not in his wildest dreams any plans to start a business in the Czech Republic, he had recently started his own venture called Simply Mortgages in Ireland. Simply was growing rapidly and needed investment, making it a perfect partner for our Czech interest and so we did a deal. My fund put in €165,000 for ten per cent of the Irish business and, in turn, gave the Irish business twenty per cent of the Czech start-up for €40,000 worth of consultancy.

We took everything from scratch, including test marketing many names, and in the end we decided to give the Czech firm the same name as its Irish counterpart. In the Czech Republic, Simply is instantly identifiable as an English word. Foreign, better by implication, and easy to translate.

We started Simply with capital and kind of only €200,000, including the €40,000 of consultancy from Peter's firm. Jan earned ten per cent of the business in the first year, another ten per cent in the second year and is still earning more shares. Two more people, Ewan Gibb and Jonathan Wilkinson, then joined the team, bringing with them €250,000 additional cash and more valuable experience. Such is the strength of the relationship, that Ewan has now joined Kilcullen Kapital Partners as a full partner and shareholder.

To our credit, Simply became the first full-service mortgage broker in the Czech Republic, dealing with commercial and residential mortgages for both nationals and non-nationals. It is also developing its own products and a mortgage fund for non-standard and sub-prime lending, bringing us further up the food chain. Although Simply started modestly with three people, I believe that Jan is exactly the right entrepreneur to make it into a multimillion euro company with hundreds of employees. By 2004, the company had over twenty staff and almost as many more in ten franchise offices around the country. For expansion, we are looking at Slovakia and then perhaps even Austria (we regard it as sleepy and uncompetitive), followed by other countries in the region.

Zoom Airways

It's probably true when they say that a good way to become a millionaire is to start in the airline business with a billion!

However, we did get into the airline business and actually made a profit from our investment. It could have been a much bigger and riskier enterprise but we got out and, in many respects, I am happy about that. People have delusions of grandeur when it comes to the aviation industry because it's one of those massive, tycoon-type things, but in reality it's a sector in flux with a lot of downward pressures.

Still, getting involved with an airline was a great, big, fascinating adventure. We flew around the place talking to potential partners and companies that dealt with aircraft leasing, airports, booking engines, pilots and so forth and, needless to say, I learned a lot about the industry. However, despite the grandiose aspects, the catalyst for the project actually came from a very mundane source.

That source was the hassle that Michal Pozar faced whenever he travelled to and from the Czech town of Brno on business. Anytime he had to get a flight, he was forced to drive all the way to Prague, around the city to the airport at the other side, fly to Germany and make his connections there.

He was fed up with it, and so were a lot of other people. Brno had a population of 600,000 people, while the greater Moravia area held 1.7 million. From these two facts, Michal concluded that an airline operating out of Brno made a lot of sense and, in 2002, brought the business plan to us.

When we met, Michal was in his late twenties with a consultant's position on his CV. Of course as soon as I heard that, the old 'those who can't do, teach' line came to mind and the first words out of my mouth to him were, 'I don't like management consultants.'

But Michal was not in that category. He had put himself through university in Chicago and had then set up his own company and sold it. Overall, he was a very motivated and competent person. Very unusual for a consultant in fact...

The business plan that Michal had given us was also the most impressive proposal that I had ever seen in terms of its research, especially for the lateral thinking it displayed. He had walked around the car parks at Prague airport and counted the car registrations to determine who was travelling and from where they had driven. Then he'd talked to travel agencies and got more of the information that was directly relevant to the proposal.

As soon as I saw the plan, I made a comparison between the Czech market and the market in Ireland and immediately recognised the potential. The size of Brno and the population of the surrounding region made the market much larger than the Irish south-west, yet it had no regional flight service.

His market argument was very strong and when that was placed alongside Michal's strength as an entrepreneur we decided to back him and his plan for what he called Trenk Airways, a name that didn't initially grab us.

There was some discussion over a better name, and for a time we had contemplated calling it Pozar Airways after Michal, however since pozar is the Czech for 'danger', we decided that it might not be the most appropriate.

In the end we gave the company the name Zoom.

Before I go on, I should outline three core sectors of the airline industry – flag carriers, low-cost and regional. The flag carriers such as Delta, British Airways, Air France and so forth have a very, *very* bad track record on investment return. On the other hand, low costs such as Ryanair, EasyJet in Europe and Southwest Airlines in the US, the original pathfinder, are expanding rapidly.

The final category, regional airlines, feeds the hubs and low-cost operators who need volume. Generally operating in smaller airports in 40–100 seat aircraft, they form local monopolies and it is not economic for the low-cost operators to compete against them, and certainly not for the flag carriers.

On doing research in the US, we learned that the regional airlines were the fastest growing and most profitable, and we decided that the same would happen in Europe. There would be consolidation and early-stage operators such as ourselves would be bought out, exactly the same objective as we'd had in the development of Globix.

Based on that, we looked around for a strategic partner to work with. Although this tactic can reduce your scope for manoeuvre later on in a project, it does lessen the risk hugely, and that was an important factor in our aviation venture. Like our success in starting the mortgage business, we started casting our net around to either pick the brains of, or partner with, somebody who was already doing it successfully.

Pádraig Ó Ceidigh of Aer Arann was the obvious choice. A man who'd spent his early days as a schoolteacher in my alma mater, Coláiste Ionaid, in Galway, Pádraig took an accounting and then a law degree before taking leave from his teaching and turning a small island hopping service in the west of Ireland into a successful regional airline.

A natural entrepreneur (in 2003 he was awarded the title of Irish Entrepreneur of the Year), Pádraig is open and receptive. In the end, because of the distance from and the growth of his existing business, Zoom was not a project for him. However, he gave us good support to the project and was very helpful to Michal, which was tremendously appreciated.

In the meantime, other regional airlines were expressing strong interest in becoming involved, however Denim Air in Eindhoven – who we originally talked to as a company to lease us aircraft – was the keenest.

Denim Air was originally started by a bunch of Dutch guys who all wore jeans and flew between Eindhoven and Stanstead. After heavy competition from low-cost carriers, they decided to refocus the company, terminate the scheduled service and lease their aircraft and crews to other airlines. This strategy proved highly successful and the company grew enormously.

It was a strange experience talking with Leen P. Jansson, CEO and owner of Denim. An industry veteran who came out of retirement to take over Denim, we eventually fell out.

Whether it was him, us, or a generation gap that was to blame, I'm not sure. Whatever happened, we did not make a comfortable team.

Then, just as we had concluded trial flights between our Czech airports and were close to doing a deal, our involvement ended as quickly as it had begun. Michal had met with the managing director of Czech Airlines and CSA's MD was so impressed with Michal's plans and knowledge of the industry that he offered Michal a seat on the board of Czech Airlines and one of the top management positions – not bad for a thirty year old.

Czech Airlines took over the project and the subsequent deal, the details of which I can't disclose, got us a good return on our investment and took us entirely out of the picture. It was an exciting and short-lived adventure, and a profitable one at that.

Since then Kilcullen has been involved in several other early stage enterprises and I'm very happy to say that the transition from entrepreneur to investor has been a satisfying one. However – having had the opportunity to both make and lose money – I've had my fill of small early stage enterprises to an extent. You cannot half-do it. It must be a full, hands-on commitment.

As the size of the investment grows I am reminded of the words of Howard Kilroy again. 'The fundamentals stay the same, you just add more zeroes.'

Implicit in Kilroy's remark is the concept of scale. You take a bigger view, hire better professionals, use more resources, do better quality research. You have to add more zeroes to your costs as well – not wastefully of course – but commensurate with the project at hand.

I like to think that I'm doing well adding zeroes, such as our €100 million renewable energy Enercap fund, now merging with our Capital Elements fund for even greater scale.

Mind you, to be clear, all these zeros are not mine – its money that investors have entrusted in an enterprise we created on their behalf. The only way we can make money is if the investors make money – and that suits them just fine.

Leverage is also a constant in the equation. You add more zeroes to your loans too, as commerce thrives on cheap, available debt. We certainly did. With increased respectability from our growing business, plus an ability to borrow from the banks we were able to achieve major acquisitions using leverage – in some cases up to 100 per cent, using agreements where the shareholder's loaned back a part of the purchase price.

This was a great deal for both parties. For the shareholders, they could unlock the value of their company, get a good price, and keep a small shareholding as security for their loan. What Kilcullen got was the company at 100 per cent finance, plus the security of a gradual transition period, as the sellers remain involved for the duration of their minority shareholding. While this 'high leverage' approach was a surprise to some, the debt can be handled well by the company. One reason is that the ability to write off bank interest can sometimes be more tax efficient than paying cash.

The downside of this available debt, as can be viewed in a dramatic way at the time of writing this updated version, is when things go wrong the further you can fall – as many respectable Western banks found to their cost. It came from the slump in US property and the disconnection between the end customer and the final product, e.g. exotic financial instruments based on poor quality assets. Several banks that were heavily exposed in this area have since collapsed. The credit lines we enjoyed before are now temporarily gone, but fortunately our investments were good and based on acquisitions whose products and services we thoroughly understood – unlike sub prime mortgage debt where the risk was sliced, diced and repackaged into synthetic forms where the final investors could not see the risk for what it really was.

What I would say about this downfall is that it shows that everything in life is dynamic, we never know what is around the corner and the only certain thing about change is change itself. The change for Kilcullen, and myself, was coming from the service sector and moving into industry and manufacturing. This has been a good experience for us, and also a challenging one. We worked with companies that had to change, compete intensely and develop, often in a very short time. In some cases we unfortunately had to shed local jobs in favour of cheaper Chinese labour – however the alternative was complete closure and no jobs at all.

Specific acquisitions facilitated by Kilcullen included ZPA (with over 200 employees) now renamed ZPA Smart Energy and a manufacturer of energy meters, TNS Servic (over 300 employees) in the automotive parts industry, and TESLA, the once famous Czech company which had 300,000 employees in its day (now only 400). Other opportunities for us included ABN AMRO's Czech asset management business that has over €200 million under management. It's now part of the Atlantic FC Group where it has a bright future.

Several of the companies we bought had many different assets, not all of which were natural partners. For example, when we acquired ZPA in Trutnov we ended up restructuring it into four companies – the lead being ZPA Smart Energy. It also brought us into contact with a wonderful group of committed people including Jarsolav Jirman, Michal Mika, Josef Krepinsky, Zdenek Stuhlik and Tim Smith, just to mention some of the great team there.

Working with this team our strategy has been to transform it from a traditional electricity meter manufacturer to a world class Energy Management Solutions provider. One was a Trutnov-based company, the other is a company that happens to be based in Trutnov. Do you understand the difference? It's about thinking local, but acting global.

At TNS Servic we were fortunate to find a company that already had a great leader and entrepreneur present. Jiri Rasner built this auto parts manufacturer from almost nothing to a €20 million company together with Jiri Vasku and Jiri Klauda – whose son, also called Jiri, is now taking over the business.

With a flexible Czech workforce and a great team it is our hope to add value to this company, maintain it as an important part of the local community and develop it for the future.

And finally, one of our most exciting opportunities was the acquisition of TESLA. Besides owning the famous TESLA brand in many countries around the world, the company has considerable property holdings that we intend to develop. Under its young Chief Executive Martin Statnik there is a new dynamic to the company. Again, it will be split into separate divisions with management teams who will enjoy more empowerment and greater focus in their specific business. Ranging from water purification systems and medical devices to communications equipment for the military, the company has enormous talent, ability and potential, and is right at the cutting edge of many growth sectors.

There is one common denominator that runs through it all, as highlighted in many ways in this book, and that is to have flexibility, an open mind and the ability and willingness to move. All Kilcullen really do is work with the best people we can find, to unleash human energy and to foster a dynamic approach to business. I'm proud to have attracted a group of people whom I respect and admire to work with Kilcullen Kapital Partners. Getting the right people in the right roles allows us to make profits for the shareholders and to keep putting something back into the community.

Oddly enough there are times when being just 'an investor' is frustrating, as you miss the opportunity to be hands on. It's ironic, because there were plenty of times when I was working flat out that I dreamed of having a more passive existence. Of course, as soon as I was able to make that a reality, I began to hunger for the creativity of making something work from scratch!

The answer was evident. I found a new purpose – one that combined my investing skills yet still offered the thrill and excitement of creating something new – by putting something back into the community. The new mission was assisting Ireland's entry to the 2008-09 Volvo Ocean Race, which was tremendously challenging in terms of time commitments and effort, but was also a hugely rewarding experience.

But now, finally and in conclusion...

Chapter nineteen

Finally, and in conclusion

I take this final chapter name from Barry Desmond's excellent political biography. For years a prominent politician at local, national and European level, Barry's book is a great read. I admire him and consider his views a good lesson in smoked salmon socialism. He confessed to me one day that he was embarrassed to have accumulated eleven different pensions!

Most recently I had contact with Barry in drafting the restructure of the Maritime Institute of Ireland, another organisation locked in a time warp – more obsessed with keeping an old church going with a mostly amateur collection of historical junk than actually executing what its name, its founders and articles of association aspire to.

Anyway, in my view most times incremental change can be painful and, like extracting a bad tooth a little bit every day, needlessly time consuming. Sometimes for real entrepreneurial change I believe you have to have the courage to just get on with it and yank the bad tooth out.

Basically you've two choices – you can wake up every day and do the same old thing or wake up and try something new. Some people are happy to wake up and go through life attending to their immediate needs, such as looking after their family, going to their job and paying off their mortgage. This is good and admirable.

Other people, in addition to doing the above as basic essentials, want to live a more creative and active life, and will make and lose money constantly in the pursuit of their passions.

I'm just a person who's in the second category. Neither group is better than the other; it's simply like putting clay into a jar of water and shaking it up. The pebbles go to the bottom, the sediment settles on top and the rest goes into layers in between. No matter how you shake that jar, the outcome will be the same.

The real question is finding out which layer you belong to. Life itself is not like the jar full of clay and water and our society is not a total meritocracy where everyone receives the position and respect they deserve. We are blocked because we are not 'in the know', or because we face corruption and prejudice, or we have the misfortune to suffer an injury, or because simple inefficiency and wastefulness destroys otherwise viable opportunities. I do not cast judgement or dare suggest how others should live their lives.

Either way, there are a lot of obstacles on the path and most of the time you have to fight for what you want. To win that fight, you must believe in yourself, and for a lot of people the struggle for self-confidence is the hardest fight that they'll ever have. But once you get there, once you accept that you have the ability, then you will succeed. Just allow your passion for whatever it is that you want to do to take over. It really is that simple.

For example if you have ten people who are equally artistic, which of those ten will succeed as artists?

Those who make the commitment to becoming one. They are the people who say to themselves, 'I don't care what anyone else says or thinks, I want to become an artist.' The fact of the matter is that for every single person who tries, they are several who either don't try or try and subsequently give up, for whatever reason.

Therefore, if you stick with it, you'll have already put yourself into the minority of winners. Naturally, there's competition between winners, and there can only be a single richest person, fastest runner, most prolific author, but so what? The most important thing in any life is for it to be lived. Do your best and you'll never regret it, regardless of where you ranked.

However, if you don't make the effort, or if you give up when things get tough, you'll never rank at all. In anything you do. It sounds harsh but that's the truth.

While the foundation of success is fundamentally a belief in oneself combined with a determination to succeed, the actual path to success is a tough pilgrimage. The road to the top is hard and lonely, you'll be making your mistakes and suffering failures – that much is assured – and you'll be learning as you go. Entrepreneurship is by its very nature a personal thing and there is no way to standardise and package the knowledge, which is why it's impossible to teach with any guarantee of success. It's impossible to give a 'get rich quick' formula to the masses.

Entrepreneurs are the singular few who have worked out ways to get above the crowd. If the entire crowd moves up a level, then there are no entrepreneurs. There's only the crowd.

The California Gold Rush is a perfect example. The masses went to dig gold out of the ground for themselves, and in truth they were averaging about $25 a day. Unfortunately, they had to pay $5 for a meal, maybe even $1 for an egg, and exorbitant prices for all the other basics, every day.

The result? Most of the prospectors made no money. Those who made the real money were the people who sold the eggs, picks, gin, clothes, etc.

The moral of this tale is that the entrepreneur is the one who has the imagination, originality and creative ability to think of a way to do something differently to everybody else, and you can't teach someone how to do that because once it becomes common knowledge, it's no longer original.

However, there are fundamentals to be observed, and that much can be taught to entrepreneurs. Some of these fundamentals are personal, some are practical, and I like to think that a lot of these things can be applied to other aspects of our lives as well. I've split them into two groups, the first being more general and the second being more specific.

1. General

Honesty

Here I have no claim to perfection, but I try. Honesty and integrity come first because so many other things spring from it. Before anything else, you have to be honest with yourself, and that means confronting all kinds of painful stuff. That you're wrong. That you've hurt somebody else. That you're acting for the sake of your pride. That you're generally making a balls of something and you should let someone else take over.

None of us like to face these things, but it has to be done because if you are not honest with yourself, you simply cannot find your path through life. Many of us succumb to peer pressure regarding who we should be or how we should live, but ultimately it's that fear that holds us back. Stop caring so much about what others think and ask yourself what you really want.

If you can't be honest with yourself, it's going to be very hard to be honest with anyone else, and then you'll find that nobody of any calibre will deal with you. In business, that means you'll have no investors, partners, employees or customers. Nothing. However, the reverse is also true. If you are honest and open, you'll build a reputation for that and people of a similar nature will interact with you.

Salespeople in particular are very likely to be dishonest in describing their products in order to make a sale. That's short-term thinking. A golden rule in any sales team I have run is that under no circumstances should salespeople tell a lie – put the best side forward, yes, but not to lie. In the end honesty and integrity always comes out top of the heap.

Besides good liars need good memories and I am forgetful...

Trust

Closely related to honesty, but having one important difference. Honesty is a thing, trust is a process. Trust is earned over a period of time where you convince somebody that they can rely upon you. Like any process, if it fails once, it will go through a period of examination and possibly disposal, so make sure that you keep your promises whenever you give them. Unfortunately I have been in situations where trust has been lost and I can tell you that it's tough in business when this happens and even tougher in personal life. Often it's lost through a misunderstanding between people of each other's position and needs.

While an absence of trust incurs the same kind of problems that come with a lack of honesty, the benefits of trust cannot be underestimated. Trust is what makes a customer buy from you in the first place, and return to you in the second place. Trust is what keeps your employees from walking out the door at the first sign of trouble. Trust is what keeps a partnership steady.

In fact, trust itself is a commodity. If you get a good service or product, one that doesn't let you down, you're inclined to pay more for it, so in that regard trust is synonymous with quality.

Learn to listen

This is again related to honesty, because in listening to other people there is the tacit understanding that you don't know everything. However, people often fail to listen because they are too caught up in other stuff, because they have things on their mind or because they are otherwise distracted. But because it's so easy not to listen, there is something of an art in learning to listen.

Listening is absolutely vital if you want to become a success at anything. The ability to listen is the ability to have meaningful conversation, to learn new things, to take advice, conduct research and find new business.

No matter what venture you get started in, chances are ninety per cent of the experience has been encountered before by other people who have tried the same thing. These people are a valuable source of information and many of them will be happy to help a newcomer. By listening to them you will avoid making common mistakes and you'll save yourself a lot of hassle.

The one other important thing is listening to yourself and, in particular, to your gut reaction. If you don't feel right about something, then don't do it. Chances are, no matter how it turns out, it wasn't for you. And that's nothing to be ashamed of. On the other hand, if you really feel good about something, you should explore it and satisfy your curiosity. It could turn out to be the best thing that ever happened to you.

Be a people person

Understanding people is vital if you wish them to support you in a project. Honesty and trust go a long way, but it's also good to know how to reward somebody who's been doing a good job, or know which buttons to press to motivate them, or get them thinking or co-operating.

Equally important is to understand which people to avoid, either because they're simply crooks or because there will be a character clash. Whichever it is, you probably won't have a very productive relationship with such a person. Its also useful to know who you can afford to get mad with and when or if to get mad in the first place.

The best way to understand people is to become a people person, and to spend time around others. You'll learn to read the vibes and understand the hidden signals. That in itself is nothing new, everybody does it. The hard part is being able to refine our abilities to the point where we can make a judgement about somebody within a short space of time, be it an interview, introduction or presentation.

The other aspect of being a people person is that you will meet a tremendous amount of very different characters from all walks of life. Some of these people might be in a position to help you in the future, whilst you might also be in a position to help them. That's the basis of networking, but remember that you should be meeting people in the right context, and that context should be to engage in common experiences or activities and have fun doing it.

Go out, join clubs, get involved with groups who enjoy doing the same things that you do. Then try a few that you've never thought of before. Do all these things and you'll be learning about people and networking at the same time.

2. Specific

If there's a market, there's a way.

If there is a genuine need for something out there and you can provide it, then people will pay you money for it. That part is not complicated. What is complicated is working out whether the market is actually worth pursuing, and that means sitting down and doing some rough figures to find out what type of margins you can make.

Now while I recommend picking a venture on the basis of returns, it's also fair to say that any involvement in business is a learning experience, and even if you start small it can be a springboard to higher things. Some of the greatest business people in the world started out with humble ventures.

So if you really believe you can make money from a venture, go and do it. That's what business is all about.

Pick ventures on the basis of returns

If you've always wanted to run a yachting magazine because that was your passion, then by all means do it. But if you always wanted to make big money, then you've got to separate your personal and commercial interests, otherwise you are in danger of doing neither one properly. You may know an awful lot about a particular industry or market, but that doesn't mean to say that there's any money in it.

I learned this the hard way when I worked intensely for several years building a boat magazine in a very small market. It was my sport, it was my passion and I made it a success. However it was tough and was not unlike extracting water from a stone.

The best way to make money is to be the first to the market with a new service or product. Competition is guaranteed to follow, but if you've established yourself correctly you'll have grabbed all the best customers. Keep moving upwards and onwards to the big deals.

Research

Always, always find out as much as you can about what you are putting your money into. You may find that the rapid burst of enthusiasm you've had may dry up once you begin to get a rounded image of what's ahead, or you may find that you really have struck gold with your business idea. Either way, there will be critical questions to be asked which can only be satisfied with decent research.

What are the long-term trends in the market? What has been the experience of others who have tried the same venture? How many competitors do you face? Are costs likely to rise or fall, and if so how long before they do? Are there any other outside factors that might have a bearing on your business?

Whenever you have a business idea that looks lucrative, research it. On one hand, your research might tell you that it's a false lead whereupon you'll have saved yourself a lot of money, time and effort. On the other hand, you might find that it's the opportunity you've been waiting for. Only your research will confirm it either way.

Many of us end up in jobs or industry more by accident than design. My core background was publishing, which was a static and declining market. But when I learned that telecoms were a high growth area (at that time) I put in the research and got straight in to where the real action was.

That's why knowledge is the most valuable commodity of all.

Calculate risk

When you are examining your market opportunity, there's more to be considered than just profit and loss. Risk management plays an important role. No matter what project you start with, there'll always be an element of having to 'make do' with some aspect of the business because you'll be operating off limited resources. Risk management comes in when you have to decide where you're going to make your trade-offs. Will it be second-hand equipment? Will it be less-than-auspicious premises? Will it be a drop in family income while you're getting started? How long before others enter the market?

There's risk involved in all of these decisions, and while the risks often can't be avoided (hit and miss, that's entrepreneurship!), at least if you understand the risks you gain a vital overall image of what you're dealing with – and if it's worth dealing with at all.

Real entrepreneurship is not about taking chances, it's about understanding the risks and minimising them.

Get the right employees

If you're thinking of hiring poor quality staff, don't. The right employees, when properly led and rewarded, will form the powerhouse of your enterprise. They will bring expertise that you lack, they will form a team for idea generation, they will buy and sell for you, they are the ones your customers will deal with, they are the ones who will keep your promises – and some day they may run the company, leaving you free for your next venture.

If none of those things convince you, just imagine how much damage the wrong employee could do to your company.

Convinced now?

Be image conscious

Business craves stability and low risk, and therefore will shy away from anything that gives a contrary appearance. Most business will avoid involvement with a terminally ill supplier, a shaky partner or a fragile start-up if they have better options. As the entrepreneur attempting to build a business, you've got to win the trust of clients and employees and convince them that you can follow through.

The right image assists in the building of trust. Because everybody's time is limited, decisions are often made on the scantiest of impressions. That's why you must take special care to project a professional and competent image at all times and to everybody.

Follow the tips in this book, and you'll be halfway there. The rest isn't that hard. Simply believe in yourself and believe in what you are offering and your conviction will carry it through. Remember, the very act of attempting to look professional makes you a professional, so it's a positive circle. Work on it and you'll quickly become more self-assured.

Build relationships with customers (and partners too)

Anything to do with your customers takes precedence over everything else. If you have no customers, you have no business. Customers are your ultimate goal and your lifeblood. Every single one of the efforts that you make to establish your business, be it in your employees, calculation of risk, image, the development of the product or service, is geared toward the accumulation of customers.

When dealing with customers, from the very first sales pitch onwards, you are building a relationship of trust. Be honest, be helpful and listen. If you do so you will be given a fair chance, and assuming that your business is offering the right product or service at the right price, you'll win customers. Never let them down and always give them what they want. That's what you're there for.

A lot of this also applies to your dealings with your business partners. You must build a relationship of trust with them and be frank in your dealings.

Beyond these simple maxims, there is one more topic I wish to discuss in some detail. I believe the subject matter is almost as important to entrepreneurship as the availability of money itself, and when used correctly is incredibly important to the growth of a successful enterprise, but when used incorrectly can lead to total disaster. The subject is...

...leverage.

Look at the simple illustrations by Conor Lynch below.

The top guy is just digging a hole for himself in pursuit of his goal. The bottom guy has used his brain and is getting on fine.

Essentially, rather than just using your own internal resources to make something happen, try to find external assistance – even if it's just a stick.

Like all forms of power, it's absolutely vital to understand how to create leverage and how to use leverage in the right way – particularly now. Using leverage in the right way can be a fantastic substitute for money. Using leverage in the wrong way is absolutely catastrophic. The widespread use of financial leveraging is at least one of the causes, and possibly the primary cause, of the global recession we are in at the time of writing.

The terms credit and leverage are often used in the same way, but there's a subtle difference, so let me just clarify my terminology before going further.

- Credit is any form of debt.
- Financial leverage is any form of credit used for the purposes of further investing, the proceeds of which should be greater than the cost of the debt. For example, any start up company would be aiming to generate income that would exceed its loan repayments.
- Non-financial leverage (in my own loose terms) is to use available resources to magnify your own efforts far beyond what you could achieve on your own. This can include using networks, access to assets or the use of relationships that carry credibility, etc.

The latter is by far the most interesting. As I made clear in my earlier discussion on credit bureaux, credit is absolutely vital to the functioning of the modern economy. What I also made clear is that *credit is inextricably linked to risk*. You cannot give credit to a person or project without some knowledge or understanding of the risk attached. Indeed as I pointed out earlier, it was only when civilization learned and understood the concept of risk that we started to advance. Prior to this everyone believed that their success was in the lap of the gods.

Leverage, therefore, is the combination of credit and risk into a simple but incredibly powerful tool. To quote J.P. Morgan again, 'Banking is not about money, it's about information.'

Earlier in the book I gave a simple example of property leverage. Here's another one. Imagine investing €250,000 of your own money, plus another €750,000 of the banks money into an €1,000,000 property, and then selling the asset at a twenty-five per cent market price increase. You would be left with the profit of €250,000 for an investment of €250,000, or a 100 per cent profit.

An example of a *highly leveraged asset* is going down to the bank and convincing them to give you the full €1,000,000 for the same property with no money down, to be secured on your own assets or income and maybe rental as well, possibly on an interest only basis. You fully intend to sell the property when it gains twenty-five per cent whereupon you have made €250,000 on an investment of zero cash, which is quite possible in a growth economy.

The difference between both becomes quite apparent when the economy goes the other way, and asset prices drop by twenty-five per cent.

The asset with the down payment drops in value, but because there was a lump sum invested at the beginning, the property could be sold again at a loss, and you walk away with a hit of €250,000. But at least you walk away, and the damage ends there.

What happens on the highly leveraged asset? There was no equity in the property, so if you sell at a loss, you are still liable for the €250,000 shortfall, which the bank will expect you to honour. This now means you have to raid your other assets and, if they are affected by the same downturn, you're really in trouble.

If you don't, that €250,000 liability will start to move down the line and gobble up all your income until it's paid or you've gone bankrupt (whereupon the loss remains with the bank, threatening the bank's survival). Financially, instead of making a profit, you've gone into reverse – big time...

When this happens on a large scale, as it has done, you have a recession.

That's a simple example of purely financial leverage, but it's a very narrow view of the concept. As an entrepreneur, you can leverage soft assets as well. You can leverage your associations, you can leverage your knowledge, you can even leverage assets that don't belong to you, as long as you have permission.

Take the following three examples that I mentioned earlier in the book.

1) One of the major reasons for the failure of Richard Branson's first trans-Atlantic record attempt was the logistics of refuelling in the mid-Atlantic and the related cost. Since the Irish Naval Service had ships patrolling the Atlantic anyway, I reckoned it would not cost them much and it would be good public relations. Lobbying the then Minister for Defence, Paddy Cooney, on my own reputation would not have been enough. However, I knew Tim Severin, who at that time had a big name in adventure. I leveraged Tim's reputation and invited him to have lunch with the Minister, and the Minister to have lunch with him...I simply turned up on the day as well. It succeeded, and we agreed the refuelling over lunch.

2) The Czech Credit Bureau was a thoroughly leveraged business from its very beginnings. I leveraged the investment and reputation of Trans Union, and I leveraged the software of CRIF. This gave a solid foundation in both investment and infrastructure. However, that alone wasn't

enough, because we still had to attract at least eighty per cent of the Czech banks to come on board. Working within existing structures and management we'd hit a brick wall. However, by persuading the CEO of one of the largest banks to host a breakfast for all the other bank CEOs, we convinced all of them to commit. I leveraged off the status of the largest bank, the status of its CEO and a free meal so to speak. Our Czech Credit Bureau was nothing more than a concept until the banks came on as clients, but the use of hard and soft leverage turned the concept into reality.

3) To get our Volvo Ocean Race stopover and yacht entry, we had to get a critical mass of decision makers together. What we needed was a big bang moment that would get all the key people in the same frame of mind, these being the organisers to bring the race to Ireland, the tourism board to back it and the government to provide seed capital. To do this we leveraged the prestige and status of Bank of Ireland, without actually committing the bank or its Governor to anything, by utilising the boardroom and a good cook for a private dinner, all thanks to Richard Burrows. On my own with Jamie Boag we could not have done it. But the powerful status of the combined group, plus the surroundings and ambience of Bank of Ireland's boardroom, made it happen.

These are all real examples of leverage. However, just like financial leverage, this sort of leverage of soft assets can also have dire consequences that can travel up the food chain. For example, if you misuse status or reputation in the pursuit of your own goals, then you will damage your own reputation in doing so. This is an even worse outcome than loss of money, and something that you cannot easily rebound from. Information travels very fast in our information age, and memories last a long time. Soft leverage is very much about trust, and you cannot abuse it.

To finalise my thoughts on leverage, financial or otherwise, you must understand that leverage is a temporary strategy. It should be used to achieve one goal at a time. You cannot build a long-term business or project on leverage because ultimately you need to cover yourself or pay down debt. If all your assets are highly leveraged, then you have a house of cards, and the failure of one will threaten all. Also, in soft leverage, you cannot keep expecting people to allow you to use and reuse their assets and goodwill. Use leverage to achieve specific goals on the way to sustainability.

The above points are my roundup of specific business and project fundamentals to help get things started. They don't amount to a magic spell, and even if you apply all of them rigorously, you may still fail on the basis of bad luck, market cycles or factors beyond your control. While the lower cost/superior service formula is without doubt the paragon in any area of business, ultimately it falls to the entrepreneur to have the creative ability to make that paragon a reality. How do you actually provide something that nobody else is able to? How can you create a product cheaper than your competitors? How can you deliver a superior service?

The entrepreneur must generally find the answers to these questions not just once, but throughout their entire involvement with a business. Sometimes you might be able to pay for the answers, but other times only the individual's leap of imagination will suffice.

That said, if you apply all of those points to the best of your ability, I guarantee it will improve your chances of success immeasurably. While you may fail once – in fact I should be honest and say you may fail considerably more times than once – if your are honest with yourself and you are prepared to learn from your mistakes, your eventual success is almost guaranteed.

Even when you have the greatest setbacks in trying something new, when your world looks like it's just about to end, I suggest you stand back, put it all into perspective and laugh. It may be all you can do!

Being an entrepreneur is about setbacks. Make no mistake; if it were easy everybody would be at it.

I never cease to be fascinated by the whole process. New ideas, new ways of doing things and new business people hit the market time after time, making things better, making money and moving up the ladder. It's human energy in action and it's like an addiction for some of us. I've often taken on too many different projects at times and have gotten far too busy, but every so often a good business idea comes along that I just can't resist. So I don't!

Ideas are also the lifeblood of the entrepreneur. While original idea generation is a bonus, it is rather the ability to make ideas happen that makes the difference. I find that travel and reading are key ingredients to finding and thinking of new ideas and I have been lucky to be able to spend a lot of time doing both. I have also been blessed with a background of cultural openness.

Entrepreneurs come from all backgrounds, races and nationalities, but I believe being Irish has given me an advantage. We have often been described as a Mediterranean culture stranded in an Anglo-Saxon environment. But the Irish travel well and that allows us to pick up ideas and get the benefit of the doubt.

A few decades ago, those who had not travelled referred to people like me as 'chancers'. Now that word has been replaced by the more fashionable term of 'entrepreneur'. However the fundamentals have not changed. We're still taking chances, or as I would prefer to say now, calculated risks.

The environment for entrepreneurs has been improving constantly, and I believe that more finance and moral support is on the way as we develop a culture that recognises and rewards individual creativity. Good entrepreneurship is the heartbeat of progressive society.

Right now, we are in a change period. Looking back into the twentieth century, capital and labour were split into two groups that viewed each other with mutual distrust and indeed, polarised themselves into totally opposing political schools of thought. One believed that labour was like all other commodities and could be bought and sold, making capital primarily important. Labour believed it could withhold itself and bargain, or if organised properly could even function without capital.

Thankfully, we have moved beyond that adversarial relationship. There's a heap of money available for the right person with the right idea. Capital and labour can be bridged by the entrepreneur and, in fact, both capital and labour need to be bridged by the entrepreneur. This statement may seem a bit outdated in recession periods, when the cheap credit of boom times has dried up and businesses are struggling, but it's not. The fact of the matter is that investors need entrepreneurs to maintain and expand their wealth, governments need entrepreneurs to drive growth and create new jobs, and society needs social entrepreneurs to build a better world.

Not everyone can play this role. Sometimes it is important to stand back. We should lead follow or get out of the way. It's amazing what can be achieved when those involved are not worried about who gets the credit.

Regarding money, while it's necessary to almost everything, I want to be clear on one thing. IT IS NOT the ultimate yardstick of success. Yes, it's a score card. Yes, it's a measure. Yes, it may actually be the end goal for a minority of entrepreneurs, but...

...the ultimate measure of success is your own personal sense of inner achievement and satisfaction, and you may not need much money for that. For most entrepreneurs, the driving force is not money, but freedom, and the accumulation of money is simply a form of self-expression. In fact, I would go so far as to say that almost all entrepreneurs are running 'lifestyle businesses', businesses whose revenue allows the founder to enjoy a particular lifestyle and no more. The scope, extent and level of luxury – if any – of that lifestyle is a completely personal choice.

Personally, I feel that we are all obliged to do what we can to make a better society. Whether this is linked to specific religious belief in a higher power and ultimate judgement on our lives, or simple humanitarian approaches grounded in charity, tolerance and forgiveness, doesn't really matter. Most of us believe that we should at least do no harm, and preferably do some good. I believe that we all have a responsibility to try and make the world a better place if we can. If we can't do this in material contribution, we can at least try with our thoughts and deeds. All the little bits add up.

Also, as I have come to learn, once you have enough money to feed and cloth, it can become fairly meaningless. Handled badly, in particular when other people have the perception that you have much more than you really do is extremely damaging.

Money itself has no intelligence. It is a dead thing. For this reason, love of money is very stupid and destructive. Accumulating money as an end in itself will ultimately lead nowhere.

The only real end is living our lives to the fullest extent of our capabilities and talents and assisting others to do the same.

That means helping artists to be artists, athletes to be athletes, doctors to be doctors, scientists to be scientists and so on, leaving last but not least (because who else will pay for it all and pull it all together), Entrepreneurs to be Entrepreneurs!

P.S. *Just remember that the secret to good navigation is to steer around the rocks. We may be unsinkable, but so was the Titanic – think about it!*

Index

A
Aer Arann 238
Afloat 72-77, 79-82, 125, 138, 149, 181, 193
Against the Gods 101
AlbumCity 230-232
Allied Irish Banks [AIB] 78, 190-191
America [USA] 5, 10, 14-15, 18, 29, 33-34, 37, 54, 67, 69, 74-75, 94, 104-105, 107, 115, 120, 128-129, 132, 134, 139,147, 184-188, 192, 198, 202, 212, 217, 231
Anchor Travel 79
Andrews, David 64
Angling and Shooting 68
Aran islands 37, 57, 63
Archer, Jeffrey 132
Argus Capital Partners 219
Armstong, Wesley 8, 63, 65
Arthur Anderson 151
Aspect 152
Aspekt Kilcullen sro, 155, 157, 161, 167, 176, 179-183, 185-187, 189, 191-192, 194, 196-197, 205, 209, 210, 213, 216, 233
Aspekt Central Group a.s., 181
Austria Telecom 220
Australia 15, 131, 197
Austrian Raiffeisen Bank 230
Austrian Erste Bank 204

B
Bahamas 105, 130-131
Baines, David 79
Bank Austria Creditanstalt 202, 203
Bank Bohemia 144-146
Bank Zachodni 190
Barroilket, Ric 162-163
Barry, Kevin 88, 89
Barry, Norman 67-68,
Bastable,Peter 235-236
Bata, Thomas 134-135
Beattie, David 19-20, 143, 153-154, 205, 235
Bermuda 14, 53, 103, 104, 129
Bernstein, Peter 101
BOC Challenge 14, 100-103
Bord Iascaigh Mhara [BIM] 93
Boston 54, 59, 148
Bourke, John 93-95, 97, 124, 211
Bourke-Kennedy, Des 97
Brannan, Sam 33-34
Branson, Richard 60-63, 65, 253
Breaking the Glass Ceiling 110
Brnak, Radek 210-214, 216-220
Brno 237-238
Broderick, Marian 63
Brodie, Ian 182-183, 185-186
Budapest Business Journal 185
Bukova, Lucie 225
Burke, Brian 131
Business and Finance 131

C
Call the Director 147
Campbell, Bobby
Canada 93-94
Carrickfergus 63
Center for Creative Leadership 110
Central European Business Weekly 182
Central European Media Enterprises 146
Ceská Sporitelna 202-204, 235
Cesky Telecom 160, 180, 194, 208, 213-214, 216
Chuck Feeney 14-15
Churchill, Lord Anthony 132
Citibank 164
Clarke, Biddy 71
Cleggan 45
Clinton, Bill 131-132, 164
Coghlan, Monica 132
Coiste an Asgard 119-121
Cólaiste Iognáid 38
Colorado 110
Connemara 37, 42, 45, 57-59
Construction Industry Federation [CIF] 35
Cooney, Paddy 61, 253
Corinthian RF Club 38
Corrib 37
Coubertain, Pierre de 130
Coveney, Hugh 85
CRIF 198-199, 205, 253
Crubeen 38
CSOB 202-203
Cudmore, Harry 84-85, 93, 94, 98
Cullen, Bill 79
Cusack, Clare 64
Czech Business Journal 183, 185-187, 192, 210
Czech Credit Bureau 126, 197, 199, 202, 204, 206, 234, 253, 254
Czech Republic 126, 134, 143, 146, 148-149, 151-152, 162, 166-167, 175, 177, 181-183, 187-191, 194, 202, 206, 210, 219, 233, 236
Czechoslovakia 134, 136, 140-141, 143, 148-149, 188

D
Data Protection Act 202
Deloitte Touche 22, 23, 151
Denemark, Thomas 197, 206
Denim Air 239
Desmond, Barry 243
Desmond, Dermot 87-92, 97, 150-151, 212
Dix, Robert 19-20, 94
Doyle, Denis 76-77
Doyle, Mary 76-77
Doyle, Tom 105
Dresdner Kleinwort Benson
Private Equity 219
Dublin 26, 31, 35, 61-62, 64, 75-76, 87-88, 92, 98, 103, 107, 132, 150-152, 179, 191, 197, 215
Dublin International Sports 130
Dublin Literary Award 131
Dún Laoghaire 64, 71, 80-81, 86, 103

E
Eindhoven 239
England 69, 94
English, Joe 84
Entrepreneurial Loop 125, 211
ESAT 212
Estonia 192
eTel 219-222
Europe 25, 48, 54, 70, 72, 98, 134, 136, 139-140, 143, 146, 148-149, 151, 153, 160, 170, 177, 181, 187, 190, 192-193, 197-198, 210, 213, 218, 226, 234, 238

F
FitzGerald, Garret 88-89
Florida 17, 104, 105, 107, 112, 129
Forbes, Conal 80
Forbes, Cyril 80
Forsa Cosanta Aitiuil [FCA] 45

G
Galway 14, 16, 20, 22, 24-26, 28-35, 37, 41, 43-44, 46, 50, 54, 59, 79, 120, 179, 233, 238

Galway Chamber of Commerce 35
Galway Oyster Festival 35
Gaughan, Frank 93
GE Capital Bank 202-203
Gemmell, Ed 181
Gherardi, Carlo 199
Gibb, Ewan 222, 236
Globix 26, 208-209, 211, 213,
Green Dragon 16, 24-25, 29, 32
Golden Pages 77, 79
Gore, Al 131
Gould, Terry 93
Greenhill Capital Partners 219
Gunning, Tim 225

H
Hardwicke, David 213
Haughey, Charlie 64-65, 85, 94, 131-134
Haughton, Frank 151
Hawaii 129
Hemmington Scott 152
Henderick, Colm 105
Henderick, Eileen 105
Hickey Boats 35
Holland 211
Holland, Ron 85, 86, 88, 90-93, 95-96
Howell, Larry 198
Howth 64, 91
Huber, Susi 104, 110
Hus, Jan 149
Huurman, Johan 225

I
IMPAC 104-105, 107-109, 112, 114, 128-136, 139-140, 169
Independent News and Media Plc 213
Intel Capital 219
Ireland Fund 131
Ireland Sailing Trust, The 87
Irish Boats and Yachting 67-68, 73
Irish Credit Bureau [ICB] 197-198
Irish Management Institute [IMI] 85, 129
Irish Ocean Youth Club 108
Irish Stock Market 152, 155
Irish Times 103-104, 107
Irish Voice 129
Irwin, Jim 104, 106, 108-109, 115, 128-131, 137, 140, 169, 171 215-223, 233, 238,
Irwin, Linda 105

J
Jansson, Leen P. 239
Jaruzelski, Gen. Wojciech 188
Jefferson Smurfit Corporation 86, 93, 94

K
Kafkova, Daniela 155, 181
Kazakhstan Bank 160-161, 165
Kennedy, Ted 133
Key 6 Business Soultions 232-234
Kilcullen Kapital Partners, 30, 181, 222, 224, 236, 242
Kilcullen Mozart Group, 204
Killeen, John 14, 19-21, 30-31, 155, 179
Kilroy, Howard 86-87, 89-94, 239
Kilroy, Jim 92-93
KISS 98 FM 151
Klaus, Václav 148
Komercni Banka 145, 193-194, 202-203, 230
Kucera, Petr 154-155, 165, 181

L
Late Late Show 61
Latvia 192
Let's Do It Global 24
Lauder, Ronald 147
Leadership 23, 45, 104, 106, 110-111, 120, 137, 142, 176, 180
Lithuania 192
Lloyds 101,103
London 14, 44, 57, 62, 83, 87, 101-102, 111, 152, 192, 208, 215, 217, 222
London Stock Exchange 152
Lynch, Brian 25, 44

M
Manhattan 54
Maritime Institute of Ireland 243

McClintock, Trevor 63, 65
McCollum, James 232-233
McGibney, Peter 129
McShane, Jimmy 153
Meciar, Vladímir 148
Melly, Seán 212-213, 217-221
Mitchell, Gay 129-131
Moravia 237
Morgan, J. P. 195, 252
Moscow 140-142, 161, 178
Moy Construction 35
Mozart Fund 223
Mozart Ventures 222
Murphy, Paul 100, 139
MUZO 199

N
National City Brokers [NCB] 87-91, 94
Nauta, Dirk 84
New York 56, 61, 83, 100, 103, 107, 129, 131, 146, 152, 192, 208, 215
Newport 102, 184
Nixon, William [Winkie] 71, 73

O
O'Brien, Denis 25, 151, 229
O'Brien, Michael 189
O'Brien, Patrick Cruise 212
O'Broin, Ann 98
Ó Ceidigh, Pádraig 238
O'Coineen, Charlie 35-36
O'Coineen, Cormac 33-35, 139
O'Coineen, Murtagh 35
O'Coineen, Suzanna 72, 103, 108, 191
O'Connor, Stephen 131
O'Donnell Sweeney 143
O'Dowd, Niall 129
O'Neill, T. P. 133
O'Reilly, Tony 55, 85, 130, 131
Ocean Youth Trust Ireland 14
Olympic project 130
Outdoor Pursuits 110

P
Paegas 233
Parks, Eric 68
Philanthrophy 13, 16-17
Phillips Innovator 84
Phoenix 96
Poland 134, 141, 143, 146, 187-192, 210, 218, 220, 231
Polish National Bank 190
Pozar, Michal 237
Prague 14-15, 23, 29, 95, 136, 143-144, 146, 148-149, 151-153, 155-157, 159, 161, 163, 165, 168, 191, 194, 197, 200, 205, 208, 210, 214-216, 225, 230, 233, 237
Prague Business Journal 185-187
Prague Post, The 182
Prague Stock Exchange 152
Prague Stock Exchange Ball 180
Prague Stock Exchange Building 206
PriceWaterhouseCooper 151
Pride of Galway 14, 120
ProntoPrint 150
Pvní Investioní Bank 161
Pyke, Dag 60, 63, 65

Q
Quinn, Feargal 94, 98

R
Rabbitt, John 34
Reuters 180

Robinson, Mary 132
Ruggario, Joe 131
Russia 140-143, 169

S
Sail and Power 68,73
Sail Ireland 82, 88, 89-92, 94-96, 98-100, 104, 108, 124, 192, 217
Sailing Alone around the World 37
San Diego 27, 29, 110
San Francisco 33, 103
Saw Doctors 233
Schrantz, Jack 230
Scoile Fhursa 38
Scotland 56, 111, 132
Security World 77-79
Severin, Tim 61, 253

Seville 120,
Signum Temporis awards 180
Simply 234, 236
Slocum, Joshua 37, 53
Slovak Credit Bureau 193, 195, 197, 199, 201, 203, 205-207
Slovakia 126,147-149
Smirnoff 63, 100
Smith, Ian 154-155, 181
Smurfit, Michael 87
Sommers, Bernard 212-213, 217
Soviet Union 139, 162, 184
Sportsmind 110
Stack, Jack 202, 235
Stacpoole, Michael 132-134
Stafford, Tom 64
Starr, Matt 210
Stentor 212
Sunday Independent 87
Svehlakova, Hana 233

T
T-Mobil 233
Tai-Pan 107, 130
TCL Telecom 212
Team-building 110, 112
Teamship 112-113
Tebbe, Klaus 233
Ted Turner 104-105
Telecom Éireann 212
Timeen Development 225
Training 14, 43, 70, 81, 93-94, 110, 112, 119-121, 167-168, 180, 183, 204, 234
Trans Union 198, 205, 253
TV Nova 146-147

U
University College Galway 41, 46, 50
Urban, Jan 14, 234
US Chamber of Commerce 146

V
Valueline 152
Volvo Ocean Race 16-17, 20-21, 28, 30-32, 242, 254

W
Warsaw 188, 191, 220
Washington 110, 131-133
Whitbread Race 17, 20, 26-27, 29, 83-85, 87-88, 92, 95, 100, 104
Wielkopolski Bank Kredytowy [WBK] 190
Wilkinson, Jonathan 236,
World Championships 92
WorldCom 212-213

Y
Yugoslavia 140, 148

Z
Zelezny, Vladimir 146-147
Zlin 134-136
Zoom Airways 237

About the Author

Born in Galway, the Author was educated at Scoil Fhursa and Coláiste Iognáid, followed by a business degree from the national University of Ireland, Galway before travelling the world and dedicating his life to business and sailing. An adventurer, entrepreneur and philanthropist, he has crossed the Atlantic several times (once single-handed in a fifteen and a half foot inflatable dinghy) and has raced and voyaged in many locations all over the world. He is the founding Chairman of Let's Do It Global Ltd, the non-profit body that brought the Volvo Ocean Race to Ireland in May 2009, as well as organising Ireland's *Green Dragon* entry.

Having set up his first businesses during the recession of the 1980s, Enda later sold his accumulated (but modest) interests in publishing, travel and insurance. Thereafter he laid the foundations for Ireland's first entry in the 1989-90 Whitbread round-the-world race, the forerunner of today's Volvo Ocean Race, before participating in the BOC single-handed round-the-world race.

In the 1990s he re-entered the business world, this time in Central Europe, where he worked mainly from Prague in the Czech Republic. Starting with a financial information firm he quickly built up a network of companies the proceeds of which ultimately formed the basis of Kilcullen Kapital, the investment management firm, that has a broad number of interests in the renewable energy, manufacturing, finance and service sectors.

The author of four books and a former correspondent for the *Irish Times*, Enda has four children, Roisin, Aisling, Saoirse and Cormac, and a large extended family. In addition to boats, business and writing, O'Coineen travels extensively and loves climbing mountains, playing tennis and chess. He is also Chairman of the Ocean Youth Trust charity of Ireland and has served on GAISCE, Coiste an Asgard and other boards.